GOURMET DISHES
from
FRANCE AND ITALY

BY ALISON BURT (FRANCE)
SONIA ALLISON AND ULRIKE BIELFELDT (ITALY)

Galley Press

This edition published 1978 by
Galley Press
In association with Cathay
Books 59 Grosvenor Street,
London W1

© 1973, 1978 Hennerwood
Publications Limited

ISBN 0 904644 52 9

Produced by Mandarin
Publishers Limited
22a Westlands Road
Quarry Bay, Hong Kong

Printed in Hong Kong

Mediterranean vegetable stew

CONTENTS

The flavour of French cooking

French cooking has, quite rightly, earned
itself the reputation of being the finest cuisine
in the world. It is made up of two different parts,
haute cuisine and cuisine bourgeoisie. The former
has evolved from the cooking of the great chefs
such as Escoffier and Câreme. The second is the
peasant cooking of the various regions of France.
You will find both types in this book, so do not
be surprised if you come across a highly
sophisticated dish in company with a simple but
delicious peasant stew.

It is fascinating finding out where the various

dishes of France have originated and how the
local produce has affected the cuisine of each
area. It is particularly useful, if you ever visit
France, to know in advance what to look out for
and the specialities to order in the local
restaurants.

Paris is the political, arts and cooking centre of
France. Every day the best and freshest of
French-grown produce, meat, fruit and vegetables
come into Runjis, near Orly airport, the vast new
market replacing Les Halles. Not only do the shops
and restaurants buy their food here, but also many

housewives who get up early one or two mornings a week to come to the market for, with true French economy in mind, they know that this is where they will get value for money. It is in the hotels and restaurants of Paris that the great chefs of France have created haute cuisine. Paris is especially noted for its gâteaux and patisserie which are varied, luscious and delicious.

Normandy to the north west of Paris and bordering on the English Channel, is a province of great natural food resources, and many great dishes originated in Normandy. It is an apple growing area and large quantities of very fine cider are made. Dishes which include apples are sometimes called 'à la Normande'. Calvados, the apple-flavoured liqueur, comes from Normandy

A selection of locally produced food

and so does Benedictine; the famous Benedictine monastery stands on the cliffs overlooking the sea. A great variety of fish are caught off the coast of Normandy and many shellfish can be gathered from the rocks. Oysters and mussels are especially good and succulent. The dairy industry thrives in Normandy and besides much good quality butter and cream, many of the most famous cheeses come from here. Together with many other regional specialities, Rouen is well known for its ducks and Caen is known for Tripe à la mode de Caen which is sold in that area but now made much in the home.

Brittany, just to the south of Normandy, is a peninsula jutting out into the Atlantic ocean. Besides being famed for its oysters, scallops, lobsters and other sea food, this is the home of the salt pastures where the lamb 'pré-sale' is raised. This young and tender lamb has a flavour all of its own which is prized throughout France. Nantes, to the south of Brittany, is a centre for cakes, biscuits and its own version of pike cooked in white wine. Breton charcuterie is well known and its shops sell a wide variety of pâtés, terrines, rillettes, sausages and so on. The autumn in Brittany brings a bountiful harvest of cereals, fruit, vegetables, honey and sweet chestnuts. Incidentally, if you come across a dish in a restaurant called 'à la Breton' it usually means that the meat will be served with a garnish of haricot beans. This has come about because haricot beans are the traditional accompaniment to the Breton gigot de pré-salé (leg of salt-meadow lamb).

The west and the south-west Basque country is rich in vines. Bordeaux is the famed wine centre of this area and it is in this region that Cognac is made. Sea food abounds in the Bay of Biscay and the Gironde estuary can boast of some of the finest caviar from locally caught sturgeons. The Landes province, at the foot of the Pyrenees, can claim many traditional dishes from Pipérade to Cassoulet, both of simple peasant origin. Bayonne is famous for its ham and this area is well-known for locally fattened Landes chickens.

Travelling east along the French border will bring you first to the **Languedoc** and then **Provence.** These two provinces both border on the Mediterranean Sea and the local cuisines are very similar. The climate is good: and fruit flourish. Apricots and peaches are regional specialities and the abundance of herbs help to scent the famous Provence honey. The well known local produce consists of olives (and olive oil), tomatoes, garlic and herbs, and if the words 'à la Provençale' appear on the menu you can be sure that the dish in question will contain at least some of these ingredients. Fish caught in the Mediterranean are naturally part of the local cuisine and it is here that the true Bouillabaisse fish stew is made. Going inland a little, the towns of Arles in Provence and Toulouse in Languedoc are noted for their sausage and charcuterie.

To the east of France are the **Alps** and the **Savoie province**. As would be expected from an alpine area, cheese and dairy produce are the local specialities. A good white wine is also produced and the charcuterie is also notable – in fact, any food that can see the people through the long snowy winters. It is in this region that Chartreuse is made.

Alsace and Lorraine are similar provinces and both have a strong German influence in their cuisine. Cheeses, pâté and other charcuterie, sauerkraut and the local wines are all reminiscent of Germany and quite unlike any other part of France. The local beer is famous, as are the locally made white brandies flavoured with wild fruit, raspberries, myrtle berries and – the most famous – cherries, known as Kirsch. The most well-known dishes are of course Quiche Lorraine and pâté de Foie gras from Strasbourg.

Coming inland on a broad front one comes to the two great wine growing regions of **Champagne and Burgundy**. These need no explanation. Dishes termed 'à la Bourguignonne' are essentially cooked in a Burgundy wine. The snails in this area are extremely good. Dijon in Burgundy is famous for its locally produced mustard.

The Midi of France is a vast area and each province boasts its own specialities. Wines are widely grown and local charcuterie is worth trying in practically every town. There are also many individual recipes for interesting stews using locally produced ingredients. The province of Périgord is famous for truffles, pâté de foie gras (which rivals that made in Strasbourg) and walnuts, from which a liqueur is made. Delicious edible fungi such as cèpes and chantrelle are found in this area. There is also an abundance of fish: carp, pike, crayfish and salmon from the many freshwater rivers and streams. To the north of the area, Orleans is known for vinegar 'à l'ancienne' which originated here, and the town of Pithiviers is known for a gâteau, sold locally, bearing the name of the town.

Basic ingredients

French cooking stands in a class of its own because French housewives take great trouble not only to use the best, freshest and most perfect ingredients but also to treat even the smallest ingredient with care and respect. At the beginning of the 18th century it was not unusual for a housewife to spend up to five or six hours preparing just one dish, but nowadays, economy and the pace of modern life has made it essential to cook the simpler dishes for everyday meals. It is still important to shop with great care, inspecting each purchase, especially of meat, fruit and vegetables. It is false economy to buy any food but the best, as you will never be able to cook a perfect French dish while the basic ingredients are inferior. Although it is not necessary to use expensive ingredients, use each one carefully, blending the flavours to produce a delicious dish.

The choice of fat and oil is important.
Whether you choose to use butter, margarine, lard,
dripping, olive oil or corn oil, use the best quality
available. Many of the regional dishes traditionally
call for goose, chicken or meat dripping. The
flavour that butter imparts is unequalled for cakes,
sauces and special dishes such as those 'au beurre'
or 'à la meunière'. Margarine is sometimes
preferred for health reasons and can be used
instead of butter as it still gives a good colour and
texture to your cooking. Oil is used frequently
instead of fat for savoury dishes and frying.
Corn oil and groundnut oil are the most economical

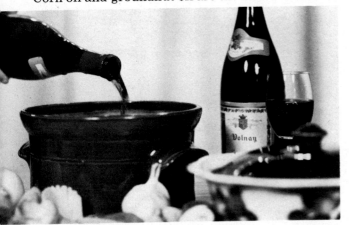

Wine used in cooking

and can be used for deep frying or added to butter
(equal quantities) when sautéing ingredients.
Using a mixture of butter and oil has the
advantage of a good butter flavour without the
butter becoming too brown. If a recipe calls for
olive oil, do make sure that you use it. Although
olive is more expensive than other cooking oils,
nothing can rival it for flavour, especially in
salad dressings or the classic vegetable stew,
rataouille.
Onions, shallots and garlic are all important
ingredients for French savoury dishes. When
gently fried and browned, they caramellize,
imparting a delicious flavour and the dish takes
on a brown colour. Always cook them slowly; if
they catch and burn the resulting flavour will be
bitter. White sauces and meat dishes are often
flavoured with onion softened but not browned.
Sometimes this is achieved by cooking a whole
bulb, studded with cloves, in with the stock, milk
or cooking liquid, to be removed before the dish
is served.
Good rich stock, whether beef, veal, chicken
or fish, is an ingredient essential to French
cooking. For a truly delicious soup or sauce, it
is worth going to all the trouble of making stock.
Rarely does one find a stock pot in anyone's
kitchen nowadays, but many cooks make stock
to store in the refrigerator and boil up every 3 or

4 days with any suitable scraps which may have
been collected since the last boil-up. Alternatively,
if you own a deep freezing unit, make your own
stock and store it frozen in a concentrated form,
the size of ice cubes. In an emergency, use a
chicken or beef stock cube, but do not expect your
cooking to retain its individual flavour.
Cheese, eggs and cream are widely used in
French cooking. If a French cheese is specified in
a recipe, try to use that one. Some cheeses are
chosen for flavour, others for their melting
properties and texture. Eggs should be as fresh as
possible. Frequently the yolks only are used and
these, in conjunction with cream, give a dish its
smoothness and richness. They are used to
thicken and add flavour to many savoury as well
as sweet dishes. Egg whites can give a light and
fluffy texture to a dish – as shown in a carefully
prepared and well-risen soufflé.
Wine plays an extremely important part in
French cooking. Use as good a quality wine as
you can afford. There are very few 'rules' as to
which colour of wine to use, as most meats can be
cooked successfully in either. It is a good idea,
however, to serve the same wine with the dish
at table as that used for cooking. Wine should
always be cooked for a long time to evaporate
the alcohol and impart its unique flavour. Add it
to stews, casseroles and to the roasting pan for
roasting meat, at the beginning of the cooking
time. If it is to be used in a dish which only has
a short cooking time, put the wine in a small
saucepan and boil it rapidly until reduced to about
$\frac{1}{3}$ of the original quantity before using it.
Herbs are best when used fresh, not dried.
Growing your own is quite simple, even if you
have no garden. Try them in a window box – they
smell superb. The most important herbs used in
French cooking are those comprising a bouquet
garni – a bay leaf, a sprig of thyme and some
stalks of parsley. Basil, tarragon and chives are
also widely used. It is useful to know that
1 tablespoon ($1\frac{1}{4}$T) fresh chopped herbs is
equivalent to 1 teaspoon dried chopped herbs.
Vinegar is used quite widely in French cooking.
The best sort to use is a good wine vinegar,
white or red, according to taste or the recipe.
Flavoured vinegars can be bought but you can
make your own if you like: e.g. Tarragon vinegar
can be made by adding a large sprig of fresh
tarragon to the bottle of vinegar. Leave for at
least 1 month before using.
Salt and pepper are essential for all cooking.
The freshly ground variety, whether rock salt, or
black or white peppercorns, have more flavour
and are distinctly preferable to the already
prepared powders.

9

Quiche Lorraine *(1)*
Tuna fish Provençale *(2)*
Pâtés *(3)*
A selection of French cheeses *(4)*
Lobster bisque *(5)*
Scallops Breton-style *(6)*
Cheese omelette *(7)*

5

6

7

Cooking utensils
(Batterie de Cuisine)

The French like to use the right tools for each job. This doesn't mean that they own a lot of gimmicky gadgets, but simple basic equipment which will perform each task quickly and with the least possible fuss. You probably possess the majority of utensils needed in your kitchen, but might like to buy just one or two of the more typically French moulds, terrines and tourtières, to complete your collection. The following utensils are those most common in French kitchens.

Pans. You would probably find a minimum of 12 pans in each kitchen. These cover every contingency from sauce-making to cooking whole fish. The following pans are a must – a set of 3 saucepans of varying size, with one large enough to hold a whole chicken.

Sauté pan	Steamer
Frying pan	Fish kettle
Deep frying pan	Preserving pan
Double saucepan	Roasting pan
(double boiler)	
Omelette pan	
(6 or 7 inch diameter)	

Copper is the best choice of metal as it is an excellent heat conductor and gives even heating over the base of the whole pan. Copper, however, can taint food and so each pan must be tin-lined. Stainless steel is a practical metal from the cleaning point of view, but a poor conductor of heat, so the base of the pans must be coated with copper. Cast iron and good quality enamelled aluminium pans are all acceptable.

Mixing bowls of all sizes are essential. It is impossible to advise on the number but the more you have, in as many different sizes, the easier life will be. If you are a really keen cook, you may like to possess the large spherical-style copper bowl which the French use only for whisking egg whites. Without a doubt you will get a better volume and a better texture to egg whites when they are whisked thus.

Knives are one of the most important elements of a good set of kitchen equipment. Always buy the best quality available and they will last for years. Steel knives can be kept sharper than stainless steel knives, although it is a good idea to have a mixture of both. Fruit discolours steel very badly and steel will rust quickly unless great care is taken.

A large French cook's knife (essential)

A vegetable knife (stainless steel)

A ham knife for cutting cold meat

A carving knife

A bread knife

A palette knife, best in stainless steel with a very flexible blade

Other useful cutting utensils are a **can opener**, a **potato peeler**, which can be used for paring fruit thinly or for removing the thin zest of citrus fruits and a mandolin for cutting wafer-thin slices of cucumber – or even cutting potatoes for game chips. **Kitchen scissors** are a must.

Large kitchen forks are useful – make sure you have at least one large carving fork.

Spoons: wooden spoons, large metal spoons for basting, slotted spoons and standard measuring spoons are a must. It is impossible to collect too many. **Wire whisks**, flat and balloon shaped, are also a help.

Three **strainers** are useful: a hair or nylon sieve in a wooden frame for puréeing fruit and vegetables, a conical 'chinois' strainer for soups and sauces, a bowl sieve for sifting dry ingredients.

A colander is a must for draining vegetables.

A cheese grater and a **nutmeg grater** are essential.

A good quality teak **chopping board** is a good investment as it will last for years and save your work surfaces. A pastry board is not now considered important as pastry can be rolled out on plastic work surfaces. The rolling pin is still a must. A marble slab is useful for making pastry the French way to keep it as cool as possible.

Weighing scales are essential, if you are a really serious cook, for accurate measuring.

A set of measuring jugs is convenient to use for measuring liquid ingredients.

Ovenproof and flameproof casseroles are available varying from very modern designs to the classic earthenware. The term 'casserole' in France denotes a wide variety of cooking utensils from saucepans to cocottes and ramekins.

A terrine is an earthenware oblong or oval dish, with a lid, which is classically used for cooking pâtés.

Many different **moulds** are used in French cooking for both sweet and savoury dishes. Some of the most common are:

Moule à manqué (a shallow cake tin with sloping sides)

Moule à charlotte (a deep oval or round mould with sloping sides)

Moule à dariole (a small round mould with tall sloping sides. Used for individual servings)

Moule à douille (this is the collective name for the many varieties of ring moulds used in French cooking)

Moule à pâté (hinged mould for raised pies)

Moule à gelée (decorative jelly mould)

Moules à madeleines (shell-shaped moulds for cooking madelines)

Timbale is yet another kind of a mould, usually round with straight or slightly sloping sides. It can be large or for individual portions and the food dish frequently includes timbale in its name e.g. Timbale de Champignon. A soufflé dish is a Timbale à soufflé.

Tart tins, (tourtières) are another must. They can be metal with a removeable base or ovenproof china. Tarts can also be made in a fluted flan ring standing on a baking tray. Savoury flans are made in a plain flan ring. Two or three baking trays are essential in every kitchen.

A loaf tin and a selection of deep and shallow cake and patty tins are useful. Biscuit cutters, both plain and fluted, and icing pipes and a bag, are desirable.

A food mixer with a blender attachment will certainly save you time.

There are many other pieces of equipment which, although not really essential, are decorative in the kitchen: a pestle and mortar for crushing spices, an hachinette for chopping herbs, a garlic press, a salt and pepper mill, au gratin dishes, a larding needle, a meat mallet and so on.

Genoise sponge in preparation

Without its famous sauces, French cuisine would be sadly lacking. It is these all-important and delicately flavoured sauces which are the basis of most of the particularly delicious dishes. French housewives know the value of taking a little extra care with the preparation and flavouring so that their sauces emerge as the final crowning glory to their cooking.

The roux sauces, such as Espagnole sauce and béchamel sauce take their flavour from the careful blending of ingredients at the beginning and then the cooking of the butter and flour roux to ensure that the sauce is neither greasy nor floury tasting. If the roux is properly cooked, it is possible to add the liquid all at once, not gradually, and still have a smooth sauce. I find that it is easier to blend a sauce if I use a wire whisk instead of a wooden spoon when adding the liquid. If you have to keep the sauce hot before serving, try pouring on a small amount of milk to cover the top of the sauce. Beat the milk in just before serving.

Sauces

Butter sauces take their flavour from the eggs and butter used in making them. They have an extremely delicate flavour which makes them generally of more use in haute cuisine than when cooking for the family. These sauces are generally served warm rather than hot.

Home made mayonnaise is superb and far preferable to the commercial variety. Before you start, make sure that all your utensils are clean, free from grease and well dried. The oil must be added very slowly at first or the mayonnaise may curdle. If this does happen, place another egg yolk in a clean bowl and add the curdled mixture to this, drop by drop, beating well all the time. Mayonnaise can be kept for a short while at room temperature – do not put it in the refrigerator as it will tend to separate.

Sweet sauces are not made as frequently as the savoury variety but they are well worth the trouble for a special dinner party. Nothing can rival the flavour of a freshly made fruit sauce or chocolate sauce.

Salmon trout in aspic (left)

Veal loaf coated in sauce chaudfroid and a layer of aspic (below)

Meat served with a white sauce (bottom)

Sauce espagnole Rich brown sauce

2 oz. (4T) butter or dripping
2 oz. (½ cup) diced bacon
½ onion, sliced
½ carrot, sliced
1 shallot, chopped
2 oz. (½ cup) plain (all purpose) flour
1 pint (2½ cups) fond brun (beef bone stock, see recipe page 30)
6 mushroom stalks
2 tablespoons tomato paste
2 tablespoons dry sherry
salt and pepper

Melt the butter or dripping in a small heavy saucepan. Add the bacon and fry until softened. Add the prepared vegetables and continue frying until they are softened but not browned. Stir in the flour and cook very gently, stirring occasionally, until the whole is a rich, russet brown (this will probably take about 20–30 minutes). Add stock and mushroom stalks. Bring to the boil, stirring, simmer for 30 minutes. Add tomato paste, sherry and seasonings, simmer for a further 15 minutes. Strain the sauce, pressing the vegetables well to extract as much liquid as possible.
Reheat. Use as required.

Sauce madère Madeira sauce

½ pint (1¼ cups) sauce espagnole
3 tablespoons (¼ cup) Madeira wine

Serve with meat and game.

Prepare the sauce espagnole, stir in Madeira wine. Reheat without boiling. Use as required.

Sauce chasseur

1 tablespoon (1¼T) oil
1 oz. (2T) butter
4 shallots, chopped
4 oz. mushrooms, finely sliced
¼ pint (⅝ cup) white wine
½ pint (1¼ cups) sauce espagnole
extra 1 oz. butter
pinch of chopped parsley
pinch of chopped tarragon

Serve with chicken, rabbit and other meats.

Heat the oil and butter in a small saucepan. Add the shallots and mushrooms and fry until the mushrooms are cooked. Pour in the wine, bring to the boil and boil until the wine is reduced by half. Stir in the sauce espagnole, butter and herbs. Simmer 2–3 minutes. Use as required.

Sauce robert

1 small onion, chopped
½ oz. (1T) butter
¼ pint (⅝ cup) vinegar
½ pint (⅝ cup) sauce espagnole
2 gherkins, chopped
2 teaspoons French mustard
1 teaspoon chopped parsley

Serve with pork, lamb, liver and kidneys.

Place the onion in a small saucepan with butter. Fry gently until softened, add the vinegar, boil until reduced by half. Add the sauce espagnole, bring to the boil and simmer for 15 minutes. Add the gherkins, mustard and parsley just before serving. Do not re-boil.

Sauce béchamel White sauce

1 shallot
1 carrot
1 stick celery
1 small bayleaf
10 white peppercorns
1 blade mace
1 pint (2½ cups) milk
2 oz. (4T) butter
2 oz. (½ cup) plain (all purpose) flour
salt

Peel and slice the shallot and carrot. Chop the celery. Place the vegetables in a saucepan with the bayleaf, peppercorns, mace and milk. Heat gently until boiling. Cover the pan and leave for 15–20 minutes. Strain the milk, discard the vegetables and spices. Melt the butter in a clean saucepan, stir in the flour and cook over a low heat until the flour is cooked but not browned (it will have a 'honeycomb' appearance), for about 2–4 minutes. Add the milk, stirring continuously, bring to the boil and simmer 5–7 minutes. Add salt to taste. Use as required.

Sauce mornay added to eggs Florentine

Sauce soubise — Onion sauce

½ pint (1¼ cups) sauce béchamel
3 onions
¼ pint (⅝ cup) fond blanc de volaille (chicken stock) (see recipe page 30)
salt and pepper
pinch of sugar

Serve with eggs, vegetables, fish or lamb.

Prepare the sauce béchamel.
Peel the onions and slice. Place in a saucepan with the stock, bring to the boil and simmer until the onions are very tender. Drain the onions and either chop finely or purée in an electric blender. Mix the onion with the sauce béchamel, adjust seasoning, add sugar. Reheat and serve as required.

Sauce aurore — Tomato cream sauce

½ pint (1¼ cups) sauce béchamel
½ pint (1¼ cups) tomato purée or sauce tomate (see page 20)
sugar
salt and pepper

Serve with fish, meat, eggs and vegetables.

Heat the sauce béchamel in a small saucepan until boiling. Add the tomato purée or sauce and bring to the boil, stirring constantly. Simmer for 3–5 minutes. Strain the sauce, reheat in a clean saucepan and adjust seasoning as necessary with sugar, salt and pepper. If the sauce is too thin, bring to the boil and continue boiling until it reaches the desired consistency. Use as required.

Sauce mornay — Cheese sauce

½ pint (1¼ cups) sauce béchamel
1 oz. (¼ cup) grated Cheddar cheese
1 oz. (¼ cup) grated Parmesan cheese
salt, pepper and mustard

Serve with eggs, vegetables, fish and pasta.

Heat the sauce béchamel in a small saucepan, stirring, until it boils. Remove from heat, whisk in the grated cheeses. Reheat, without boiling, whisking until the cheese is melted. Add salt, pepper and mustard to taste. Use as required.

Sauce béarnaise

**3 tablespoons (1¼ cup) white
wine vinegar
6 peppercorns
1 shallot, chopped
¼ pint (⅝ cup) sauce béchamel
2 egg yolks
1 oz. (2T) butter
salt and pepper**

Serve with vegetables, fish and grilled meat.

Place the vinegar, peppercorns and shallot in a small saucepan.
Bring to the boil and boil until the vinegar is reduced to 1
tablespoon. Strain. Put the sauce béchamel in a bowl, add the
reduced vinegar and the egg yolks. Place the bowl over a saucepan of
simmering water (do not allow the bowl to touch the water). Stir
continuously with a wooden spoon.
Add the butter in small pieces, heating continuously. Do not
overheat the sauce or it will curdle. If this happens, add 1 tablespoon
of very cold water and beat well again. When sauce is the
consistency of thick mayonnaise, season to taste.
Use as required.

note: a different flavour can be achieved if 2 tablespoons wine
vinegar and 1 tablespoon tarragon vinegar are used. A few drops of
chilli vinegar can also be added.

Timbale de champignon

Savoury egg custard with mushroom sauce

**3 eggs
¾ pint (approx. 2 cups) milk
3 oz. (¾ cup) grated
Cheddar cheese
salt and pepper
¼ teaspoon dry mustard
½ pint (1¼ cups) sauce béchamel
(see recipe page 16)
4 oz. (1 cup) button mushrooms**

A timbale is a type of mould. The word timbale in a recipe title
generally means that the dish is cooked in a timbale and served
unmoulded.

Beat the eggs lightly, add the warmed milk and cheese and stir to
mix. Season to taste with salt, pepper and mustard. Pour egg mixture
into a small soufflé dish or charlotte mould. Stand mould in a
roasting pan, add water to about 1 inch depth. Bake in a moderately
slow oven (325°F. Mark 3) for 50 minutes or until set.
Prepare the béchamel sauce. Slice the mushrooms finely, stir them
into the sauce and cook for a further 2–3 minutes.
Turn the timbale out of the mould on to a heated serving dish, pour
the sauce over the top and serve immediately.

note: this can also be made in individual dariole moulds. Reduce the
cooking time to about 25 minutes.

serves 4

Sauce choron

**1 quantity sauce béarnaise
1 tablespoon tomato paste**

Serve with fish, particularly salmon.

Prepare the sauce béarnaise.
Whisk in the tomato paste just before the sauce is completed. Use as
required.

Sauce valois

**1 quantity sauce béarnaise
1 tablespoon (1¼T) tomato paste**

Serve with chicken or veal.

Prepare sauce béarnaise.
Add the warmed beef extract just before the sauce is completed.
Use as required.

Sauce velouté

1 oz. (2T) butter
6 white peppercorns
3 parsley stalks
1 oz. (¼ cup) plain (all
purpose) flour
¾ pint (approx. 2 cups) fond
blanc or fond blanc de volaille
(white stock or chicken stock,
see recipes page 30)
4 mushroom stalks
juice of ¼ lemon
salt
1 tablespoon (1¼T) single
(light) cream

Melt the butter in a small saucepan. Add the peppercorns, parsley stalks and flour. Cook gently, stirring continuously, until the flour is cooked but not browned (it will have a 'honeycomb' appearance) about 2–4 minutes. Add the stock, stirring, and bring to the boil. Add the mushroom stalks, lemon juice and salt to taste. Simmer gently for 20–25 minutes, stirring occasionally. Strain the sauce, add the cream and reheat without boiling. Use as required.

Sauce hollandaise

juice of ½ a lemon
1 teaspoon water
2 egg yolks
4 oz. (8T) butter
salt and cayenne pepper

Serve with vegetables, fish and eggs.

Place the lemon juice and water in a small bowl. Put the bowl over a saucepan of simmering water (do not let it touch the water). Add the egg yolks and ½ oz. butter. Whisk very thoroughly until stiff enough to retain the marks of the whisk.
Remove the saucepan from the heat and add the remaining butter in very small pieces, whisking well all the time.
Season to taste with salt and cayenne pepper.
Use as required.

Sauce verte
Green sauce

1 quantity sauce hollandaise
4 oz. (½ cup) finely chopped
cooked spinach
salt and pepper

Serve with seafood.

As soon as the sauce hollandaise is cooked, whisk in the spinach, off the heat. When thoroughly combined, reheat very carefully without boiling. Adjust the seasoning. Use as required.

Sauce bercy

½ oz. (1T) butter
2 shallots, chopped
¼ pint (⅝ cup) white wine
1 pint (2½ cups) fond blanc,
fond blanc de volaille or fond de
poisson (white stock, chicken
stock or fish stock, see recipes
page 30)
salt and pepper
juice of ½ lemon
1 tablespoon (1¼T)
chopped parsley
extra ¾ oz. (scant ⅛ cup)
butter, softened
¾ oz. (scant ¼ cup) plain (all
purpose) flour

Serve, according to the stock used, with eggs, veal, vegetables and fish.

Melt the butter in a saucepan, add the shallots and cook gently until softened but not browned. Add the wine and boil. Cook until the wine is reduced by half.
Add the stock, seasoning, lemon juice and parsley. Bring to the boil, then remove from the heat.
Cream the extra butter and flour together well. Add to the saucepan in very small pieces, stirring until well blended. Bring to the boil, simmer 1–2 minutes.
Use as required.

Sauce de tomates provençale
Tomato sauce Provençale-style

2 lb. tomatoes
2 tablespoons (2½T) olive oil
1 clove garlic, crushed
1 bayleaf
1 small onion finely chopped
1 small carrot, finely chopped
1 stick celery, finely chopped
bouquet garni
salt, pepper and sugar

Serve with meat or fish.

Skin the tomatoes, remove the seeds and chop roughly.
Heat the oil in a saucepan, add the tomatoes, garlic, bayleaf, vegetables and bouquet garni. Cover the pan tightly and simmer for 30 minutes.
Remove the bouquet garni and bayleaf. Season with salt, pepper and sugar to taste. Sieve the sauce or purée in an electric blender if a smooth sauce is desired. Use as required.

Mayonnaise

2 egg yolks
2 tablespoons (2½T)
tarragon vinegar
¼ teaspoon each salt, pepper and
mustard
pinch of sugar
½–¾ pint (1¼-approx. 2 cups)
olive oil

Place the egg yolks, vinegar, salt, pepper, mustard and sugar in a clean bowl. Whisk with a fork or beat with a wooden spoon until creamy.
Add the oil, drop by drop, beating well all the time. When half the oil has been added, add the remainder in a slow but steady stream. Beat until a smooth thick sauce is formed. If it becomes too thick, add a little boiling water.

note: mayonnaise will keep, if stored in a clean screw-top jar, for about 1 month.

Sauce tartare

½ pint (1¼ cups) mayonnaise
1 teaspoon chopped capers
1 teaspoon chopped gherkins
1 teaspoon chopped mixed herbs
1 hard-boiled egg white, chopped
salt and pepper

Serve with grilled or fried fish.

Combine all the ingredients together. Season to taste. Use as required.

Sauce aïoli　Garlic sauce

Serve with cold meats, fish and shellfish.

Make the mayonnaise as described above, using a scant ½ pint (1¼ cups) olive oil. Add 3–4 well crushed cloves of garlic to the egg yolks before adding the oil.

Sauce vinaigrette　Vinaigrette dressing

¼ teaspoon each, salt, pepper and dry mustard
3 tablespoons (3¾T) olive oil
1 tablespoon (1¼T) vinegar

Serve with salads and cooked meats.

Place the seasonings in a bowl, add a little oil and mix to a smooth paste, add the remaining oil and then the vinegar. Whisk very briskly until the sauce is emulsified and the vinegar and oil thoroughly mixed.
Use as required.

note: add 1 clove garlic, crushed, 1 teaspoon mixed chopped dried herbs and 1 small onion, finely chopped, for a more flavoursome dressing.

Aspic

2 pints (5 cups) well flavoured stock (beef, veal or fish, according to the dish to be decorated)
¼ pint (⅝ cup) sherry
1 tablespoon (1¼T) vinegar
2 oz. (6 tablespoons) gelatine
2 egg whites

Aspic jelly (jello) plays a big part in French cold cookery. It can be used for setting savoury ingredients in a mould or for giving the dish a glazed appearance. It is nearly always used to line a mould before the savoury mousse or cream is put in to set. Alternatively, half-set aspic jelly (jello) is spooned over the dish.
It is possible to buy commercially prepared aspic jelly (jello) crystals but for a special occasion you may feel it would be worthwhile making your own.

Place the cold stock, sherry, vinegar and gelatine in a large saucepan. Heat slowly over a gentle heat, stirring occasionally. Whisk the egg whites until frothy, add them to the saucepan and whisk, over a low heat, until boiling. Allow the mixture to boil to the top of the pan without whisking, draw the pan aside. Repeat the boiling and drawing aside process twice more. Put aside for 5 minutes.
Strain the mixture through a scalded jelly (jello) bag or several thicknesses of muslin.
Use as required.

Sauce chaudfroid

¾ pint (approx. 2 cups) sauce béchamel (see recipe page 16) (make this sauce using 1 oz. (2T) butter, 1 oz. plain (all purpose) flour, ¾ pint milk)
2 tablespoons (2½T) aspic, made double strength
2 tablespoons (2½T) single (light) cream
salt and pepper

For coating cold fish, eggs and chicken.

Combine all the ingredients together thoroughly. Cool, stirring frequently to keep the sauce smooth.
When set to the consistency of thick cream, use for coating the cold foods.

note: for Chaudfroid brown sauce, use sauce espagnole (see recipe page 16) instead of sauce béchamel. Use for coating cold game, duck, cutlets and so on.

Sauce au chocolat   Chocolate sauce

2 oz. plain dark chocolate
2 tablespoons (2½T) water
1 teaspoon cornflour
(cornstarch)
¼ pint (⅝ cup) milk
1 teaspoon castor
(superfine) sugar
½ teaspoon vanilla essence
1 tablespoon (1¼T) single (light)
cream, optional

Grate the chocolate into a saucepan, add the water and heat gently, without boiling, until chocolate has melted and combined with the water.
Mix the cornflour with the milk, add to saucepan. Bring to the boil, stirring constantly, simmer 4–5 minutes.
Add the sugar and vanilla essence and stir until the sugar is dissolved. Stir in the cream when the sauce has cooled slightly, do not reboil.
note: for a thicker sauce, halve the amount of milk used.

Sauce d'abricots   Apricot sauce

3 tablespoons (¼ cup)
apricot jam
8 fl. oz. (1 cup) water
½ tablespoon arrowroot
lemon juice and sugar to taste

Place the apricot jam and water in a saucepan. Bring to the boil, stirring constantly. Mix the arrowroot with a very little extra water, add to the saucepan, bring to the boil and cook until clear, stirring constantly.
Add the sugar and lemon juice to taste. Sieve the sauce.
Use as required.

Sauce aux fruits   Fruit sauce

Fruit purée
sugar
arrowroot

Place the fruit purée in a saucepan. Bring to the boil, add sugar to taste and stir until the sugar is dissolved. If the purée is very thin, thicken with 1 teaspoon arrowroot for every ½ pint (1¼ cups) purée. Mix the arrowroot with a little fruit juice or water before adding it to the pan. Bring to the boil and stir until the sauce clears. Serve as soon as possible.

Choux buns with fruit sauce

Pears with ice cream and chocolate sauce

note: the following fruits are most suitable for this sauce: currants, stoned (pitted) fruits, apples, berries.

Ham mousse

Hors d'oeuvres

'Hors d'oeuvres' is the French for appetizers. This means all the light delicious dishes which can precede the main course of a luncheon or dinner party. Sometimes hors d'oeuvres can be served as well as a soup although this does not always follow. The hors d'oeuvres is served before a soup course.

An hors d'oeuvres should never be served in large portions. It is merely a small daintily prepared dish to tempt your guests towards what is to come. Choose the dish carefully so that it will not clash with the other courses on the menu. Avoid serving more than one fish dish, or more than one course featuring the same meat or vegetable. Select the hors d'oeuvres to complement the menu in colour, texture and taste.

Some hors d'oeuvres can be served as a light luncheon on their own. Other chapters in the book include recipes which (if made in smaller quantities) could be served as hors d'oeuvres.

Hors d'oeuvres variés should be a selection of daintily prepared cold dishes of meat, fish, egg, fruit and vegetables. Serve at least four together, making sure that each complements the other in colour, flavour and texture. A suitable choice might be: rice salad, sardines, tomato, egg, radish; or sliced Continental sausage, orange sections, potato salad, cucumber. All the dishes must be carefully prepared and the food served in iced water, vinegar, a vinaigrette dressing or home made mayonnaise (see recipes pages 21 and 20), as appropriate to prevent it becoming dry. Guests help themselves to a little of each dish.

Tomato Skin and slice tomatoes thinly. Arrange them in a dish, sprinkle with vinaigrette dressing and a little finely chopped parsley.

Cucumber Score the skin at intervals with the prongs of a fork. Slice thinly, arrange in a dish and cover with vinaigrette dressing or vinegar. Decorate with thin slices of radish.

Celeriac Cut washed celeriac into julienne strips. Add enough home made mayonnaise to moisten. Serve.

Beetroot Peel and slice beetroot thinly. If you have some aspic cutters, cut the slices in fancy shapes. Arrange in a serving dish, sprinkle with vinaigrette dressing. Garnish with snipped chives.

Radish Slice washed and trimmed radishes very thinly. Arrange in a dish, cover with iced water. Garnish with fine cress.

Potato Dice cooked potato and mix it with enough home made mayonnaise to moisten. Serve garnished with chopped parsley or snipped chives.

Rice Mix hot cooked rice with enough vinaigrette dressing to moisten. Leave to cool. Add a little finely chopped red and green capsicum. Toss and serve.

Macedoine of Vegetable Mix diced cooked vegetables together gently (carrot, parsnip, celery, sweetcorn, peas, for example). Add enough home made mayonnaise to moisten. Serve garnished with finely chopped parsley.

Pineapple Cut pineapple in neat dice, chill. Serve topped with chopped mint.

Orange Peel orange, remove all the pith. Either slice thinly or cut into segments. Arrange in a dish, sprinkle with vinaigrette dressing and garnish with chopped mint. (This dish is extra delicious with a few halves of peeled and stoned grapes added.)

Cold Sausage (Charcuterie) Remove skin if necessary and slice thinly. Arrange in a serving dish and either sprinkle with vinaigrette dressing or coat in home made mayonnaise.

Ham Dice cooked ham, add enough home made mayonnaise to moisten. Serve garnished with chopped parsley or a sprinkling of cayenne pepper.

Sardines Arrange whole drained sardines in a dish. Sprinkle with vinaigrette dressing. Garnish with finely chopped parsley and cayenne pepper in lines.

Egg Hard boil an egg, allow to become cold. Slice in thin rounds. Arrange slices in a dish on a bed of shredded lettuce. Coat with home made mayonnaise and serve garnished with a sprinkling of cayenne pepper.

Shrimps or Prawns Peel shrimps or prawns, add enough home made mayonnaise to moisten. Serve on a bed of shredded lettuce garnished with fine cress and some of the heads.

Asperge à la hollandaise
Asparagus with hollandaise sauce

4 bundles asparagus (about 10 stalks in each)
sauce hollandaise (see recipe page 19)

Trim the asparagus, remove any hard woody stem and clean well in cold water. Cook in boiling salted water to cover for 15–20 minutes or until just tender. Drain. Remove the string tying the bundles. Serve each bundle of asparagus on a heated serving plate with a spoonful of sauce hollandaise at one end. It is possible to buy special asparagus dishes on which to serve asparagus, with a separate place for the sauce.

note: each asparagus stalk is picked up individually with the fingertips, dipped in the sauce and then eaten. Supply finger bowls of iced water.

variation: an equally delicious but simpler way of serving asparagus is to serve it with melted butter instead of sauce hollandaise.

serves 4

Avocat vinaigrette
Avocado pear with vinaigrette dressing

2 ripe avocado pears
4 tablespoons (good ¼ cup) sauce vinaigrette (see recipe page 21)
lettuce for serving

Cut the avocado pears in half lengthways. Remove the stones carefully. Spoon a little sauce over the cut surfaces to prevent them from discolouring.
Place each half of avocado pear on a bed of lettuce on individual serving dishes. Spoon the remaining sauce vinaigrette into the hollows left by the stone.
Serve chilled.

variation: mix the sauce vinaigrette with 8 oz. (2 cups) peeled prawns (shrimp) and fill into the avocado pear halves.

serves 4

Salade de melon et jambon
Melon and ham salad

1 small honeydew melon
4 slices Bayonne ham
lettuce
8 black olives

Remove the melon flesh from the skin with a parisienne (melon-ball) cutter and cut into dice. Roll the ham up and secure each roll with a cocktail stick.
Place a bed of lettuce in each of 4 individual serving dishes or on plates. Put the melon on the lettuce and top with the ham. Garnish each dish with 2 black olives.
Serve chilled.

note: bayonne ham is a raw smoked ham prepared in the South West of France. If it is not available, use parma, prosciutto or westphalia ham as they are very similar.

serves 4

Pamplemousse au gingembre
Grapefruit with ginger

2 large grapefruit
sherry
¼ teaspoon each ground ginger and ground nutmeg
1 tablespoon (1¼T) finely chopped preserved ginger (in syrup)
2 glacé cherries
serves 4

Peel the grapefruit and remove all the pith. Cut them into segments, carefully removing all the skin.
Arrange the segments in individual serving glasses. Sprinkle with sherry, ground ginger and ground nutmeg, mixed together. Decorate each glass with chopped ginger and half a glacé (candied) cherry.
Serve chilled. Serve sugar separately, if necessary.

Tomates farcies aux crevettes
Tomatoes stuffed with shrimps

4 large firm tomatoes
6 oz. (1½ cups) peeled shrimps
½ teaspoon dried basil
½ pint (1¼ cups) home made mayonnaise (see recipe page 20)
lettuce for serving

serves 4

Skin the tomatoes and stand them firmly, stalk end underneath. Cut off the tops, scoop out the pulp and pips carefully with a teaspoon. Combine shrimps and basil with the home made mayonnaise, then spoon into the tomato cases.
Place a bed of lettuce on 4 individual serving plates and top with the stuffed tomatoes.

note: skin the tomatoes by plunging them in boiling water for 1 minute. Place in cold water until cool enough to handle, then peel skin off with a knife.

Salade de tomates
Tomato salad

6 firm red tomatoes
3 tablespoons (¼ cup) sauce vinaigrette (see recipe page 21)
1 teaspoon chopped capers
1 teaspoon finely chopped gherkin
1 teaspoon finely chopped parsley
serves 4

Tomato salad is a very popular appetizer for a meal in France, especially around the Mediterranean where the tomatoes are large and luscious.

Skin the tomatoes and slice thinly. Arrange the slices in a serving dish.
Mix the sauce vinaigrette with the capers, gherkin and parsley. Pour over the tomatoes. Serve.

Escargots au beurre
Snails in butter

4 dozen snails
3 cloves garlic
3 oz. (6T) butter
3 tablespoons (¼ cup) chopped parsley
2 tablespoons (scant ¼ cup) fine white breadcrumbs
freshly ground black pepper

serves 4

Wash the snails, place them in a large saucepan and cover with cold water. Bring to the boil, simmer 15–20 minutes. Remove the snails from their shell, rinse shells and put back the snails. Crush the cloves of garlic, then add the butter, parsley, breadcrumbs and black pepper. Beat until smooth.
Place a little butter mixture into each shell on top of the snails.
Place snails on a heatproof dish and place in a very hot oven (450°F. Mark 8) until the butter is sizzling.
Serve immediately in the shells.

note: snails must be fasted for a week before cooking if they are gathered fresh. They have sometimes eaten things which would be poisonous to man. The day before cooking, wash them well and cover with salted water until needed.

Grenouilles à la Lyonnaise
Frog's legs lyonnaise

2×3⅔ oz. cans or 8 oz. fresh frogs legs
flour
salt and pepper
1 onion
2 oz. (4T) butter
1 teaspoon wine vinegar
chopped parsley for garnish

serves 4

Although frog's legs are not always considered such a delicacy outside France, they are nevertheless an ideal way to start a typical French meal. They can be cooked in a very wide variety of ways but the following recipe is particularly delicious.

Drain canned frog's legs. If fresh frog's legs are used, remove feet, skin them and skewer; soak in iced water for 6–8 hours, changing the water every 2 hours.
Season the flour with salt and pepper. Coat the frog's legs in flour. Slice the onion very thinly.
Melt the butter in a frying pan, add the onion rings and fry them until softened. Add the frog's legs to the pan and continue cooking for 2–3 minutes.
Place the onion and the frog's legs in a heated serving dish. Add the vinegar to the butter in pan and reheat. Sprinkle the frog's legs with parsley, pour the butter over and serve immediately.

Spooning half-set aspic over veal galantine

Galantine de veau Veal loaf

8 oz. minced lean veal
4 oz. pork sausage meat
4 oz. streaky bacon, chopped
3 oz. (1 cup) soft white breadcrumbs
salt and pepper
¼ teaspoon ground nutmeg
½ teaspoon dried mixed herbs
1 egg
2 tablespoons water
3 hard-boiled eggs, shelled
sauce chaudfroid (see recipe page 21)
extra aspic jelly (jello)
cucumber and radish for garnish

Mix together thoroughly the veal, sausage meat, bacon, breadcrumbs, salt and pepper, nutmeg, herbs, egg and water. Scald a pudding cloth by pouring boiling water through it. Spread the meat mixture on to the cloth and lay the eggs in the centre. Form into a short thick roll. Tie pudding cloth firmly. Cook in boiling water, to cover, for 2–2½ hours.
Press under a heavy weight until cold. Place on a cake rack and spoon the sauce chaudfroid over. When the sauce is set, cover with a layer of aspic. Garnish with thin rounds of cucumber and radish, dipped in aspic jelly (jello).

note: Veal Galantine can be made in a terrine or loaf tin. Cook as for Terrine de campagne (*overleaf*). The sauce chaudfroid and aspic may be omitted.

Blanchaille au naturel Fried whitebait

1 lb. whitebait
flour
salt
pepper
oil or fat for deep frying
lemon wedges and thin slices of brown bread and butter for serving

Whitebait are too small to be drawn, so make sure that they are as fresh as possible. They are a considered delicacy on the French coast—where they are prepared as soon as the day's catch of fish is sold. Do not wash them unless absolutely necessary and handle them as little as possible.

Remove weed and any grit from the whitebait. Mix the flour with salt and pepper and dredge the whitebait with it
Heat the oil until 375°F. (a ¼ inch dice of bread will brown in less than a minute) or fat until a faint blue haze rises from the surface. Place a handful of whitebait in the frying basket and fry for 2 minutes. Drain on absorbent kitchen paper. Continue until all the whitebait has been fried.
Just before serving, reheat oil or fat and refry all the whitebait together for 1–2 minutes or until crisp but not dry. Drain on absorbent kitchen paper.
Serve on individual heated serving plates sprinkled with extra salt and pepper. Garnish with lemon wedges. Serve the brown bread and butter separately.

serves 4

27

Mousse au jambon — Ham mousse

8 oz. ham
1 teaspoon tomato paste
¾ oz. (2¼ tablespoons) gelatine
¼ pint (⅝ cup) fond blanc (white stock, see recipe page 30)
¼ pint (⅝ cup) sauce béchamel (see recipe page 16)
salt and pepper
¼ pint (⅝ cup) double heavy cream
2 egg whites
serves 4

Mince the ham twice and beat very thoroughly with the tomato paste. Press through a wire sieve or cream in an electric blender. Dissolve the gelatine in the heated stock and allow to cool. Beat the béchamel sauce into the ham mixture with the stock and gelatine, season. Allow to cool until beginning to set. Half whip the cream. Whisk the egg whites until stiff. Fold the cream and egg whites into the ham mixture.

Spoon into individual serving dishes or a prepared soufflé case (see page 43).

Put in a cool place until set. Garnish as desired.

Pâté normand — Pâté Normandy-style

8 oz. minced pork
8 oz. minced veal
4 oz. minced pigs tongue
4 oz. minced pigs liver
4 oz. minced bacon
2 oz. minced pork fat
3 cloves garlic, crushed
¼ teaspoon each ground nutmeg, ground cloves, dried thyme, dried basil
½ teaspoon salt
¼ teaspoon freshly ground black pepper
¼ pint (⅝ cup) dry sherry
8 rashers streaky bacon

Mix all the ingredients, except the rashers of streaky bacon, thoroughly. Line a terrine with 6 of the bacon rashers, fill with the meat mixture and press down very firmly. Cover with the remaining bacon rashers. Cover the pâté with aluminium foil and cook in a moderate oven (350°F. Mark 4) for 1½ hours.

Cool. Place cooked pâté in a cool place or in the refrigerator for 6–8 hours before turning out and cutting.

note: the meats may have to be minced 2–3 times to get the necessary smoothness.

Rillettes de Porc — Potted pork

1 lb. belly pork
8 oz. pork fat
1 clove garlic, crushed
1 teaspoon chopped mixed herbs
½ teaspoon salt
¼ teaspoon freshly ground black pepper
3 tablespoons (¼ cup) water

Chop the meat into short thin strips. Dice the pork fat. Mix with all the remaining ingredients and pile into an earthenware or enamelled dish. Cover with aluminium foil.

Bake rillettes in a very slow oven (275°F. Mark 1) for 3–4 hours.

The pork should be very soft and swimming in its own fat. Adjust the seasoning.

Drain off all the fat. Mash rillettes thoroughly with a fork. Pack into small earthenware pots, covering with the fat. Cover with aluminium foil and store in the refrigerator.

Terrine de campagne — Terrine country-style

8 oz. fat belly pork, minced
4 oz. minced lean veal
8 oz. minced chicken livers
2 tablespoons (scant ¼ cup) dry white wine
2 tablespoons (scant ¼ cup) brandy
1 oz. pork fat, diced
3 black peppercorns
3 juniper berries
1 clove garlic, crushed
¼ teaspoon ground mace
½ teaspoon salt
8 rashers streaky bacon

A terrine is the mould in which a pâté is sometimes cooked. Hence the word terrine in a recipe title indicates that it is a pâté cooked in a terrine.

Mix all the ingredients (except the bacon rashers) together very thoroughly.

Line a terrine with 6 rashers of the bacon. Fill with the meat mixture, press down well. Top with the remaining bacon rashers. Stand terrine in a roasting pan with water 1 inch deep. Cook in a slow oven (300°F. Mark 2) for 1½ hours or until the meat starts to shrink away from the edge.

Cool, press with a heavy weight and store in the refrigerator. Seal with melted pork fat if the terrine is to be kept for more than a week.

Soups

There are too many French soups to be able to mention them all but certainly the French can claim some of the most delicious in the world. Every French housewife knows the value of having some good stock always on hand. She is then ready to produce, almost at a moment's notice, practically any soup you can mention with its own individual home made flavour. (See introduction).

Soup is served with nearly every meal in France. Whether it is the lightest lunch or the most elaborate dinner party, there is a suitable soup for the occasion: a substantial garbure for a winter supper or a vichyssoise for a smaller luncheon, consommé en gelée for a summer dinner party or potage à la hollandaise for a formal winter dinner – the suggestions are almost endless.

A tureen is the best container in which to serve soup as it can sit decoratively on the table and you can serve second helpings if required. It is a good idea to have two types of soup dishes, one for the family soups, with a wide top, and small bouillon cups for lighter, more delicate soups.

Fond brun   Beef bone stock

2 lb. beef bones
1 onion
1 carrot
1 turnip
1 leek
4 pints (10 cups) water
½ teaspoon salt
4 peppercorns
½ teaspoon meat extract

Wash the bones and trim off excess fat. Prepare the vegetables and chop them into large pieces. Place all the ingredients in a large saucepan.
Bring the stock to the boil, cover and simmer slowly for 4–5 hours. Skim frequently.
Strain the stock. Either allow it to become cold and remove the fat or lay strips of absorbent kitchen paper across the surface of the hot stock to remove excess fat.
Use as required.

note: for a richer stock, add 4 oz. shin of beef, minced or finely chopped.

Fond blanc   White or veal stock

2 lb. veal bones
4 oz. veal, chopped
½ teaspoon salt
4 white peppercorns
4 pints (10 cups) cold water
1 onion
1 stick celery
1 carrot

Wash the bones, remove excess fat. Place the bones, meat, salt, peppercorns and water in a large saucepan. Bring to the boil slowly, skim.
Prepare the vegetables and chop roughly. Add to the pan. Cover the saucepan tightly. Simmer the stock 3–4 hours.
Strain the stock and cool it. Remove the fat when the stock is cold.

note: more water may be added to the bones and vegetables to make a 'second stock'. Simmer for a further 2–3 hours.

Fond blanc de volaille   Chicken stock

carcass of 1 cooked chicken
2 pints (5 cups) water
1 teaspoon salt
4 peppercorns
1 carrot
1 onion stuck with 4 cloves
1 stick celery
bouquet garni

Prepare the stock as for fond blanc (above). Break the chicken carcass into small pieces if necessary. Simmer for 1–1½ hours.

Court bouillon

1½ pints (3¾ cups) water
½ pint (1¼ cups) white wine
1 onion, sliced thinly
2 shallots, chopped
bouquet garni
1 teaspoon salt
6 white peppercorns

An aromatic liquor in which meat, fish and various vegetables are cooked.

Place all the ingredients into a saucepan. Cover, bring to the boil and simmer for 30–40 minutes. Strain.
Use as required.

note: the wine can be omitted and ¼ pint (⅝ cup) vinegar used instead.

Fond de poisson   Fish stock

Make the court bouillon as shown above but add a fish head and some bones to the saucepan.

Consommé

2 pints (5 cups) fond brun (beef bone stock)
2 egg whites
2 washed egg shells, crushed
4 oz. beef (lean shin is good), finely chopped
4 peppercorns
½ teaspoon salt
3 tablespoons (¼ cup) sherry
meat extract if necessary

serves 4

(Enriched, concentrated and clarified meat stock)
Allow the stock to become cold, then remove any fat.
Half whisk the egg whites.
Place the stock in a large saucepan and heat it slowly until nearly boiling.
Add the meat, egg whites, egg shells, peppercorns and salt. Bring the stock to the boil, whisking constantly with a fork or wire whisk. Simmer very gently, without whisking, for 1 hour. Strain through a scalded jelly (jello) cloth or bag into a scalded bowl. Add the sherry. The consommé should be a clear deep amber colour. A little meat extract can be used to adjust the colouring if necessary. Reheat, then add the chosen garnish. Serve very hot.

note: jelly (jello) cloths and bags can be bought from shops selling good kitchen equipment. Scald by pouring boiling water through.

Consommé brunoise

Beef bone consommé

1 tablespoon (1¼T) finely diced carrot
1 tablespoon (1¼T) finely diced turnip
1 tablespoon (1¼T) finely diced leek
1 tablespoon (1¼T) finely diced celery
1 quantity consommé
serves 4

Prepare the vegetables and cook in boiling water until tender.
Place a little of each vegetable in the bottom of 4 soup cups. Pour on piping hot consommé. Serve as soon as possible.

Consommé à la julienne

1 tablespoon (1¼T) matchstick shreds carrot
1 tablespoon (1¼T) matchstick shreds turnip
1 tablespoon (1¼T) matchstick shreds green leek
1 tablespoon (1¼T) matchstick shreds celery
1 quantity consommé
serves 4

Prepare and serve as for consommé brunoise.

Consommé au vermicelle

½ oz. vermicelli
1 quantity consommé
serves 4

Cook the vermicelli in boiling water until tender. Rinse well in hot water. Put a little vermicelli in each of 4 soup cups, pour in very hot consommé and serve as soon as possible.

Consommé en gelée

Cold jellied consommé

serves 4

Make the consommé as given above. When making the fond brun add a veal bone to the beef bones. Consommé gelée should gel on its own accord with no added gelatine. The veal bone will help in this.
Serve cold but not chilled, garnished with slices of lemon.

Consommé madrilène
Consommé with tomatoes

1 lb. red tomatoes
1 quantity consommé
½ oz. vermicelli, cooked
chervil

Chop the tomatoes roughly and place them in a saucepan with a little water, if necessary. Heat until boiling, cook, stirring until the tomatoes are pulpy and leave the sides of the pan.
Make the consommé as shown above. Add the cooked tomatoes 15 minutes before the cooking time is completed. Strain in the usual way. Place a little vermicelli and a pinch of chervil in the bottom of each of 4 soup cups. Pour the hot consommé on top, serve as soon as possible.

serves 4

Bisque de homard
Lobster bisque

1 large carrot
1 large onion
2 oz. (4T) butter
1 small lobster
3 tablespoons (¼ cup) brandy
½ pint (1¼ cups) white wine
4 oz. (½ cup) rice
3 pints (7½ cups) court bouillon
(see page 30)
¼ pint (⅝ cup) single (light) cream
salt and cayenne pepper
parsley for garnish

Peel and chop the carrot and onion into small pieces. Melt 1 oz. butter in a large saucepan, add the vegetables and cook gently, stirring, 2–3 minutes. Split the lobster in half lengthways, remove the coral and place the lobster, cut side down, on the vegetables. Cover the pan, cook 2 minutes.
Heat the brandy, ignite and pour over the lobster with the wine. Cover the saucepan tightly and cook very gently for 15 minutes, lightly shaking the pan occasionally.
Cook the rice in 1 pint (2½ cups) boiling court bouillon for about 30 minutes or until very soft.
Shell the lobster, cut up the meat and place in a bowl with the coral, drained vegetables (reserve liquor), and rice. Pound very thoroughly to a soft pulp. (This can be done in an electric blender; add the reserved liquor for this process.) If done by hand, add the reserved liquor after the pounding is completed. Add ½ pint (1¼ cups) court bouillon and sieve.
Add the remaining court bouillon, pour into a clean saucepan. Reheat and whisk in the remaining 1 oz. butter in small pieces. Add the cream, then season with salt and cayenne pepper. Reheat, if necessary, without boiling.

serves 6–8 Serve hot, garnished with a small sprig of parsley.

Potage à la hollandaise
Hollandaise soup

1 oz. (2T) butter
1 oz. (¼ cup) plain (all purpose) flour
1 pint (2½ cups) fond blanc (white stock)
1 onion
bouquet garni
1 egg yolk
¼ pint (⅝ cup) single (light) cream
cucumber, carrot, celery and peas for garnish

Melt the butter in a saucepan, add the flour and cook gently, stirring constantly, until the roux has a 'honeycombed' appearance but is not browned. Add the stock and bring to the boil, stirring, then add the whole onion and the bouquet garni and simmer for 10–15 minutes. Remove the saucepan from the heat, cover and put aside for 10 minutes. Remove and discard the onion and bouquet garni. Mix the egg yolk with the cream, add to the soup and reheat very gently without boiling.
Cut the cucumber and carrot into small balls with a ball-cutter. Dice celery finely. Make about 1 tablespoon of each vegetable and add 1 tablespoon peas. Cook the carrot in boiling salted water for 2 minutes, add celery, cook another 3 minutes, add cucumber and peas and cook a further 2 minutes. Drain and rinse the vegetables in cold running water.
Add the garnish to the soup and reheat without boiling.

serves 4 Serve piping hot.

French onion soup

Crème de concombres — Cream of cucumber soup

1 large cucumber
1 pint (2½ cups) fond brun (white stock)
¾ oz. (1½T) butter
¾ oz. (3 tablespoons) plain flour
3 tablespoons (¼ cup) milk
3 tablespoons (¼ cup) single (light) cream
salt and pepper
green colouring
watercress for garnish

Wash the cucumber. Removing about ¾ of the skin, chop the cucumber into large pieces. Bring a large saucepan of water to boiling point, add the cucumber, cook for 1 minute, then drain well. Pour the stock into a saucepan, add the cucumber and bring to the boil. Simmer, covered, for about 20 minutes or until the cucumber is very tender. Rub through a sieve or purée in an electric blender. Melt the butter in a clean saucepan, add the flour and cook, stirring constantly until the flour is cooked (the roux will have a 'honeycomb' appearance). Add the cucumber purée, bring to the boil, stirring constantly, and simmer 3–4 minutes.
Cool slightly, stir in the milk and cream. Season with salt and pepper to taste. Add a little green colouring if necessary. Reheat without boiling.

Serve very hot, garnished with sprigs of watercress or thin rounds of cucumber.

serves 4–6

note: Crème de Concombres can also be served chilled.

Soupe à l'oignon — French onion soup

1 lb. onions
2 oz. (¼ cup) butter
salt and black pepper
½ teaspoon mustard
2 teaspoons plain flour
1½ pints (3¾ cups) fond brun (beef bone stock)
¼ pint (⅝ cup) white wine
4–6 slices French bread, lightly toasted
2 oz. (½ cup) grated Parmesan cheese

serves 4–6

Peel and finely slice the onions. Melt the butter in a large saucepan, then add the onion rings, salt, pepper and mustard. Cook over a very gentle heat, stirring occasionally until onion is browned (this will take 20–30 minutes).
Add the flour and stir until smooth. Add the stock and white wine, stirring constantly, then bring to the boil and simmer for 30 minutes. Taste and adjust seasoning.
Place slices of toasted bread on the bottom of a soup tureen or in individual soup bowls, sprinkling with cheese. Pour hot soup carefully on to bread.
Place under a hot grill until the cheese is beginning to brown. Serve immediately.

Crème vichyssoise   Cold leek soup

1 lb. potatoes
4 leeks (white part only)
1 onion
2 oz. (4T) butter
2½ pints (6¼ cups) fond blanc (white stock)
¼ pint (⅝ cup) double (heavy) cream
1 tablespoon snipped chives
pinch of nutmeg
salt and pepper to taste

serves 4–6

Prepare the vegetables, slice thinly.
Melt the butter in a large saucepan, then add the leeks and the onion. Fry, stirring, until softened. Add the stock and the potatoes, bring to the boil, cover the pan and simmer for 30–40 minutes. Press the soup through a sieve with a wooden spoon, or purée in an electric blender. Allow to become quite cold.
Stir in the cream and chives. Season with nutmeg and salt and pepper to taste. Add a little extra stock if the soup is too thick.
Serve cold in chilled soup cups.

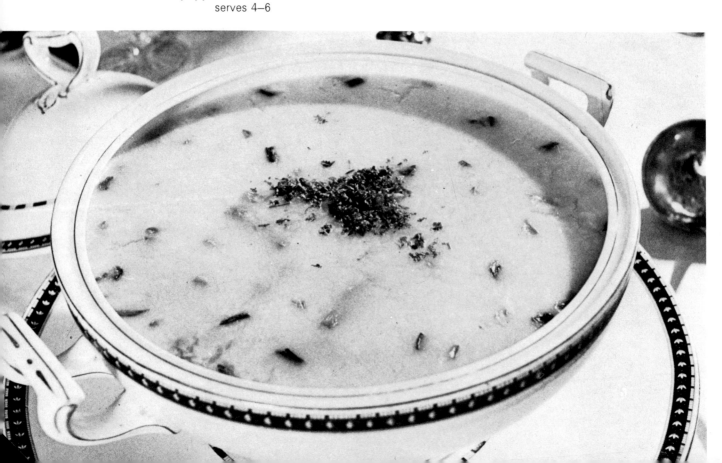

Garbure
Classic peasant vegetable soup

2 carrots
2 onions
1 small turnip
¼ cabbage
2 leeks
4 sticks celery
2 potatoes
1 oz. (2T) butter
2 tablespoons (2½T) olive oil
7 oz. (1 cup) cooked haricot beans
4 pints (10 cups) fond brun (beef bone stock)
6 slices French bread
2 oz. (½ cup) grated gruyère cheese
salt and pepper
serves 6

Prepare the fresh vegetables and slice thinly. Melt the butter with 1 tablespoon (1¼T) of olive oil in a large saucepan, then add the prepared vegetables. Cover the saucepan and cook very gently for 20–25 minutes. Add the beans and stock. Cover the saucepan, bring to the boil and simmer 20–30 minutes or until vegetables are very tender. Press the soup through a sieve with a wooden spoon or purée in an electric blender. Return it to the saucepan and continue simmering, uncovered, until it begins to thicken.

Heat the remaining 1 tablespoon (1¼T) oil in a small frying pan and fry the slices of bread until golden on both sides. Spread each slice with a little soup and sprinkle with cheese.

Season the soup. Pour into a soup tureen or on to individual soup plates. Serve piping hot topped with the croûtes of bread and cheese.

Purée de tomate
Thick tomato soup

2 lb. tomatoes
1 oz. (2T) butter
1 oz. bacon, chopped
1 onion, chopped
1 carrot, chopped
1 stick celery, chopped
2 pints (7 cups) fond blanc (white stock)
1 bayleaf
10 white peppercorns
3 tablespoons (¼ cup) cornflour (cornstarch)
3 tablespoons (¼ cup) milk
1 tablespoon (1¼T) single (light) cream
salt and sugar to taste
finely chopped parsley for garnish
serves 4–6

Wash the tomatoes and chop them roughly. Melt the butter in a large saucepan, add the bacon and fry until softened. Add the onion, carrot and celery and fry gently until softened but not browned. Add the tomatoes, stock, bayleaf and peppercorns. Bring to the boil and simmer very gently in an uncovered pan for 1½ hours.

Sieve the soup, pressing it through the sieve well with a wooden spoon. Mix the cornflour with the milk. Place the tomato purée and cornflour in a clean saucepan, bring to the boil and simmer 3–4 minutes, stirring constantly. Add the cream, taste and adjust seasoning, adding salt and sugar as necessary.

Reheat without boiling. Serve piping hot, garnishing with chopped parsley.

Velouté de volaille
Creamed chicken soup

1 pint (2½ cups) fond blanc de volaille (chicken stock)
½ oz. (2 tablespoons) cornflour (cornstarch)
¼ pint (⅝ cup) milk
2 egg yolks
3 tablespoons (¼ cup) double (heavy) cream
nutmeg, salt and pepper
1 breast of chicken, cooked
serves 4

Strain the stock, pour it into a saucepan and bring it to the boil. Mix the cornflour with the milk and gradually add to the stock. Re-boil, then cook 2–3 minutes.

Mix the egg yolks with the cream, adding the nutmeg, salt and pepper. Add to the saucepan, reheat and cook gently until it begins to thicken, without boiling.

Cut the chicken breast into julienne strips, and add to the soup. Adjust seasoning.

Serve in a hot tureen or individual soup cups.

Preparing and chopping the leeks

Cold leek soup

Eggs play a tremendous part in French cuisine. They are
not necessarily served at breakfast time (we all know that
a French petit déjeuner consists of a large cup of coffee
and rolls and butter) but are sometimes served for lunch
or supper or as part of a dinner party menu.
Omelettes, soufflés, pancakes and savoury flans can all be
served as hors d'oeuvres. They also make a superb
luncheon if teamed with crisp French bread, a green
salad with homemade mayonnaise and perhaps a
steaming hot bowl of soup to start.
The number of recipes is endless, but all of them produce
a light dish, under rather than overcooked and extremely
nutritious.

A selection of egg dishes

Oeufs au beurre noir
Fried eggs with black butter

4 oz. (8T) butter
4 eggs
½ tablespoon (¾T) wine vinegar
1 tablespoon (1¼T) finely chopped parsley

serves 4

Melt 3 oz. (6T) butter in a frying pan. Break the eggs into the pan and cook gently, basting the eggs with the butter to cook the tops. Place the cooked eggs on a heated serving plate. Add the remaining butter to the pan and cook until a deep brown (be careful it does not burn). Add vinegar and parsley, stirring quickly, then pour over eggs. Serve immediately.

Oeufs sur le plat
Eggs cooked on a plate

2 oz. (4T) butter
4 eggs

This dish is traditionally cooked in a shallow copper or earthenware dish with handles or 'ears'. There are innumerable variations on the basic recipe. Serve as a light lunch or supper dish.

Melt 1 oz. (2T) of the butter in a heatproof dish (individual dishes can also be used), and heat until sizzling. Melt the remaining butter in a small saucepan.
Break each egg carefully into the heatproof dish and spoon a little melted butter over each yolk. Bake in a very hot oven (450°F. Mark 7) for 3–4 minutes or until the whites are just set and the yolks still runny.

serves 4

Serve immediately.

Niçoise
Chop roughly 2 sticks celery, 2 tomatoes (skinned and deseeded) and 2 anchovies. Cook with 1 tablespoon olive oil in the heatproof dish, until softened. Add eggs and bake as above.

Bercy
Cook eggs as above. Pour over a little sauce bercy (see recipe page 20) and serve immediately.

Lorraine
Remove the rind and rust from 2 rashers of bacon. Cut into dice and cook in boiling water for 3–4 minutes. Heat the butter in the base of the heatproof dish, add a layer of bacon then a layer of 1 oz. grated gruyère cheese. Add the eggs, pour the melted butter over, season. Bake for 5–7 minutes in a moderate oven (350°F. Mark 4).

note: for a richer dish, substitute a teaspoonful of cream for the melted butter poured over the egg yolks.

Eggs Lorraine

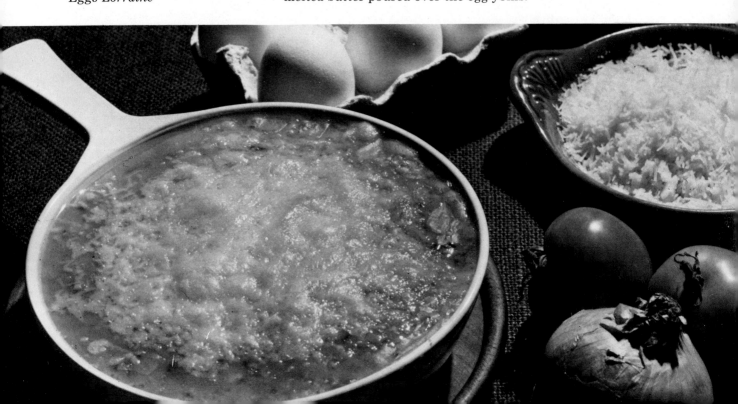

Oeufs florentine Eggs with spinach

12 oz. (1½ cups) frozen or cooked spinach
½ oz. (1T) butter
salt, pepper and ground nutmeg
oil for frying
6 eggs
½ pint (1¼ cups) sauce mornay (see recipe page 17)

Cook the spinach in the minimum of water, in a large saucepan. Drain very thoroughly, beat in the butter and season to taste.
Heat a little oil in a frying pan, add an egg and fry it gently, spooning a little of the hot oil over the yolk to set the top. Remove and drain well. Cook all the remaining eggs in the same way.
Place the eggs carefully on the spinach in a heatproof serving dish. Coat the entire dish with the prepared sauce mornay. Grill quickly under a hot grill until beginning to brown.
Serve immediately.

variations: use other bases under the fried eggs. Oeufs Niçoise and Oeufs Lorraine can be made using the ingredients given as variations in Oeufs sur la Plat and using them as above. If you like, sprinkle extra grated cheese on the top before grilling.

serves 6

Oeufs en cocotte à la crème Eggs baked with cream

4 tablespoons (5T) cream
8 eggs
½ oz. (1T) butter
salt
freshly ground black pepper

Cook these eggs in individual heatproof dishes or 'cocottes'.

Heat the cream in a small saucepan until boiling. Warm the cocottes and pour 1 tablespoon (1¼T) of cream into each. Add the eggs carefully (2 to each cocotte) so as not to break the yolks. Dot each egg with small pieces of butter. Season.
Stand the cocottes in a roasting pan with hot water coming halfway up the sides. Cover with aluminium foil.
Bake in a moderate oven (350°F. Mark 4) for 6–8 minutes or until the whites are set and the yolks are creamy.
Serve immediately.

serves 4

Oeufs au gratin Eggs baked with breadcrumbs and ham

2 oz. ham
4 tablespoons (good ¼ cup) fresh white breadcrumbs
salt and freshly ground black pepper
¼ teaspoon dry mustard
1 oz. (2T) butter
1 tablespoon (1¼T) hot milk
4 eggs

Chop the ham and mix with the breadcrumbs and seasonings. Melt ½ oz. of the butter and add it to the ham mixture with the milk. Mix well.
Reserve 2 tablespoons (2½T) of the ham mixture, then place the remainder in the base of a heatproof dish. Make four indentations and break an egg carefully into each. Scatter reserved mixture on top. Dot with small pieces of remaining butter.
Bake in a moderate oven (350°F. Mark 4) for 5–7 minutes or until eggs are set.
Serve immediately.

serves 4

Oeufs brouillés aux tomates Scrambled eggs with tomatoes

2 tomatoes
1 tablespoon (1¼T) olive oil
1 shallot, finely chopped
1 oz. (2T) butter
1 tablespoon (1¼T) milk
4 eggs
salt and pepper
chopped parsley for garnish

Blanche the tomatoes in boiling water, remove skin and pips. Chop roughly. Heat the olive oil in a small saucepan, fry the shallot until it has softened then add the tomatoes. Cook for 2–3 minutes, stirring constantly.
Melt the butter in a saucepan. Beat the milk and eggs together and season. Add the eggs to the butter and cook, stirring constantly over a low heat, until the mixture is creamy.
Place the scrambled eggs on a heated dish, make a hollow in the centre. Spoon the tomato mixture on to the eggs and garnish with finely chopped parsley.
Serve immediately.

serves 4

Oeufs mollets à la crécy

Soft-boiled eggs with carrots

3 carrots
2 oz. (4T) butter
½ pint (1¼ cups) sauce béchamel
(see recipe page 16)
4 eggs
salt and pepper
2 tablespoons fresh white
breadcrumbs
1 tablespoon (1¼T) melted butter

serves 4

Oeufs mollets can be served in many ways. 'A la Crécy' they make a good light supper dish or can be served as an appetizer.

Peel the carrots and grate. Place the butter in a small saucepan, melt it gently then add the prepared carrot. Cover pan and cook very, very gently for 10–15 minutes or until the carrot is soft. Prepare sauce béchamel.

Boil a large saucepan of water. Add the eggs (in their shells) and cook them for exactly 4 minutes. Immerse them in cold water. Carefully remove the egg shells.

Season the carrots and place an equal amount in each of four small individual heatproof dishes. Place the cooked eggs on top and coat with the sauce béchamel. Sprinkle the breadcrumbs on the sauce and pour a little melted butter over.

Place dishes under a very hot grill until tops are lightly tinted brown. Serve immediately.

Piperade

Basque egg and vegetables

12 oz. tomatoes
2 green peppers
1 shallot
2 tablespoons (scant ¼ cup)
olive oil
2 cloves garlic, crushed
4 eggs
3 tablespoons (¼ cup) milk
salt and pepper
4 rounds fried bread
serves 4–6

Skin the tomatoes, remove the seeds and chop. Remove seeds and membranes from the peppers and cut into dice. Peel and chop the shallot finely. Heat the olive oil and fry the shallot and garlic until beginning to colour. Add the peppers, cook gently for 4–5 minutes. Add the tomato and simmer uncovered until the tomato is pulpy, stirring occasionally.

Beat the eggs and milk together, season, add them to saucepan and cook gently, stirring, for 2–4 minutes or until the eggs are creamy. Spoon the egg mixture on to the rounds of fried bread. Serve immediately on a heated serving plate.

Crêpes

Pancakes

4 oz. (1 cup) plain (all
purpose) flour
salt
1 egg
½ pint (1¼ cups) milk
4 tablespoons (¼–½ cup) clarified
butter or lard

makes about 8×7 inch crêpes

Savoury crêpes are made from exactly the same pancake batter as sweet crêpes. They can be served with a wide variety of fillings as appetizers or for a light lunch or supper dish.

Sift the flour with a pinch of salt into a mixing bowl. Make a well in the centre and add the egg. Using a wooden spoon, mix the egg and gradually incorporate the flour from around the well. Beat, adding the milk gradually until all the flour is blended. Stir in the remaining milk.

Heat about ½ tablespoon clarified butter in a 7 inch diameter frying pan. Drain off excess.

Add about 1 large tablespoon of batter to the frying pan, tilting pan to spread the batter evenly and cook until the surface is bubbly.

Slide a palette knife under the crêpe, loosen and then turn it over. Cook until underside is lightly browned.

Cool the cooked crêpes on a clean tea towel. They can be stacked in piles of 4 or 6 for storage in the refrigerator and also freeze well if required.

Crêpes florentine — Pancakes with spinach

8 cooked crêpes (see above)
2 onions, finely chopped
2 rashers streaky bacon, cut into strips
1½ oz. (3T) butter
1×14 oz. packet frozen chopped spinach
1 oz. (¼ cup) plain (all purpose) flour
¼ pint (⅝ cup) milk
2 tablespoons (2½T) single (light) cream
salt and pepper

serves 4

Prepare the crêpes.
Place the onion, bacon and ½ oz. (1T) of the butter in a saucepan. Fry until the onion and bacon are softened. Add the frozen spinach, cover pan tightly and cook for 5 minutes on a high heat. Uncover, stir and cook for a further 4 minutes, stirring occasionally until dry. (It will hiss loudly when sufficiently dry.)
Melt the remaining 1 oz. (2T) butter in a clean saucepan, stir in the flour and cook for 2 minutes. Remove from the heat and add the milk gradually, stirring constantly. Return to the heat, bring to the boil and boil for 2 minutes, stirring constantly. Add the prepared spinach mixture with the cream. Season to taste and combine thoroughly.
Place the filling on the crêpes, down the middle. Roll up carefully. Serve immediately or reheat by placing the crêpes in an ovenproof dish, cover with foil and place in a moderate oven (350°F. Mark 4) for 15 minutes.

Crêpes aux crevettes provençale — Prawn pancakes provençale

8 cooked crêpes (see above)
1 onion, finely chopped
1 oz. (2T) butter
1 green pepper, chopped
8 oz. tomatoes, skinned and chopped
6 oz. peeled prawns (shrimp)
1 clove garlic, crushed
salt and freshly ground black pepper
6 black olives, pitted
serves 4

Prepare the crêpes.
Place the onion and butter in a small saucepan. Fry the onion gently until softened. Add the pepper and continue cooking for 5 minutes. Add the tomatoes, prawns (shrimp), garlic and seasonings. Cover the cook gently for 10 minutes.
Place the filling equally on each cool or cold pancake. Roll up and place in a greased ovenproof dish. Cover with foil and cook in a moderate oven (350°F. Mark 4) for 15 minutes.
Serve garnished with chopped black olives.

Crêpes aux rognons — Kidney pancakes

8 cooked crêpes (see above)
4 lambs' kidneys
6 rashers streaky bacon
oil if necessary
1 onion, thinly sliced
½ oz. (2 tablespoons) plain (all purpose) flour
¼ pint (⅝ cup) chicken soup
salt and freshly ground black pepper
1 tablespoon (1¼T) tomato paste
1 tablespoon (1¼T) sherry
¼ teaspoon chopped dried basil
chopped parsley and bacon rolls (rashers of bacon rolled up and secured with a toothpick) for garnish
serves 4

Prepare the crêpes.
Skin the kidneys, remove the cores and slice thinly. Remove the rind from the bacon and cut into dice. Fry the bacon in a saucepan until golden. Remove, add the kidneys and cook quickly for 2–3 minutes, remove. Add a little oil if necessary, fry the onion until browned, sprinkle with the flour and continue cooking for 2–3 minutes, stirring constantly. Add stock, bring to the boil and simmer for 1 minute. Add all the remaining ingredients (except garnish) to the pan, including the bacon and kidneys, bring to the boil, cover and simmer for 15–20 minutes.
Place the filling equally on each cooled or cold crêpe. Roll each crêpe and place in an ovenproof dish. Cover with aluminium foil and reheat in a moderate oven (350°F Mark 4) for 15 minutes.
Serve garnished with chopped parsley and grilled bacon rolls.

Cooking an omelette
(a) With a fork the egg mixture is drawn from the
sides to the middle of the pan, allowing the
omelette to cook quickly.

(b) The cooked omelette is folded over in half,
then gently shaken out on to a heated plate.

Omelette

2 eggs
1 tablespoon (1¼T) water
salt and pepper
½ oz. (1T) butter

Break the eggs into a bowl and whisk very lightly with a fork until
the whites and yolks are mixed but not frothy. Stir in the water and
seasonings.
Melt the butter in an omelette pan (use one with a 6 inch diameter
base) and heat until just beginning to brown. Add the egg mixture
and cook rapidly, using a fork to stir the mixture. Bring some of the
cooked mixture to the centre, allowing the uncooked egg to come
into contact with the pan. Continue cooking until the top is lightly
set and the underside is a light golden brown. Fold the omelette in
half, slide it on to a heated serving plate.
Serve immediately.

note: a filling is frequently added to an omelette just before it is
folded. An omelette 'aux fines herbes' however has the chopped mixed
herbs actually added to the egg mixture before cooking.

serves 1

Omelette au fromage

Cheese omelette

Add 1 oz. (¼ cup) finely grated cheese to the omelette, just before
folding.

Omelette au jambon et champignon

Ham and mushroom omelette

Melt ½ oz. (1T) butter in a small saucepan, add 1 oz. (¼ cup) finely
diced ham, fry for 2–3 minutes. Wash 1 oz. button mushrooms, slice
thinly, add to the pan and continue cooking for a further 2–3
minutes. Season to taste, add 1 teaspoon finely chopped parsley. Add
filling to the omelette just before folding.

Omelette parmentier

Potato omelette

Cut a small cooked potato into thin slices. Melt 1 oz. (2T) butter in a
frying pan and fry potato until crisp and golden. Sprinkle with
¼ teaspoon chopped dried rosemary. Add to the omelette just before
folding.

Omelette aux crevettes

Prawn (shrimp) omelette

Prepare the prawn (shrimp) filling as for Crêpes aux Crevettes
Provençales. Add the filling to the omelette just before folding.

Soufflé au fromage — Cheese soufflé

2½ oz. (5T) butter
2 tablespoons (2½T) fresh white breadcrumbs
1½ oz. (⅜ cup) plain (all purpose) flour
scant ½ pint (1⅛ cups) milk
4 egg yolks
2 oz. (½ cup) grated Parmesan cheese
1 oz. (¼ cup) grated gruyère cheese
pinch cayenne pepper
pinch freshly ground black pepper
½ teaspoon salt
5 egg whites

serves 4

Using ½ oz. (1T) of the butter, grease a 6 inch soufflé dish. Cut a double strip of greaseproof paper, long enough to go around the soufflé dish and wide enough to stand 2 inches above the edge of the dish. Grease the top 2 inches of one side of the paper. Tie the paper around the dish, greased side inside. Sprinkle the breadcrumbs around the inside of the dish.

Melt the remaining butter in a saucepan, add the flour and cook gently, stirring constantly for 2–3 minutes until 'honeycombed' in appearance but not browned. Add milk, bring to the boil, stirring constantly and simmer 2–3 minutes. Cool slightly, beat in the egg yolks one at a time, then add the grated cheeses and seasonings. Whisk the egg whites until they stand in stiff peaks. Beat 1 tablespoon (1¼T) egg white into the saucepan mixture. Then gently fold in the remaining egg whites.

Pour the soufflé mixture into the prepared dish.

Bake in a moderately hot oven (375°F. Mark 5) for 35–40 minutes or until well risen, firm and golden. Remove greasproof paper. Serve immediately.

Soufflé aux épinards — Spinach soufflé

Omit cheeses, breadcrumbs and cayenne pepper. Use instead 1 lb. spinach (cooked, well-drained and very finely chopped), 2 oz. (½ cup) grated gruyère cheese, 1 shallot (peeled and grated), and ¼ teaspoon grated nutmeg.

Soufflé aux champignons — Mushroom soufflé

Omit breadcrumbs, gruyère cheese and cayenne pepper. Use instead 8 oz. mushrooms (finely chopped and sautéd in a little butter), 1 shallot (peeled and grated), 1 teaspoon lemon juice and ¼ teaspoon grated nutmeg.

Making a soufflé
(a) Milk is added to a mixture of flour and melted butter.
(b) The egg yolks, grated cheeses and seasoning are gradually added.
(c) The egg whites are whisked until very stiff, then folded into the sauce mixture.
(d) The mixture is poured into the prepared soufflé dish, three-quarters filling it, then baked in the oven.
(e) The finished soufflé should be well risen, firm and golden.

a

b

c

d

e

Quiche lorraine
Cheese, egg and bacon flan

4 oz. pâte brisée (see recipe page 119)
2 eggs
2 oz. (½ cup) grated gruyère cheese
¼ pint (⅝ cup) single (light) cream
salt and pepper
1 oz. (2T) butter
4 rashers streaky bacon, diced
1 onion, finely sliced

serves 4–6

Make the pastry and line a 7 inch diameter plain flan ring standing on a baking tray.

Beat the eggs and cheese together with the cream, salt and pepper.

Melt the butter in a frying pan and fry the bacon and onion until beginning to brown.

Spread the bacon and onion over the base of the uncooked flan, then pour in the egg and cream mixture. Bake in a moderate oven (350°F. Mark 4) for 20–25 minutes or until golden brown and firm to the touch.

Serve immediately, while still puffed up.

Tarte à l'oignon — Onion tart

4 oz. pâté brisée (see recipe page 119)
1½ lb. onions
2 eggs
1 egg yolk
¼ pint (⅝ cup) single cream
¼ teaspoon grated nutmeg
¼ teaspoon freshly ground black pepper
2 oz. (4T) butter
1 tablespoon olive oil
ham for garnish

serves 4–6

This dish is from Alsace.

Make the pastry and line a 7 inch diameter plain flan ring standing on a baking tray.
Peel the onions and slice very thinly. Beat together the eggs, egg yolk, cream and seasonings.
Heat the butter and oil in a saucepan, add the onions and cook (very gently), uncovered, until soft and golden. This must be done very slowly to prevent the onions from burning. Stir occasionally. Mix the onions into the cream mixture, then spoon into the prepared uncooked flan case. Bake in a moderate oven (350°F. Mark 4) for about 30 minutes or until well risen and browned.
Serve immediately, garnished with strips of thinly sliced ham.

Gougère au poulet et jambon — Cheese choux pastry flan with chicken and ham

¼ pint (⅝ cup) water
2 oz. (4T) butter
2½ oz. (good ½ cup) plain (all purpose) flour
2 eggs
2 oz. (½ cup) coarsely grated gruyère cheese
salt and pepper
1½ tablespoons (⅛ cup) olive oil
2 shallots, chopped
2 mushrooms, chopped
extra ½ tablespoon plain (all purpose) flour
¼ pint (1¼ cups) chicken stock
4 oz. (1 cup) chopped cooked chicken
2 oz. (½ cup) chopped cooked ham
1 tomato, skinned and chopped
1 tablespoon (1¼T) grated Parmesan cheese
1 tablespoon (1¼T) brown breadcrumbs
1 teaspoon finely chopped parsley

serves 4–6

Gougère is a dish from the Burgundy region of France. It has become very popular and is now made in all parts of the country.

Place the water and butter in a saucepan, heat until the butter is melted and the water is boiling. Add the flour, off the heat, and beat until the mixture is smooth.
Allow the mixture to cool, then add the eggs one at a time. Beat very well after each addition. Continue beating until the mixture is smooth. Add the gruyère cheese and mix well. Season. Place the olive oil in a saucepan, add the shallots and fry them until softened. Add the mushrooms and cook for 2 minutes. Add the extra flour, cook, stirring constantly 2–3 minutes. Add the stock, bring to the boil and simmer for 5 minutes. Add chicken, ham and tomato.
Arrange the cheese choux pastry in spoonfuls around a greased ovenproof dish. Pile the filling into the centre, sprinkle with Parmesan cheese and breadcrumbs.
Bake in a hot oven (400°F. Mark 6) for 30–40 minutes or until well risen, golden, firm to the touch and cooked through. (Avoid opening the oven door before 30 minutes is up).
Serve as soon as possible, garnished with chopped parsley.

Croque monsieur — Cheese toasted sandwich

2 thin slices bread (from a sandwich loaf)
½ oz. (1T) butter
1 slice gruyère cheese
1 slice cooked ham
clarified butter for frying

serves 1

Serve this as an easily prepared snack or an unusual appetizer.

Remove crusts from the slices of bread. Butter both on one side only. Place the gruyère cheese on the buttered side of one piece of bread, top with the ham and cover with the second slice of bread. Fry the sandwich in hot clarified butter until it is golden. Drain well and serve very hot.

Quiche Lorraine

Fish

Fish has always played a large part in French cooking; the French border is three quarters sea and there are also a great number of inland rivers and waterways rich in fish. Atlantic, Mediterranean and fresh water fish are all popular, especially in the local areas, for it is important that the fish be cooked when at its freshest.

Whether fish is being prepared for an extra special dinner party or simply for the family, the method of cooking is always simple. Fish is extremely nutritious and as tender as the finest beef steak. Long cooking is unnecessary and in fact would spoil the fish. Some of the most famous methods of cooking fish come from France, for instance 'à la meunière' and 'moules marinière'. There are also some great French classic fish dishes such as bouillabaisse and la bourride which, although difficult to make without Mediterranean fish, can be copied with reasonable success.

Fish can only be kept successfully for a very short time unless frozen. Frozen fish can be very good, since it is frozen immediately the catch is in and all the flavour, texture and goodness are preserved. Only freeze your own fish if they are very fresh indeed. Preparing fish can be a laborious and difficult job. Ask your fishmonger to clean, skin and fillet your purchase (as necessary). After all, he is the expert.

Filets de merlan à la meunière
Fillets of whiting meunière

4×12 oz. whiting
4 oz. (8T) clarified butter
flour
salt and pepper
1 egg, beaten
2 teaspoons chopped parsley
1 tablespoon (1¼T) lemon juice

serves 4

Fillet the fish:— Remove the heads and fins along the sides and bottom of the fish. Insert a very sharp knife to one side of the backbone and with long smooth cuts, ease the fillet away from the bones. Turn the fish over and remove the other fillet. Trim. Clarify the butter. Mix the flour with a little salt and pepper. Dip the fillets in the flour and then into the beaten egg. Heat the butter in a large frying pan and fry the fillets until golden brown on both sides, turning once.

Place the whiting on a heated serving plate. Pour off all the butter in the pan except 2 tablespoons (2½T), add the parsley and lemon juice, reheat and pour over fish. Serve immediately.

La brandade de morue
Creamed cod

1 lb. dried salt cod (or 1½ lb. fresh cod, tablespoon (1¼T) salt and 1 teaspoon lemon juice)
½ pint (1¼ cups) sauce béchamel (see recipe page 16)
8 fluid oz. (1 cup) olive oil
1 small clove garlic, crushed
freshly ground black pepper
croûtes of fried bread

serves 6

This is a traditional dish from the Mediterranean. It is a speciality of both Languedoc and Provence. Unfortunately, due to the long preparation, it is not made in the home as frequently as it used to be, but is bought ready made. If you own an electric mixer or blender, however, this certainly takes all the hard work out of this recipe. Use 1½ lbs. fresh cod if the dried salt cod is not available.

Soak the dried salt cod in cold water for 24 hours, changing the water once. Rinse well. Place in a large saucepan, cover with fresh cold water, bring to the boil and simmer for 30 minutes. (Fresh cod must be sprinkled with salt, left for 30 minutes and then, after the excess liquid and salt have been removed, covered and baked in a moderate oven (350°F. Mark 4) for 15–20 minutes.) Prepare the sauce béchamel and keep warm. Heat the olive oil gently in a small pan until almost boiling.

Beat the cooked cod with the garlic until smooth. This is a laborious and long job when done by hand but can be done with equal success in a mixer. It can also be successfully done in an electric blender. Add a little of the sauce béchamel when you begin to moisten it. When smooth, and all the fish fibres have been broken down, add about 3 tablespoons (3¾T) sauce béchamel, continue beating and add 3 tablespoons olive oil. Continue in this way until all the sauce and the oil are smoothly blended in. Season with black pepper. Reheat, serve in a heated dish, surrounded with fried croûtes of bread.

Thon à la provençale
Tuna fish Provençale

2×7 oz. cans tuna
juice of ½ lemon
salt and freshly ground black pepper
4 anchovy fillets
1 tablespoon olive oil
1 onion, chopped
4 ripe tomatoes, skinned, deseeded and chopped
1 clove garlic, crushed
bouquet garni
¼ pint (⅝ cup) white wine
chopped parsley for garnish

serves 4

Tuna fish are found in both the Mediterranean Sea and the Atlantic Ocean, off the French coast. If you are lucky enough to be able to get fresh fish, use a middle cut, marinate it in olive oil, then continue with the following recipe.

Remove the tuna from the cans very carefully so that they stay in shape and place side by side on an ovenproof serving dish. Sprinkle them with the lemon juice and season lightly with salt and pepper. Arrange the anchovy fillets on the top.
Heat the olive oil in a small saucepan, add the onion and cook until softened. Add tomatoes, garlic, a bouquet garni and wine. Bring to the boil and boil rapidly, uncovered, until reduced and thickened. Pour the sauce over the tuna, cover and bake in a moderate oven (350°F. Mark 4) for 10–15 minutes. Remove bouquet garni. Serve sprinkled with chopped parsley.

Trout with almonds

Filets de plie mornay — Plaice fillets in cheese sauce

2×12 oz. plaice
court bouillon (see recipe
page 30)
1 slice lemon
½ pint (1¼ cups) sauce mornay
(see recipe page 17)
grated Parmesan cheese

serves 4

Skin the plaice, fillet and cut each fillet in half lengthwise. Fold the pieces of fish in three and place them in a greased ovenproof dish. Add the court bouillon to a depth of ½ inch and the lemon slice. Cover and bake in a moderate oven (350°F. Mark 4) for 10–15 minutes. Drain the fillets.

Arrange the cooked plaice in a heated serving dish. Make the sauce mornay and coat the fish with it. Sprinkle the top with Parmesan cheese and place under a hot grill until the cheese is melted. The top may be browned if you prefer, but this is not essential. Serve very hot.

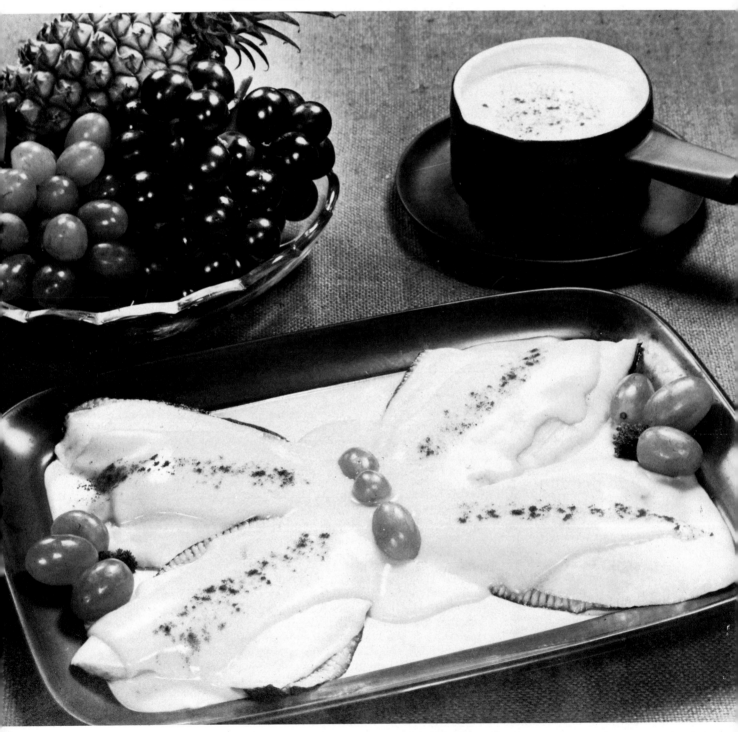

Plaice fillets in cheese sauce (above)   Herrings Brittany-style (right)

Filets de sole orly   Fillets of sole Orly

4 sole fillets

marinade
1 tablespoon (1¼T) olive oil
½ tablespoon (⅔T)
tarragon vinegar
1 teaspoon lemon juice
1 teaspoon chopped parsley
1 teaspoon finely chopped shallot
pinch each of cayenne pepper
and salt

batter
2 eggs
2 oz. (½ cup) plain (all
purpose) flour
salt
2 tablespoons milk
1 tablespoon (1¼T) oil
oil for deep frying
sauce de tomate Provençale
(see recipe page 20)
for serving
serves 4

Wipe the fillets, skin them, cut in half lengthwise then each half into thirds, diagonally.

Mix all the marinade ingredients together, add the sole pieces and marinate for 30 minutes.

Separate eggs. Sift the flour and salt into a mixing bowl, add egg yolks, milk and oil, beating well all the time. Whisk egg whites until stiff and fold into the batter just before using.

Heat oil for deep frying until 375°F. (a ¼ inch dice of bread will brown in less than a minute). Dip marinated sole pieces in the batter and deep fry until golden. Drain well on absorbent kitchen paper. Serve hot. Serve tomato sauce separately.

note: if sole is not available, use flounder or plaice fillets.

Filets de sole Veronique

Fillets of sole with grapes

2×12 oz. lemon or Dover sole
salt and freshly ground
black pepper
4 oz. white grapes
¾ pint (scant 2 cups) sauce
velouté (see recipe page 19)
paprika pepper for garnish

Skin and fillet the soles. Place bones and skin in a saucepan with
1 pint (2½ cups) water. Bring to the boil, covered, and simmer for 30
minutes. Strain.
Cut each fillet in half down the centre lengthwise and season well.
Fold in 3, skin side inside. Place in a greased ovenproof dish with the
prepared fish stock. Cover and bake in a moderate oven (350°F.
Mark 4) for 15 minutes.
Drain the sole, keeping hot, and pour the stock into a saucepan. Boil
the stock rapidly until reduced to 2 or 3 tablespoons (2½ or 3¾T).
Make the sauce velouté and add the reduced fish stock. Skin and
depip the grapes, heat in a little water.
Arrange the fish on a heated serving dish, coat with the sauce and
garnish with the hot grapes. Sprinkle a little paprika pepper on top
of each sole fillet.

serves 4

note: white wine may be used instead of fish stock and for heating
the grapes. Use plaice or flounder if sole is not available.

Sole à la colbert

Fried sole with maître d'hôtel butter

4×8 oz. soles
flour
salt and pepper
lemon juice
2 eggs, beaten
fine white dried breadcrumbs
oil for deep frying
sprigs of parsley
2 thin slices lemon
2 oz. (4T) maître d'hôtel butter

Wash, clean and skin the soles, leaving the heads on. On the 'white'
side, make a cut down the centre to the bone, 1 inch in from the top
and bottom. Carefully slice the fish away from the bones on each side
and roll the flesh of the fillet back. Using scissors, carefully snip
through the rib bones in the opening. Mix the flour with salt and
pepper. Sprinkle the soles with lemon juice and coat in seasoned
flour.
Dip each sole carefully in beaten egg and then coat in the
breadcrumbs. Heat the oil for frying to 375°F. (a ¼ inch slice of bread
will brown in less than a minute). Deep fry the soles, one at a time,
until golden. Drain well on absorbent kitchen paper. Remove the
bones from the opening.
Fry dry sprigs of parsley until they are crisp, about 30 seconds. Serve
the soles on a heated dish, then put the fried parsley and

serves 4

maître d'hôtel butter in the opening. Garnish with lemon butterflies.

Mâitre d'hôtel butter

Cream 2 oz. (4T) butter with a wooden spoon until soft. Add 2
teaspoons lemon juice and 2 teaspoons of finely chopped parsley with
salt and pepper. Beat well until they have thoroughly combined.
Make into a long 'sausage', wrap in aluminium foil and chill until
needed.

Fillets of sole Orly

Sole normande Sole Normandy-style

4 sole fillets
¼ pint (⅝ cup) cider (hard)
¼ pint (⅝ cup) water
salt and pepper
2 oz. button mushrooms
2 oz. (4T) butter
1 oz. (¼ cup) plain (all purpose) flour
1 egg yolk
1 teaspoon lemon juice
12 mussels, cooked
watercress for garnish

Sole Normandy-style   serves 4

Wipe the fillets, skin them and cut in half down the centre. Fold each piece of fish in half and place it in a greased ovenproof dish. Add the (hard) cider and the water and season. Cover and bake in a moderate oven (350°F. Mark 4) for 15–20 minutes. Drain and keep hot, reserving the cooking liquor (liquid).

Cut the mushrooms in half. Melt 1 oz. (2T) of the butter in a small frying pan and cook mushrooms gently until tender. Drain well. Melt the remaining 1 oz. (2T) butter in a saucepan, add flour and cook, stirring constantly until 'honeycombed' in appearance but not browned, 2–3 minutes. Add the reserved cooking liquor (liquid), bring to the boil, stirring, and simmer 3–4 minutes. Add the egg yolk, lemon juice, seasonings, mushrooms and mussels. Reheat without boiling.

Arrange fillets in a heated serving dish and pour the sauce over. Garnish with watercress.

Sole niçoise   Fillets of sole Nice-style

2×12 oz. lemon or Dover sole
salt and freshly ground
black pepper
lemon juice
3 tablespoons (¼ cup) béchamel
sauce (see recipe page 16)
¼ teaspoon cayenne pepper
½ pint (1¼ cups) court bouillon
(see recipe page 30)
1 pint (2½ cups) sauce de tomates
Provençale (see recipe page 20)
chopped gherkin and 4 pitted
black olives for garnish

Skin the soles and fillet. Cut each fillet in half down the centre and trim.

Season each fillet with salt, freshly ground black pepper and a little lemon juice. Chop the trimmings and mix with the sauce béchamel and cayenne pepper. Spread an eighth of the sauce mixture on each fillet and roll up from head to tail, keeping the cut side straight. Place the paupiettes (cut side downwards) in an ovenproof dish with the court bouillon. Cover and bake in a moderate oven (350°F. Mark 4) for 20 minutes.

Drain the fish, place it on a heated serving dish. Have the tomato sauce piping hot and coat the sole with it. Garnish with chopped gherkin and place half a black olive on each paupiette. Serve as soon as possible.

serves 4   **note:** use plaice or flounder if sole is not available.

Truites amandines — Trout with almonds

4 trout
salt and pepper
4 oz. (8T) clarified butter
2 oz. (½ cup) blanched almonds

This dish is at its best when eaten in the Grenoble area. Here there is an abundance of rivers coming down from the Alpes and the river trout are delicious, especially when freshly caught.

Wipe the trout, but do not remove the heads. Sprinkle with salt and pepper.
Heat the clarified butter in a large frying pan and fry the trout until cooked and golden, about 10–15 minutes. Drain the fish and place on a heated serving dish.
Slice the almonds into shreds and fry in butter in the pan until browned. Pour the butter and almonds over the trout and serve immediately.

serves 4

Truite saumonée en aspic — Salmon trout in aspic

1 × 3–4 lb. salmon trout
1½–2 pints (3¾–5 cups) court bouillon (see recipe page 30)
2 pints (5 cups) fish stock (see recipe page 30)
2 egg whites
2 oz. gelatine
3 tablespoons (¼ cup) sherry
prawns (shrimp), cucumber and lemon for garnish
mayonnaise for serving

Wash the trout, clean the cavities and rub with salt, then rinse. Curl the trout and place it in a deep ovenproof dish. Add the court bouillon and cover with a lid or aluminium foil, making sure it does not touch the fish. Bake in a moderately slow oven (325°F. Mark 3) for 40–50 minutes, basting frequently. Cool in the cooking liquid. Remove the skin. Make a cut on either side of the back bone, snip at each end and remove the back bone carefully. Place the fish stock in a large saucepan; an enamel or tin lined pan is best. Add egg whites and gelatine and whisk with a wire or balloon whisk. Bring slowly to the boil, whisking constantly. Remove from the heat and leave for 20 minutes. Strain through a scalded jelly bag or cloth. Stir in sherry and allow to cool.
Spoon the aspic carefully over the cooked salmon trout until it is glazed with a thin layer of jelly. Pour a thin layer of jelly in the base of a serving plate; allow to set. Very carefully lift the fish on to the serving dish. Garnish with chopped aspic, prawns (shrimp), cucumber and lemon slices. Serve the mayonnaise separately.

note: salmon may be prepared in the same way, but frequently they are too large and can only be served in individual steaks. It is sometimes easier to lift the fish on to the serving dish with the back bone still intact. Remove it when the salmon trout is actually on the dish.

serves 6

Mayonnaise de poisson — Fish mayonnaise

1 small lettuce
sauce vinaigrette (see recipe page 21)
1 lb. cooked white fish or shellfish
½ pint (1¼ cups) home made mayonnaise (see recipe page 20)
6 anchovy fillets
milk
capers
6 stuffed olives
1 tomato, skinned and sliced
1 hard-boiled egg, sliced

Wash the lettuce, dry it and cut it into thin shreds. Toss the lettuce in a little sauce vinaigrette and drain again. Remove all skin and bones from the fish; flake.
Arrange the lettuce in a serving dish and place the cooked fish on top. Coat the fish evenly with home made mayonnaise. Soak the anchovies in milk for 20 minutes, drain. Garnish the home made mayonnaise with strips of anchovy fillet arranged in a trellis with a caper in each space. Place halved stuffed olives, tomato slices and hard-boiled egg around the edge.
Serve as soon as possible.

serves 4

Coquilles St. Jacques à la breton
Scallops Breton-style

1 lb. Mediterranean, Pacific or Atlantic scallops
4 oz. (8T) melted butter
8 tablespoons (¾ cup) fine browned breadcrumbs
½ clove garlic, well crushed
1 teaspoon finely chopped parsley
salt and freshly ground black pepper

Scallops are readily available (when in season) in nearly all parts of the world. There are many ways of serving them but this extremely simple recipe is one of the best ways. Scallops also vary in size so although 2–3 scallops will be more than enough for one person when they come from the Atlantic, you will need 4–5 Pacific or Mediterranean scallops for each serving.

Trim the scallops and remove the strip of skin and muscle on the outside. Rinse, drain and slice the scallops into thick pieces. Grease 4 scallop shells or small ovenproof dishes with a little of the melted butter. Sprinkle with half the breadcrumbs. Divide the sliced scallops equally between the four shells.

Mix the remaining breadcrumbs with the garlic and parsley, season. Cover the scallops with the breadcrumb mixture and pour the remaining melted butter over the top. Bake, uncovered, in a moderately slow oven (325°F. Mark 3) for 15–20 minutes.

serves 4   Serve in the shells.

Crab garni
Dressed crab

1 medium sized crab, cooked
2 tablespoons (2½T) browned breadcrumbs
salt, pepper and dry mustard
2 hard-boiled egg yolks, chopped or grated

Remove the small claws and reserve. Remove the large claws, crack them open and remove all the flesh. Separate the upper and lower parts of the crab shell by pulling them apart, holding them with a clean tea towel. Remove the small sac on top of the big shell near the head, the spongy gills and any green matter in the big shell.

Scrape out the brown creamy meat which lies around the sides of the big shell. Mix it with browned breadcrumbs, salt, pepper and mustard. Break the crab body in half and remove all the white meat carefully. Use a skewer and be careful not to break off any shell. Mix all the white meat together and chop. Season.

Scrub the main body shell, rinse and dry thoroughly. Arrange the crab meat in the shell in rows with the egg yolk. Put a wide band of dark meat down the centre, egg yolk on either side and then two rows of white meat, one each side.

Serve as soon as possible. Serve a salad, home made mayonnaise and thin slices of brown bread and butter, separately.

note: if you are fortunate enough to have a freshly caught crab, first kill it by plunging it into boiling water. Cook it in court bouillon (see recipe page 30) allowing 15 minutes for each lb. weight.

serves 2–4

Dressed crab

Bouillabaisse Provençale fish stew

2–3 lb. fish *Use a mixture of at least 5 varieties: John Dory, whiting, turbot, bass, mullet, conger eel, hake, halibut, cod, lobster and red or grey snapper are all suitable. Also include some langoustine or king prawns (shrimp)*
3 tablespoons (¼ cup) olive oil
1 onion, chopped
3 red tomatoes, skinned, deseeded and chopped
2 cloves garlic, crushed
bouquet garni
salt and pepper
pinch of saffron
2 pints (5 cups) water, boiling
¼ pint (⅝ cup) white wine, optional
8 slices French bread
2 tablespoons (2½T) finely chopped parsley
serves 6–8

Bouillabaisse can really only be made properly with fish and shellfish which come only from the Mediterranean Sea. It is possible, however, to make a very good imitation with fish that are available elsewhere.

Wash the fish, removing all the bones and any skin. Cut into thick slices (but not the prawns [shrimp]).
Heat the olive oil in a large saucepan, add the onion and cook until softened, stirring constantly. Add the tomatoes, garlic and bouquet garni. Season, then add the saffron and the boiling water. Add the firm-fleshed fish (not the prawns [shrimp], John Dory or whiting).
Bring to the boil again and cook rapidly, uncovered, for 10 minutes. Add the prawns (shrimps), soft fish and wine. Continue cooking for another 5 minutes. Shake the pan occasionally to prevent the fish from sticking.
Place the slices of bread in a deep, heated serving dish, pour the cooking liquid in and make sure that it is all absorbed. Arrange the fish, according to variety, on the bread. Serve immediately, sprinkled with chopped parsley.

note: the bread may be served separately if liked.

Prawn butter balls

Provençale fish stew

Trout with almonds

Homard thermidor
Lobster thermidor

2×12 oz. lobsters
1 oz. (2T) butter
½ teaspoon each dried chervil, tarragon and parsley
1 shallot, chopped
¼ pint (⅝ cup) white wine
¼ pint (⅝ cup) double (heavy) cream
¼ pint (⅝ cup) sauce béchamel (see recipe page 16)
¼ pint (⅝ cup) fish stock (see recipe page 30)
¼ teaspoon paprika pepper
½ teaspoon dry mustard
salt
3 oz. (¾ cup) grated Parmesan cheese

serves 4

Split the lobsters in half lengthwise, removing all the meat from the shells and from the claws. Chop roughly.
Melt the butter in a saucepan, then add the herbs and shallot and cook for 1 minute. Add the wine and simmer 5 minutes. Add the cream and sauce béchamel, bring to the boil and simmer until thick and creamy. Add the fish stock, reheat, season with paprika pepper, mustard and salt. Stir in half of the cheese.
Mix the lobster meat with the hot sauce. Pile the meat back into the shell halves, sprinkle with remaining cheese and brown the tops under a hot grill.
Serve as soon as possible.

note: use fresh herbs if available; 1 teaspoon, chopped, of each herb is enough.

Moules marinière
Mussels in wine sauce

4 dozen mussels
¼ pint (⅝ cup) white wine
½ pint (1¼ cups) water
bouquet garni
1 carrot, thinly sliced
2 shallots, chopped
1 clove garlic, crushed
6 black peppercorns
salt to taste
1 tablespoon (1¼T) chopped parsley
3 tablespoons (¼ cup) single (light) cream
2 egg yolks

serves 4

Wash the mussels, remove weed and discard any that have opened. Place them in a large saucepan with the wine, water, carrot, shallots, garlic and peppercorns. Bring to the boil, slowly, then simmer for 5 minutes, shaking the pan gently until all the shells have opened. Arrange the mussels in a serving dish and keep them warm. Strain the cooking liquid and return it to the saucepan. Bring to the boil and continue boiling rapidly until the liquid has reduced to a third of the quantity. Mix the cream with the egg yolks and add to the pan with the salt and parsley. Cook, without boiling, until slightly thickened.
Pour sauce over the mussels and serve immediately.

note: the egg yolks may be omitted. They can also be replaced by a beurre manié.
Cream ½ oz. (2T) flour with ½ oz. (1T) butter, add to the pan in small pieces, bring to the boil and cook 2–3 minutes. Only add enough beurre manié to obtain a creamy sauce. Add the cream afterwards; do not boil.

La bourride
Fish in garlic sauce

1½ lb. white fish (use 3 different kinds as available e.g. John Dory, turbot, bass)
1 fish head and bones
court bouillon (see recipe page 30)
½ pint (1¼ cups) sauce aïoli (see recipe page 21)
2 egg yolks
8 rounds toasted French bread for serving
chopped parsley for garnish

serves 4

Although this is a Provençale dish, it can be easily reproduced using fish other than those caught only in the Mediterranean. The essential part of this recipe is the garlic sauce. Make sure that your guests like garlic before serving it to them!

Wash the fish, remove any bones and skin and cut it into thick slices. Place the fish head and bones in a saucepan with court bouillon. Bring to the boil and simmer for 10 minutes. Put the fish into a saucepan, add the strained court bouillon, to the depth of ½ inch, bring to the boil, cover and poach the fish gently for about 15 minutes or until just cooked. Drain, keep hot. Boil the stock in a pan until 3 tablespoons (3¾T) remain.
Place half of the prepared sauce aïoli in the top of a double boiler (or in a bowl) over hot water. Heat gently, add the egg yolks and cook, stirring, until it begins to thicken. Beat in the reduced fish stock. Put the drained fish in a heated serving dish, pour over the sauce. Serve with rounds of toasted French bread and garnished with chopped parsley. Serve the remaining sauce aïoli separately.

note: a piece of orange peel and a sprig of fennel can be added to the court bouillon, if available.

Harengs breton
Herrings Brittany-style

3 oz. (6T) butter
4 dessert apples, cored
3 sticks celery, chopped
½ onion, grated
½ pint (1¼ cups) cider (hard)
salt and pepper
4 herrings, cleaned, with heads
and fins removed
sprigs of parsley for garnish

serves 4

Melt 1 oz. (2T) of butter in a large frying pan. Chop 2 of the apples and add them to the pan with the celery and onion. Fry gently for 10 minutes. Add the (hard) cider, salt and pepper and simmer, uncovered, for a further 10 minutes. Place the cider mixture on a serving plate and keep hot.

Melt the remaining 2 oz. (4T) butter in cleaned pan. Slice the remaining apples and fry them for 3 minutes on each side. Remove from the pan and keep hot. Fry the prepared herrings in the same frying pan for 4–5 minutes on each side. Drain the cooked herrings and place on the cider mixture on the serving plate. Garnish with fried apple slices and sprigs of parsley.

Serve very hot.

Rougets provençales
Red mullet with garlic and herbs

4×12 oz. red mullet
salt
3 tablespoons (¼ cup) lemon juice
3 tablespoons (¼ cup)
chopped parsley
1 clove garlic, crushed
1 oz. butter, softened
2 tablespoons French mustard
pinch of mixed dried herbs
extra lemon juice

serves 4

Clean the mullet, season, and place them in an oiled roasting pan. Sprinkle them with lemon juice and the parsley and garlic mixed together. Bake, uncovered, in a moderately hot oven (375°F. Mark 5) for 20 minutes.

Blend together the butter, mustard, herbs and a little extra lemon juice. Make it into a roll, wrap in greaseproof paper and chill, then slice into rounds.

Serve the mullet on a heated serving plate, topped with the herbed butter.

Huîtres
Oysters

Oysters are mainly found around the Normandy and Brittany coast. They are at their best when served raw.

Open them just before they are to be served. Serve the oyster in the deep half of the shell and stand the shells on a bed of crushed ice. Sprinkle each oyster with a little cayenne pepper and garnish with a lemon wedge. Serve thinly sliced brown bread and butter separately. Allow 6–12 oysters for each person.

Meat

Meat is expensive compared with other foods, and nowhere is this more true than in France. It is because of the price of meat that the French housewife buys it with such care and, in consequence, the French butchers have developed their own style of presenting their meat. All the excess fat and sinews are trimmed off so that the housewife can see exactly what she is buying. Joints are neatly tied, cutlets have the top inch of bone bare (Frenched) ready for a cutlet frill. Tournados steaks have a piece of bacon or a thin strip of fat tied around the outside, to keep them moist. If the cut of meat to be roasted is rather dry, such as topside or aitchbone, the butcher will 'lard' it by threading thin strips of fat into the meat with a special 'larding needle'. You can buy larding needles in this country or alternatively, simply bard the meat with rashers of fat bacon. Pork is the fattest of the meats and almost never has to be larded. It is pork fat that is most commonly used for larding beef and veal. Lamb cuts rarely need larding.

The cuts of meat used in France are not always available elsewhere. I have given the more familiar cuts which your butcher will understand. Buy them with care and cook them carefully following the recipe – you will achieve a truly French dish.

In the average French home, meat is not eaten every day, for economy reasons. If, however, it is served at a dinner party, you will frequently find that it appears twice on the menu, once as the entrée which is a made dish, and once as a joint to be carved at the table – this course is called the relevé. Naturally, a dinner such as this would be extremely formal and on most occasions meat would only be served at one course, either for the entrée or the relevé.

Some of the recipes in this chapter are ideal for family meals. Try your family with a pot-au-feu or côte d'agneau à la Bretonne; you will receive praise indeed!

Preparing meat

La daube de boeuf Provençale

Provençale beef stew

2 lb. stewing beef; chuck, round or blade are all suitable
½ pint (1¼ cups) red wine
3 tablespoons (¼ cup) olive oil
bouquet garni
thin strip orange peel
2 rashers streaky bacon, diced
2 carrots, sliced
2 onions, sliced
2 oz. button mushrooms
4 tomatoes, skinned, deseeded and chopped
2 cloves garlic, crushed
1 tablespoon chopped parsley
salt and freshly ground black pepper
½ pint (1¼ cups) fond brun (beef bone stock) (see recipe page 30)
12 black olives, pitted
serves 4–6

There are many different recipes for this dish. It must, however, include wine, herbs and garlic. The remaining ingredients (except the beef) may include whatever is available at the time. This is an old farmhouse recipe.

Cut the beef into large cubes and place in a bowl with the wine, olive oil, bouquet garni and orange peel. Marinate the beef for 3–4 hours.

Place the bacon in a flameproof casserole. Heat, and fry the bacon until softened, add the carrots, onions, mushrooms, tomatoes, garlic, parsley and seasonings. Stir, then cover the casserole and cook very gently for 5–10 minutes. Add the beef and the marinade, to the stock, bring to the boil, then cover the casserole tightly and place in a slow oven (275°F. Mark 1) for 2½–3 hours. Add the olives 30 minutes before cooking time is completed. Remove the bouquet garni and the orange peel.

Serve hot, in the casserole.

note: this dish is frequently served with noodles. Toss the cooked noodles with a little of the gravy before serving.

Boeuf bourguignonne

Beef cooked in Burgundy wine

2 lb. topside steak (rump pot roast)
4 oz. pickled pork
2 oz. (4T) butter
2 tablespoons (2½T) oil
12 very small onions or shallots
1 oz. (¼ cup) plain (all purpose) flour
¼ pint (⅝ cup) fond brun (beef bone stock, see recipe page 30)
2 cloves garlic, crushed
bouquet garni
salt and freshly ground black pepper
½ bottle (13 fluid oz.) red Burgundy wine
4 oz. button mushrooms
croûtes of fried bread
chopped parsley for garnish
serves 4–6

This dish is one of the great classics. It came originally from the Burgundy province in eastern France but is now cooked all over the country. Red Burgundy wine is still an essential ingredient.

Trim the meat, removing excess fat. Cut the beef into 2 inch cubes. Put the pork in a small saucepan, cover with water, bring to the boil and simmer for 5 minutes. Drain and slice the pork into thin strips.

Heat 1 oz. (2T) of the butter with the oil in a flameproof casserole. Add the peeled onions and fry gently until browned all over. Remove and drain. Add the beef and pork and fry until browned. Remove and drain. Add the flour to the casserole and cook, stirring constantly for 2–3 minutes. Add the stock, garlic, bouquet garni and seasonings, then return the meat to the casserole. Heat the wine in a small saucepan, ignite and pour over the beef.

Cover the casserole and cook in a slow oven (300°F. Mark 2) for 1½–2 hours.

Heat the remaining 1 oz. (2T) butter in a small frying pan and fry the mushrooms for 3–4 minutes. Add the mushrooms and onions to the casserole 30 minutes before cooking time is completed.

Serve hot, in the casserole, garnished with croûtes of bread and chopped parsley.

Boeuf à la mode   Beef à la mode

1×4 lb. piece top rump beef
2 oz. (¼ cup) dripping
½ pint (1¼ cups) red wine
fond brun (beef bone stock)
(see recipe page 30)
4 rashers streaky bacon
1 small calf's foot
3 carrots
3 onions
bouquet garni
salt and freshly ground
black pepper

Wipe the meat. Heat the dripping in a heavy, flameproof casserole and fry the beef until browned all over. Pour off excess fat. Add the wine, bring to the boil and simmer until the quantity of the wine is reduced by half. Add enough stock to almost cover the beef.
Cut the bacon into strips and place in a small saucepan with the calf's foot. Cover with cold water, bring to the boil and simmer for 4–5 minutes. Drain and rinse in cold water. Add the bacon, calf's foot, whole peeled vegetables, bouquet garni and salt and pepper to the casserole.
Cover the casserole tightly and cook in a very slow oven (275 °F. Mark 1) for 5 hours.
Place the meat on a serving dish, strain the gravy and pour it over. If the meat is to be served cold, place the beef in a bowl, pour over the strained gravy and allow it to become a jelly (jello).

note: do not serve the cooking vegetables; by now, they will be very overcooked.

serves 8–10

Pot-au-feu   Boiled beef and soup

3 lb. rolled rib of beef
1 lb. veal bones
½ tablespoon salt
2 carrots
2 leeks
2 onions
4 cloves
1 turnip
2 sticks celery
bouquet garni
freshly ground black pepper

This classic French dish is the basis of an excellent soup, or can serve as a strong stock for use in soups (with additional ingredients) or even for consommé. The beef is served as a separate course, accompanied by the vegetables.
Place the beef in a large saucepan with the veal bones and salt. Add 6 pints (15 cups) of water. Bring slowly to the boil and remove the scum with a metal spoon. Skim again as necessary. Simmer gently for 30 minutes.
Prepare the vegetables, cutting them in half or quarters if large, otherwise leaving them whole. Stick the cloves into one of the onions. Add the vegetables to the pan with the bouquet garni and some freshly ground black pepper. Continue cooking for a further 2–2½ hours or until the meat is tender.
Serve the beef on a heated dish, surrounded by the vegetables. Return the soup to the heat and continue cooking for a further 1 hour. Use as required.

note: originally, pot-au-feu was simply a stockpot. Today it is considered too wasteful to use 3 lb. beef only for stock so it is removed when tender and not left in the pan for the complete cooking time.

serves 4–6

Chateaubriand

A chateaubriand steak is also cut from the middle of the fillet. It usually weighs 1 lb. or more and is almost a small joint. It is always grilled, however, and this must be done very carefully so that the outside does not become over-brown before the middle is cooked.
First seal the outside quickly under a very hot grill, then reduce the temperature and continue cooking for about 20 minutes, (or until cooked to your liking). Baste the steak occasionally with melted butter. Serve the chateaubriand with maître d'hôtel butter (see recipe page 51) or sauce béarnaise (see recipe page 18). Chateaubriand originally got its name from the château potatoes which are the traditional accompaniment. The recipe for these is on page 88.

serves 2–3

Fillet steaks béarnaise (above)

Loin of lamb with haricot beans (right)

Beef cooked in burgundy wine (far right)

Tournedos de boeuf   Fillet steaks

4×4–6 oz. tournedos steaks
salt and freshly ground
black pepper
2 oz. (4T) clarified butter
4 croûtes fried bread

The middle of the fillet, when cut into a 1½–2 inch slice, is called a tournados. It is the most tender piece of the whole animal and should be cooked with extreme care. Try cooking it at the table, pouring 2 tablespoons (2½T) of warmed brandy over the top and igniting.
Serve when the flames die down.

Trim the steaks, removing the skin from around the edge. Cut away the majority of the fat. Sprinkle each steak with salt and freshly ground black pepper.
Heat the butter in a large heavy frying pan, add the prepared steaks and cook for 3–4 minutes on each side, turning once. This cooking time will give a rare to medium-rare steak; allow a little more time for frying each side for a medium or well-done steak, if preferred.

serves 4   Serve each steak on a fried croûte of bread.

Tournedos à la pompadour

Pour a little of the butter in the frying pan over the steaks, place a slice of grilled tomato on top and a small piece of mâitre d'hôtel butter (see recipe page 51) on top of this.

Tournados à la béarnaise

Place 2 teaspoons of sauce béarnaise (see recipe page 18) on each steak. Garnish with sprigs of watercress.

Tournedos chasseur

Place 2 teaspoons of sauce chasseur (see recipe page 16) on top of each steak. Garnish with a little chopped parsley.

Tournedos provençale

Omit the fried croûtes of bread and use instead ¼–½ inch slices of aubergine. Sprinkle them with salt, leave for 30 minutes, rinse and drain well. Fry in butter until golden. Top each steak with a little sauce de tomate provençale (see recipe page 20).

Tournedos au poivre

Crush 1 tablespoon (1¼T) whole peppercorns (black or white) with a rolling pin. (It is easiest if you put the peppercorns between two pieces of greaseproof paper.) Press the crushed peppercorns into the tournados on both sides, before cooking. Cook in the usual way. Serve the tournados on croûtes. Add 1 tablespoon (1¼T) brandy to the juices in the pan, ignite, and pour the flaming brandy over the top.

Tournedos jardinière

Serve the steaks on a bed of freshly cooked mixed vegetables. Use new potatoes, carrots, peppers and peas. Cook them individually and toss together with a little melted butter and seasonings.

Filet de boeuf dubarry
Roast beef fillet with cheese and cauliflower

1 × 3 lb. fillet of beef
2 oz. (4T) butter
4 rashers streaky bacon
freshly ground black pepper
1 cauliflower
1 pint (2½ cups) sauce mornay
(see recipe page 17)
2 oz. (½ cup) grated
Parmesan cheese
parsley for garnish

serves 6

This recipe was reputedly a favourite of Madame Dubarry, a famous courtesan at the court of King Louis XIV.

Trim the excess fat from the fillet. Heat the butter in a roasting pan, place the fillet in the pan and lay the rashers of bacon on top. Baste with the butter and sprinkle with freshly ground black pepper. Roast in a hot oven (425°F. Mark 7) for 30–40 minutes or until the fillet is cooked medium-rare. (If you like well cooked meat, extend the cooking time accordingly.)
Meanwhile, cut the cauliflower into florets. Cook the cauliflower in a saucepan of boiling salted water for 10 minutes or until tender. Place the cauliflower around the fillet on a heated serving plate and coat with sauce mornay. Sprinkle the top with Parmesan cheese and place under a hot grill until golden. Garnish with sprigs of parsley and serve immediately.

Filet de boeuf en croûte
Fillet of beef in pastry

1 × 3 lb. fillet of beef
salt and freshly ground
black pepper
2 oz. (4T) butter
8 oz. pâte feuilletée (see recipe page 119)
1 egg yolk

serves 6–8

Rub the fillet with salt and pepper. Melt the butter in a frying pan and fry the fillet until browned all over. Use a pair of tongs or 2 spoons to turn it so as not to pierce the outside. Remove and cool. Roll out the pastry on a lightly floured surface to ⅛ inch thick and large enough to enclose the whole fillet. Trim the pastry and place the beef in the centre. Fold the pastry around the meat, brush a little egg yolk along the edges and seal the pastry around the meat. Cut pastry leaves from the trimmings and stick them on to the top of the pastry with egg yolk. Brush the pastry and leaves all over with egg yolk.
Bake in a very hot oven (450°F. Mark 8) for 15 minutes. Reduce the heat to moderate (350°F. Mark 4) for a further 15–20 minutes. Serve as soon as possible.

note: the meat will be rare. If you like your meat medium or well-done, extend the cooking time accordingly.

Alouettes sans Têtes
Stuffed beef rolls

1 lb. topside (round) steak
1 onion, sliced
1 carrot, sliced
1 stick celery, sliced
2 rashers streaky bacon, chopped
salt and black pepper
¼ pint (⅝ cup) red wine
½ pint (1¼ cups) fond brun
(beef bone stock see page 30)
1 teaspoon tomato paste
bouquet garni
choppped parsley for garnish

stuffing:
1 oz. (¼ cup) finely chopped ham
1 clove garlic, crushed
2 teaspoons chopped parsley
3 tablespoons (¼ cup) breadcrumbs
1 teaspoon grated lemon rind
salt and pepper
pinch of ground nutmeg
milk

serves 4–6

Literally, 'alouettes sans têtes' means 'larks without heads'!

Slice the beef into very thin slices, place each slice between 2 pieces of polythene and beat well with a rolling pin until wafer thin.
Cut the slices into pieces about 2 inches by 4 inches.
Mix all the stuffing ingredients together, adding sufficient milk to bind. Place a teaspoon of the stuffing on each piece of beef, roll up and tie with thread.
Place the onion, carrot and celery with the bacon in the base of an ovenproof dish. Put the 'alouettes' on top and season with salt and pepper. Pour in the wine and the stock, mixed with the tomato paste and add the bouquet garni.
Cover the dish with greased greaseproof paper and cook in a moderately slow oven (325°F. Mark 3) for about 2 hours, or until very tender. Remove the 'alouettes', then untie and discard the cotton. Strain the gravy into a saucepan, reheat and add the 'alouettes' to the pan. Simmer 2–3 minutes.
Serve in a heated dish, sprinkled with chopped parsley.

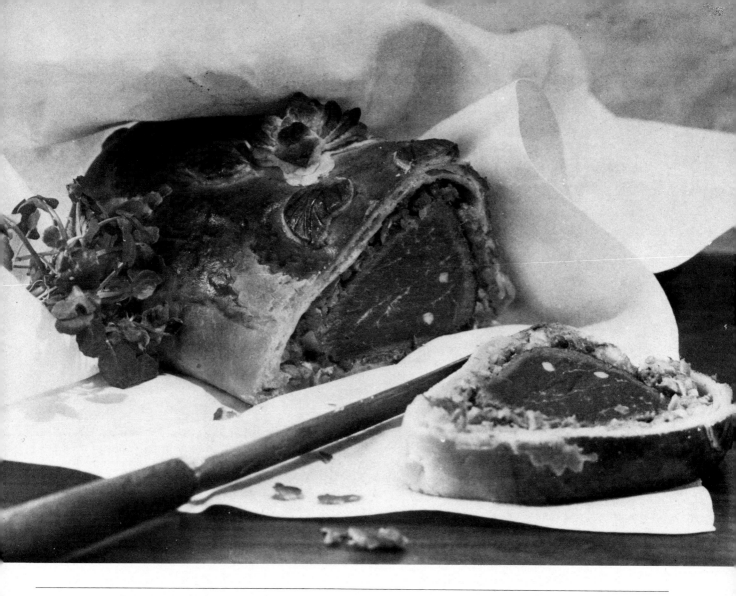

Le fricandeau   Braised veal

1½ lb. veal
4 rashers streaky bacon
4 oz. pickled pork, diced
1 large onion, sliced
1 large carrot, sliced
¼ pint (⅝ cup) white wine
1 pint (2½ cups) fond blanc
(white stock) see recipe
page 30)
bouquet garni
salt and pepper
chopped parsley for garnish

Le fricandeau is a long sliver of veal which is cut from under the 'nut' of veal which is the top of the leg. It is usually about 1½ inches thick and is cut along the grain of the meat. This recipe is the classic for cooking 'le fricandeau'.

Cut the veal into 1½ inch slices (see above). Cut the bacon into long strips. Place the pickled pork in the base of a large, heavy, flameproof casserole, add the vegetables and then the veal and cover with the bacon. Heat the casserole very gently, cover and cook for 20–25 minutes. Add the wine, cover, and cook for 15–20 minutes. Add ¼ pint (⅝ cup) of the stock, cover and cook for 15–20 minutes or until the liquid is well reduced. Add another ¼ pint (⅝ cup) of stock and cook as before. Pour in the remaining stock, cover the casserole tightly and cook in a moderately slow oven (325 °F. Mark 3) for 1½ hours.

Remove the meat and strain the gravy. Place the meat in a saucepan, pour over the gravy, adjust seasonings and cook rapidly, turning the meat over occasionally, until the liquid is reduced to ¼–½ pint (⅝–1¼ cups).

Serve the meat with the thickened gravy poured over it. Garnish with chopped parsley.

note: at no time should this dish be allowed to brown. The veal should be extremely tender when cooked and the gravy should give a good glaze.

serves 4

Escalopes de veau à la savoyard
Veal escalopes with cream sauce

4 × 4–4½ oz. veal escalopes
salt and pepper
lemon juice
2 oz. (4T) butter
6 tablespoons (½ cup) dry
white vermouth
6 tablespoons (½ cup) double
(heavy) cream
4 slices of lemon for garnish

serves 4

This delicious recipe comes from the Alpine Savoie department of France. Savoie is famed for its dairy produce and the capital town of Chambery is also known for the locally produced dry white vermouth.

Trim the escalopes and place them between two sheets of polythene. Using a small mallet or a rolling pin, beat the veal until it is about ⅛ inch thick. Season with salt, pepper and lemon juice.
Melt the butter in a very large frying pan until very hot, add the escalopes and fry until they are beginning to brown, turning once. Add the vermouth and bring to the boil. Add the cream and continue cooking, shaking the pan occasionally, until the vermouth and cream are combined and thickened.
Serve on a heated serving dish, garnished with slices of lemon.

note: if your frying pan is not large enough to take the 4 escalopes all at once, fry them 2 at a time and return the first to the pan just before adding the vermouth.

Blanquette de veau
Veal stew

1½ lb. stewing veal
10 small onions or shallots
2 oz. (4T) butter
2 oz. (½ cup) plain (all
purpose) flour
1½ pints (3¾ cups) fond blanc
(white stock) see recipe page 30)
bouquet garni
6 white peppercorns
4 oz. mushrooms
2 teaspoons lemon juice
¼ pint (⅝ cup) single
(light) cream
salt
croûtes of fried bread
small grilled bacon rolls (rashers
of bacon rolled up and secured
with a tooth pick)
chopped parsley

serves 4

Trim the meat and cut it into 2 inch cubes. Peel the onions. Heat the butter in a saucepan, add the meat and fry until it has changed colour, but do not allow it to brown. Remove and drain the meat, add the onions and fry for 4–5 minutes, without browning.
Remove and drain. Stir the flour into the saucepan and cook gently, stirring constantly, until the roux is 'honeycombed' in appearance but has not browned, 3–4 minutes.
Add stock and heat, stirring, until boiling. Add the bouquet garni, peppercorns and the washed stalks from the mushrooms. Simmer for 20 minutes.
Strain the gravy into a clean saucepan, add the veal and onions, cover, and continue cooking for 1–1½ hours or until meat is tender. Add the chopped mushrooms (or whole button mushrooms) 15 minutes before cooking time is finished. Add the lemon juice and cream, taste and adjust the seasoning.
Reheat without boiling.
Serve in a heated dish garnished with croûtes of bread, bacon rolls and chopped parsley.

Stuffed ham rolls (right)

Provençale beef stew (far right)

Longe de veau rôti Roast loin of veal

1 × 3 lb. loin of veal, boned
salt and pepper
1 teaspoon dried
rosemary chopped
4 rashers streaky bacon
3 tablespoons (¼ cup) olive oil
serves 4

Rub the veal all over with salt and pepper. Tie it firmly in a roll. Place the meat in a roasting pan, sprinkle with rosemary and place the bacon over the top. Roast in a moderate oven (350°F. Mark 4) for 2 hours (allowing 40 minutes for each lb.). Baste with oil every 20 minutes.
Serve sliced on a heated serving dish.

Gigot d'agneau en croûte Roast leg of lamb in pastry case

1 × 4 lb. leg of lamb, boned
4 lambs' kidneys
3 oz. (6T) butter
1 clove garlic, crushed
salt and pepper
8 oz. pâte feuilletée (see recipe page 119)
1 egg yolk
serves 6

Wipe the leg of lamb and trim off the excess fat. Skin the kidneys, cut in half and remove the tubes. Melt 1 oz. (2T) of the butter in a frying pan and fry the kidney with the garlic until tender, 3–4 minutes. Season with salt and pepper and place the kidney mixture into the cavity. Tie securely with fine string. Place in a roasting pan, rub with the remaining 2 oz. (4T) butter and roast in a hot oven (425°F. Mark 7) for 1 hour (allowing 15 minutes cooking time for each lb.). Remove and allow to cool.
Roll out the prepared pastry to a size which will envelop the leg of lamb. Place the lamb on the pastry, moisten the edges and wrap the meat up firmly, pressing the edges together. Brush the pastry with the egg yolk. Bake in a hot oven (as before) for 15–20 minutes, or until golden and crisp.
Serve, ready for carving, on a heated plate.

Navarin d'agneau Lamb stew

1½ lb. lean lamb, shoulder or middle neck
3 tablespoons (¼ cup) oil
4 onions
4 carrots
1 turnip
1 oz. (¼ cup) plain (all purpose) flour
1 pint (2½ cups) fond blanc (white stock, see recipe page 30)
bouquet garni
1 tablespoon tomato paste
1 clove garlic, crushed
salt and pepper
parsley for garnish
serves 4

Trim the meat and cut it into 1 inch cubes. Heat the oil in a large heavy saucepan and fry the meat until it has changed colour. Peel and slice the onions, peel and dice the carrots and turnip. Add the vegetables to the saucepan and fry until beginning to brown. Stir in the flour and cook, stirring constantly for 3–4 minutes.
Return the lamb to the saucepan, add the stock, bouquet garni, tomato paste, garlic, salt and pepper. Cover the saucepan. Bring to the boil and simmer very gently for 1½–2 hours or until the meat is very tender. Serve in a heated dish, garnished with sprigs of parsley.

note: if mutton is used, adjust the cooking time to 2–2½ hours, or until the meat is very tender.

Noisettes d'agneau béarnaise Noisettes of lamb with béarnaise sauce

2 lb. best end of neck
salt and pepper
½ teaspoon dried basil
½ pint (1¼ cups) sauce béarnaise (see recipe page 18)
croûtes of fried bread
serves 4

Ask the butcher to chine the meat. Remove the chine bone, rib bones and the skin. Sprinkle the meat with salt, pepper and basil. Roll the meat up tightly, starting with the thick side. Tie the meat securely in 1½ inch lengths and slice into noisettes.
Grill the noisettes under a hot grill, turning once, until the meat is sealed. Reduce the heat of the grill and continue cooking for 5–10 minutes or until the lamb is just cooked.
Serve each noisette on a croûte of bread. Top with a spoonful of sauce béarnaise. Place on a heated dish and serve immediately.

note: noisettes can also be prepared and served as for lamb cutlets.

Lamb cutlets

Côtelettes d'agneau soubise

Lamb cutlets with onions

8 lamb cutlets, from the best end of neck
1 oz. (2T) butter
1 small onion, sliced
salt and pepper
bay leaf
¼ pint (⅝ cup) white wine
¾ pint (approx. 2 cups) sauce soubise (see recipe page 17)
fried onion rings for garnish (see recipe page 93)
serves 4

Trim the cutlets. Heat the butter in a large saucepan, add the cutlets and brown all over. Remove the cutlets, add the onion and fry until golden. Return the cutlets to the saucepan and add salt, pepper, a bay leaf and white wine. Cover the pan and simmer very gently for 15–20 minutes.
Serve the cutlets on a heated serving plate, coat in sauce soubise and garnish with fried onion rings.

Côtelettes d'agneau provençale

Omit the sauce soubise and the fried onions from the above recipe. Use instead ¾ pint (approx. 2 cups) sauce de tomate provençale (see recipe page 20).

Côtelettes d'agneau savoyard

Omit the sauce soubise and the fried onions from the above recipe. Use instead ¾ pint (approx. 2 cups) sauce mornay (see recipe page 17) and garnish with 4 oz. mushrooms, sliced and fried gently in 1 oz. (2T) butter.

Côte d'agneau à la bretonne

Loin of lamb with haricot beans

8 oz. dried haricot beans, soaked overnight
1 carrot
1 onion
bouquet garni
1 × 2 lb. loin of lamb, boned
salt
1 clove garlic
½ pint (1¼ cups) fond brun (beef bone stock, see recipe page 30)
2 large red tomatoes, skinned, deseeded and chopped

serves 4

Brittany is renowned for producing delicious lamb. There are large expanses of salt meadows where lambs are pastured and it is these that give the meat its distinctive flavour.

Place the beans in a large saucepan with salted cold water to cover. Add the carrot, onion and bouquet garni. Bring to the boil and simmer for 2 hours or until tender.
Meanwhile, wipe the lamb, rub it all over with salt and insert slivers of garlic in various places just under the skin. Roll and tie with fine string.
Place the lamb in a greased roasting pan with the stock, cover with greased greaseproof paper and roast in a moderately hot oven (375°F. Mark 5) for 50 minutes. After 20 minutes remove the paper and baste with the stock in the pan; baste 2–3 more times during cooking and remove the paper completely for the last 10 minutes to allow the lamb to brown.
Place the meat on a heated serving plate and keep hot. Drain the cooked beans, remove and chop the onion and carrot. Mix the beans with the tomato, carrot and onion and a little of the meat stock, to moisten.
Spoon the beans around the lamb and serve.

71

Côte de porc normande
Pork chops in cider

1 oz. (2T) butter
2 teaspoons oil
4 oz. button onions, peeled
4 pork chops
8 oz. tomatoes, skinned and quartered
2 sticks celery, cut into 1 inch lengths
2 dessert apples, cored and sliced
4 oz. button mushrooms, washed
¾ oz. (3 tablespoons) plain (all purpose flour)
¾ pint (scant 2 cups) fond blanc (white stock, see recipe page 30)
4 tablespoons (good ¼ cup) still cider (hard)
1 tablespoon dried thyme
salt and freshly ground black pepper
chopped parsley for garnish

serves 4

Heat the butter and oil together in a flameproof casserole. Add the onions and fry gently until golden brown. Add the pork chops and fry until browned on both sides. Mix the remaining vegetables and apple slices, add to the casserole and cook, stirring, for 3 minutes. Stir in the flour, cook 2–3 minutes. Pour in the stock and (hard) cider, add the thyme and season to taste.
Cover the casserole tightly and cook in a moderate oven (350°F. Mark 4) for 45 minutes.
Serve garnished with chopped parsley.

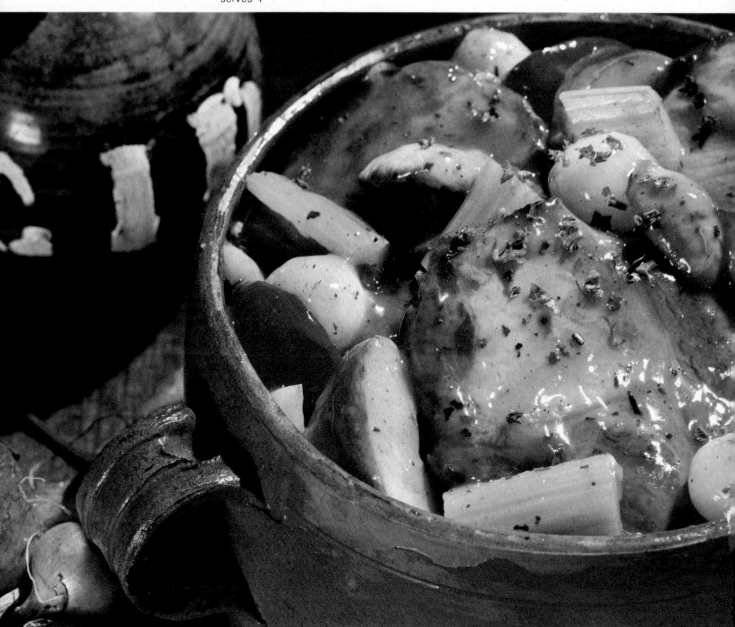

Carré de porc provençale
Loin of pork with garlic and herbs

1 × 3 lb. loin of pork
1 clove garlic
salt and pepper
½ teaspoon chopped dried thyme
¼ pint (⅝ cup) red wine
3 tablespoons (¼ cup) soft white breadcrumbs
3 tablespoons (¼ cup) finely chopped parsley

serves 4–6

Ask your butcher to chine the loin of pork. Cut off the skin but leave the fat unless it is very thick. Cut the garlic into thin slivers and insert them in various places, close to the bone. Rub salt and pepper into the pork then place it in a dish with the thyme and red wine. Marinate the meat for 2–3 hours.

Place the pork and the marinade in a roasting pan, fat side up. Cover with greased greaseproof paper or aluminium foil and roast in a moderate oven (350°F. Mark 4) for 1¼ hours. Remove the paper, mix the breadcrumbs and parsley together and press on to the pork fat with a palette knife. Baste with the cooking liquid and continue cooking in a slow oven (300°F. Mark 2) for 45 minutes. Baste occasionally.

Serve on a heated plate ready for carving into chops.

note: traditionally, this dish is served with pommes mousseline (see recipe page 88).

Pork chops in cider (left)   Cold meat and relishes (below)

Rôti de porc à la boulangère

Roast pork with sliced potatoes and apples

2 lb. boned and tied hand of
pork (boneless pork joint)
1½ lb. medium sized potatoes
3 apples
2 oz. (4T) butter
1 teaspoon dried
rosemary, chopped
salt and black pepper
serves 4–6

Wipe the meat and trim if necessary. Peel and slice the potatoes into
¼–½ inch slices. Peel and thinly slice the apples.
Cut the butter in small pieces and scatter them over the base of a
shallow roasting pan. Put apple slices on top of the potatoes,
overlapping in lines. Top with pork and sprinkle with rosemary and
salt and pepper. Roast in a hot oven (400°F. Mark 6) for 1 hour
(allowing 30 minutes cooking time for each lb.). Baste frequently.
Serve in the roasting pan in which it is cooked.

Jambon à la bourguignonne

Ham in red Burgundy wine

1 × 3 lb. gammon ham
1 onion
4 cloves
4 peppercorns
bouquet garni
1 carrot
½ bottle (13 fl. oz.) red Burgundy
½ tablespoon arrowroot

serves 6–8

Soak the ham overnight, if necessary, in cold water to cover. Next
day, drain and place it in a large saucepan, cover with fresh water
and add the onion, stuck with cloves, the peppercorns, bouquet garni
and carrot. Bring slowly to the boil and simmer for 1 hour.
Drain the ham and remove the skin. Place in an ovenproof casserole
with red wine and 1 pint (2½ cups) of the cooking liquid. Roast in a
moderately slow oven (325°F. Mark 3) for 1 hour, basting
occasionally. Remove the ham and strain the gravy into a saucepan.
Mix the arrowroot with a little water and add to the saucepan. Bring
to the boil, stirring constantly, and simmer 2–3 minutes.
Carve the ham into slices, arrange on a serving plate and pour over
the gravy.

Paupiettes de jambon

Stuffed ham rolls

8 slices cooked ham
2 sticks celery
2 apples
2 oz. (¾ cup) walnuts
1 tablespoon (1¼T)
chopped chives
1 tablespoon (1¼T) lemon juice
¼ pint (⅝ cup) home made
mayonnaise (see recipe page 20)
salt and pepper
4 oz. terrine de campagne (see
recipe page 28)
serves 4

Cut ham slices thinly and as large as possible. Chop the celery, peel,
core and chop the apples, chop the walnuts. Mix all these together
with the chives and lemon juice. Add home made mayonnaise, taste
and adjust the seasoning.
Spread each slice of ham with pâté. Divide the home made mayonnaise
mixture between the slices and roll up.
Serve the paupiettes on a bed of salad or garnished with parsley and
lemon slices.

Foie d'agneau farci

Stuffed lamb's liver

1 lb. lamb's liver
6 tablespoons (½ cup) white
breadcrumbs
1 oz. (2T) butter, melted
2 teaspoons chopped parsley
1 teaspoon grated lemon rind
½ teaspoon mixed dried herbs
1 shallot, finely chopped
salt and freshly ground
black pepper
¾ pint (approx. 2 cups) fond
brun (beef bone stock, see recipe
page 30)
4 rashers streaky bacon
serves 4

Wash, trim and slice the liver into ½–¾ inch slices. Arrange the slices
in an ovenproof serving dish.
Mix the breadcrumbs with butter, parsley, lemon rind, herbs,
chopped shallot and the seasonings. Divide into 4 and pack in 4
separate piles on top of the liver.
Pour the stock around the liver. Remove the rind from the bacon and
place on top of the stuffing. Cover with greased greaseproof paper or
aluminium foil and bake in a moderately hot oven (375°F. Mark 5)
for 1 hour. Remove the paper 15 minutes before cooking time is
completed to crisp the bacon.
Serve hot.

Foie de veau en brochette
Calves' liver kebabs

1½ lb. calves' liver
4 rashers bacon
4 small tomatoes, skinned
salt and black pepper
juice of ½ a lemon
1 teaspoon chopped dried basil
or marjoram
olive oil

serves 4

Wash the liver, trim and cut it into 1 inch cubes. Remove the rind from the bacon and cut into 1 inch pieces. Slice each tomato into 4. On each of 4 long skewers, thread first a piece of liver, then bacon and finally tomato. Continue until all the ingredients have been used. Sprinkle each brochette with salt, pepper, lemon juice, basil and oil. Cook under a moderately hot grill for 7–10 minutes, turning once. Serve on a heated plate.

note: this is delicious when served on ratatouille (see recipe page 93).

Rognons sauté turbigo
Fried kidneys with mushrooms and sausages

8 lamb's kidneys
1 oz. (2T) butter
4 oz. button mushrooms
12 small onions or shallots
4 thin pork sausages
½ pint (1¼ cups) sauce espagnole
(see recipe page 16)
salt and black pepper
croûtes of fried bread
chopped parsley for garnish

serves 4

Cut the kidneys in half lengthwise, cutting out the tubes and skin. Heat the butter in a saucepan, fry the mushrooms until tender, 2–3 minutes, remove and drain. Add the onions and fry them until browned all over, then remove. Cut the sausages into 1 inch lengths and fry, with the prepared kidneys, until browned. Return the onions to the saucepan and add the sauce espagnole. Cover the saucepan and simmer very gently for 15 minutes, stirring occasionally. Add the mushrooms and continue cooking for 5 minutes.
Serve in a heated dish, surrounded by croûtes of bread and sprinkled with chopped parsley.

Rognons de veau au vin blanc
Veal kidneys in white wine

4 small veal kidneys
1 oz. (2T) butter
1 tablespoon (1¼T) oil
1 onion, finely chopped
2 oz. mushrooms, sliced
½ pint (1¼ cups) fond brun
(beef bone stock see recipe
page 30)
¼ pint (⅝ cup) white wine
1 teaspoon tomato paste
salt and pepper
1 tablespoon (1¼T) arrowroot
chopped parsley for garnish

serves 4

Skin the kidneys and slice thinly. Heat the butter and oil in a saucepan and fry the kidneys until well browned, then remove them from the pan. Add the onion and fry until golden. Add the mushrooms and fry for a further 2–3 minutes. Pour in the stock and the wine, bring to the boil, add tomato paste and seasonings, then simmer for 5 minutes.
Add the fried kidneys. Mix the arrowroot with a little water and add to the pan, stirring. Bring to the boil, stirring constantly and simmer 2–3 minutes.
Serve in a heated dish, sprinkled with chopped parsley.

Ris de veau à la suprême
Sweetbreads in sauce velouté

1 lb. calves' sweetbreads
¾ pint (approx. 2 cups) sauce
velouté (see recipe page 19)
4 oz. button mushrooms
1 oz. (2T) butter
4 large croûtes of fried bread
chopped parsley for garnish

serves 4

Soak the sweetbreads in cold salted water for 1–2 hours. Bring a large saucepan of salted water to the boil, add the sweetbreads and cook for 3–4 minutes. Remove the sweetbreads from the pan and immerse in cold water to stop them cooking any further. Skin, then place them between two plates until cold.
Place in an ovenproof dish with ¼–½ inch depth of water. Cover with aluminium foil or greased greaseproof and cook in a moderate oven (350°F. Mark 4) for 20–25 minutes.
Prepare the sauce velouté. Fry the mushrooms in butter until cooked. Drain the sweetbreads and cut into ½ inch slices. Place them in a heated serving dish on the croûtes of bread and pour the sauce over the top. Arrange the mushrooms on either side of the dish and serve sprinkled with chopped parsley.

Langue de boeuf chasseur
Ox tongue with chasseur sauce

1 ox tongue, salted 1 carrot 1 onion 1 stick celery 1 bay leaf 6 peppercorns ¾ pint (approx. 2 cups) sauce chasseur (see recipe page 16) pommes mousseline (see recipe page 88) serves 6	Soak the tongue in cold water to cover for 8 hours or overnight. Place in a large saucepan with water to well cover, together with the whole cleaned vegetables, the bay leaf and the peppercorns. Bring to the boil slowly, cover and simmer for 4 hours. Allow to cool for 1 hour in the saucepan, then remove from the pan, skin, remove any bones and allow to cool. Slice the tongue and place in a saucepan with the sauce chasseur. Reheat very gently. Arrange the pommes mousseline on a heated serving dish, top with the slices of ox tongue and pour the remaining sauce over the top.

Ragoût de queue de boeuf
Oxtail stew

1 × 3 lb. oxtail 2 onions 4 carrots 2 sticks celery 1 oz. (2T) butter 1 tablespoon (1¼T) oil 2 rashers streaky bacon, diced 1 oz. (¼ cup) plain (all purpose) flour 2 pints (5 cups) fond brun (beef bone stock, see recipe page 30) bouquet garni salt and pepper 1 turnip 10 shallots or small onions 1 small cabbage chopped parsley for garnish	Ask the butcher to chop through the oxtail at the joints. Put them in a bowl with cold water to cover and soak them overnight. Next day, place them in a saucepan, cover with fresh water and bring slowly to the boil, skimming the top as necessary. Simmer for 10–15 minutes. Drain well. Slice the onions, 2 of the carrots and the celery. Heat the oil and butter in a large heavy saucepan, add the oxtail and brown very well all over. Remove from the pan. Place the prepared vegetables and the bacon in the saucepan and fry them until they begin to brown. Pour off the excess fat and add the flour, then cook, stirring, until the flour is a light brown. Add the stock, bouquet garni and salt and pepper to taste. Bring to the boil, stirring constantly. Return the oxtail to the pan, cover and simmer very gently for 3–4 hours or until very tender. Meanwhile, cut the remaining carrots and the turnip into ½ inch dice. Peel the shallots and leave whole. Place in a small saucepan of boiling, salted water and cook until tender. Drain well. Remove the outer leaves from the cabbage and cut the heart into quarters. Cook the cabbage in boiling, salted water until tender. Drain well. Remove the cooked oxtail from the gravy and place on a heated serving plate, piled high. Strain the gravy into a clean saucepan, bring to the boil, skin and boil rapidly until thickening slightly. Pour the gravy over the oxtail and garnish with the prepared vegetables around the edge and the parsley sprinkled over the top.
serves 4	

Veal stew (above)   Coq au vin (right)

Poultry and game

Poultry and game have always been popular in France, especially for peasant cookery, as poultry are kept on the local farms and wild game used to abound in the countryside. Some of the greatest French classic dishes will be found in this chapter; they include such favourites as chicken Marengo and coq-au-vin. Other less known recipes are included, such as partridge with cabbage, which has its origin in peasant cookery and was cooked when the man of the house brought home two partridges, one young and tender, the other old and tough. This recipe is a good solution to the cook's problem of how to cook them both to perfection.

All poultry, chicken, turkey, goose and duck are now all easily available, and can be bought ready-drawn and trussed for the oven, all the year round. Game is usually only available in season. It is possible to buy this, too, ready prepared. You may have to pluck and draw game yourself if you are presented with a newly killed bird, however, First, hang the birds for a week or ten days and then prepare them for the oven. Hares should also be hung for about this time before skinning. Collect the blood, if possible, for thickening the gravy.

Poultry and game, but game in particular, are rich and filling. Try to serve them with vegetables and accompaniments which will contrast both the texture and the flavour. Salads are crisp and light and make an ideal accompaniment. Fruit jellies and sauces, which are slightly tart, are a good foil for the rich meat.

Poulet à la vallée d'auge

Chicken with apples and cider

1 × 3–3½ lb. chicken
4 oz. (8T) butter
6 firm apples
salt and pepper
¾ oz. (3 tablespoons) plain (all purpose) flour
¾ pint (scant 2 cups) draught cider (hard)
bouquet garni
¼ pint (⅝ cup) double (heavy) cream
chopped parsley for garnish

The Vallée d'Auge is a region in Normandy to the North of France.

Cut the chicken into 4 portions. Melt 2 oz. (4T) of the butter in a flameproof casserole, add the chicken and brown the portions all over. Remove and drain.
Peel, core and slice 2 of the apples, sprinkle with salt and pepper and fry in melted butter until beginning to brown. Sprinkle in the flour and cook gently, stirring occasionally until the flour is a light brown. Add ½ pint (1¼ cups) of the (hard) cider and bring to the boil, stirring constantly. Replace the chicken pieces and add the bouquet garni. Cover with greaseproof paper and a tightly fitting lid. Cook in a moderately hot oven (375°F. Mark 5) for 1 hour.
Meanwhile, peel, core and cut into quarters the remaining 4 apples. Melt 1 oz. (2T) butter in a frying pan and fry the apple until browned lightly. Place in an ovenproof dish with 3 tablespoons (¼ cup) water. Cover and place in the oven under the casserole, until needed.
When the chicken is cooked, remove it from the casserole and place it on a heated serving dish, to keep hot. Bring the sauce to the boil, add the remaining ¼ pint (⅝cup) of the (hard) cider, return to the boil and boil rapidly for 10 minutes. Strain and return to the rinsed saucepan. Add the apples and the cream. Stir in the remaining 1 oz. (2T) butter in small pieces. Reheat very gently without boiling Adjust seasoning. Pour over the chicken.

serves 4   Serve garnished with chopped parsley.

Poulet à la marengo

Chicken Marengo

1 × 3–3½ chicken
3 tablespoons (¼ cup) oil
½ pint (1¼ cups) sauce espagnole (see recipe page 16)
8 oz. tomatoes, skinned, deseeded and chopped
1 clove garlic, crushed
3 tablespoons (¼ cup) sherry
12 button mushrooms
4 croûtes of fried bread
chopped parsley for garnish

This famous French classic is thus named because it was first eaten by Napoleon after the battle of Marengo in 1800.

Cut the chicken into 4 portions. Heat the oil in a large frying pan and fry the chicken on both sides until golden. Drain, keep warm. Prepare the sauce espagnole, then add the tomatoes and garlic. Bring to the boil and simmer, stirring occasionally, for 10 minutes. Add the sherry and cook for a further 5 minutes. Add the mushrooms and fry the chicken on both sides until golden. Drain, keep warm. Place the croûtes of bread on a heated serving dish, placing a chicken quarter on each.
Pour the sauce over and serve sprinkled with chopped parsley.

Poulet veronique

Chicken with grapes

2 oz. (4T) butter
4 chicken breasts
1 onion, chopped
1 pint (2½ cups) fond blanc de volaille (chicken stock, see recipe page 30)
1 oz. (¼ cup) plain (all purpose) flour
½ pint (1¼ cups) white wine
salt and pepper
2 oz. (1 cup) white grapes, peeled, halved and pipped
¼ pint (⅝ cup) soured cream
extra white grapes for garnish
serves 4

Melt 1 oz. (2T) of the butter in a large saucepan and fry the chicken breasts until lightly browned. Add the onion and the chicken stock. Bring to the boil and simmer, covered, for 30 minutes. Drain and reserve the stock.
Melt the remaining 1 oz. (2T) butter in a clean saucepan, stir in the flour off the heat and blend in ¼ pint (⅝ cup) of the reserved stock. Bring to the boil, stirring continuously and cook for 1 minute. Stir in the wine, seasonings, grapes and soured cream.
Reheat carefully, without boiling, stirring constantly.
Arrange the chicken breasts on a serving dish and coat evenly with the sauce. Serve garnished with the extra grapes.

Poulet paysan Chicken peasant-style

1×3–4 lb. boiling fowl
3 carrots
3 onions
bouquet garni
6 black peppercorns
salt
3 oz. (6T) butter
2 oz. mushrooms, sliced
2 leeks
clove garlic, crushed
2 rashers streaky bacon, diced
1 oz. (¼ cup) plain (all purpose) flour
¼ pint (⅝ cup) red wine
1 tomato, skinned, deseeded and chopped
1 turnip

serves 4–6

Place the chicken in a large saucepan and cover with water. Add 1 carrot, 1 onion, bouquet garni, peppercorns and 1 teaspoon salt. Cover the pan, bring to the boil and simmer for 1 hour. Drain, reserving the cooking liquor (liquid).
Melt 2 oz. (4T) of the butter in a large saucepan. Fry the chicken gently all over until golden. Remove and drain. Reserve the stock. Slice 1 carrot and 1 onion into thin slices and add to the saucepan with the mushrooms, leeks, garlic and bacon. Fry for 5–7 minutes. Add the flour and cook, stirring, 2–3 minutes. Add the wine, tomato, and 1 pint (2½ cups) of the chicken stock. Bring to the boil, stirring, add the chicken, cover and simmer slowly or cook in a moderate oven (350°F. Mark 4) for 1 hour or until the chicken is tender. Slice the remaining carrot and onion into very thin rounds and slice the turnip thinly. Melt the remaining 1 oz. (2T) butter in a saucepan, add the prepared vegetables and ½ pint (1¼ cups) chicken stock. Cover and simmer very gently until the vegetables are tender, about 20 minutes. Drain.
Carve the chicken in large pieces: wings, drumsticks, breast. Place on a serving dish and keep warm. Strain the gravy into a saucepan, bring to the boil and boil rapidly until it begins to thicken. Pour the gravy over the chicken and place the vegetables in rows down each side of the chicken.
Serve very hot.

Poulet à la doria Chicken with cucumber

Roast the chicken as above using half stock and half white wine in the roasting pan. Peel and chop 1 cucumber. Peel and trim 6 spring onions. Blanche them in boiling water, then cook in 1 oz. (2T) butter over a very low heat until soft and very tender. Stir in 1 tablespoon chopped mint.
Carve the chicken and serve garnished with the cucumber and spring onions on a heated serving plate. If liked, thicken the gravy with a little arrowroot and pour over the chicken. Otherwise serve it separately in a gravy boat.

Coq-au-vin Chicken in red wine

1×3–3½ lb.
3 oz. (6T) butter
8 small onions or shallots
4 rashers streaky bacon
3 tablespoons(¼ cup) brandy
½ pint (1¼ cups) red wine
½ pint (1¼ cups) chicken stock (see recipe page 30)
salt and freshly ground black pepper
bouquet garni
2 cloves garlic, crushed
4 oz. button mushrooms
1 oz. (¼ cup) plain (all purpose) flour
chopped parsley and fried croûtes of bread for garnish

serves 4

Translated literally, coq means cockerel. It is, however, permissable to use any chicken – not just a young cock!

Cut the chicken into 4 portions. Melt 2 oz. (4T) of the butter in a large saucepan and fry the chicken until golden, then remove and drain. Peel the onions, remove the rind and dice the bacon. Fry the onions and bacon in butter until golden, stirring occasionally. Return the chicken to the pan, pour in the brandy and ignite. When the flames have died down add the wine, stock, salt, freshly ground pepper, bouquet garni, garlic and mushrooms. Bring to the boil, cover, and simmer gently for 35–45 minutes or until the chicken is tender. Remove, and discard the bouquet garni.
Mix the remaining butter with the flour to a smooth paste (beurre manié). Remove the chicken from saucepan and place the portions on a heated serving plate, keeping hot. Bring the cooking liquor (liquid) to the boil and add the beurre manié in small pieces, stirring constantly. Add enough beurre manié to form a slightly thickened consistency. Allow the gravy to boil for 2–3 minutes.
Pour the gravy over the chicken, sprinkle with chopped parsley and arrange the croûtes around the edge of the plate. Serve very hot.

Poulet bonne femme
Chicken with white wine and mushrooms

1 × 3–3½ lb. chicken
2 oz. (4T) butter
12 small onions or shallots
4 oz. bacon, diced
½ oz. (2 tablespoons) plain (all purpose) flour
4 oz. button mushrooms
¼ pint (⅝ cup) white wine
¼ pint (⅝ cup) chicken stock (see recipe page 30
bouquet garni
salt and freshly ground black pepper
chopped parsley and croûtes of fried bread for garnish, optional
serves 4

Cut into 4 portions. Melt the butter in a large saucepan and fry the chicken pieces until brown all over. Remove and drain. Add the onions and bacon and fry until softened. Add the flour and cook, stirring, for 2–3 minutes. Add the mushrooms, wine, stock, bouquet garni, salt and pepper.
Bring to the boil and simmer for 35–45 minutes or until the chicken is tender.
Remove and discard the bouquet garni. Serve the chicken in a heated dish, pouring over the sauce and garnishing with chopped parsley and croûtes, if desired.

Poulet rôti au beurre
Chicken roasted in butter

1 × 3–3½ lb. chicken
salt and pepper
few sprigs rosemary or tarragon
2 oz. (4T) butter
2 rashers streaky bacon
½ pint (1¼ cups) chicken stock (made from giblets)

serves 4

Wipe the chicken and season inside with salt and pepper. Put sprigs of rosemary and tarragon into the bird with ½ oz. (1T) of the butter. Truss the chicken and rub the outside with the remaining butter. Place the chicken in a roasting pan, remove the rind from the bacon and place it across the breast. Pour the stock into the base of the pan. Roast in a moderate oven (350°F. Mark 4) for 20 minutes per lb. Turn the chicken over twice during the cooking time so that it will be evenly browned. Baste occasionally.
Strain the juices in the cooking pan into a small saucepan, bring to the boil and boil rapidly for 3–4 minutes. Skim. Serve in a gravy boat. Serve the chicken on a heated serving plate, ready for carving.

80

Vol-au-vent au volaille
Chicken vol-au-vent

8 oz. pâte feuilletée (see recipe page 119)
1 egg, beaten
8 oz. (2 cups) cold cooked chicken
½ pint (1¼ cups) sauce béchamel
1 egg yolk
juice of half a lemon
4 oz. button mushrooms
1 oz. butter
¼ teaspoon ground nutmeg
salt and pepper to taste

Roll out the pastry on a lightly floured board to ½ inch thickness. Use a saucepan lid of 6–7 inch diameter and place a sharp knife into the pastry. Cut round the lid with the knife sloping slightly outwards. Turn the round over and place on a damp baking tray. Make a circle in the middle of the round, using smaller saucepan lid or a saucer as a guide, but cut only half way through the pastry. Mark a criss-cross pattern on the centre circle with a knife. Allow the pastry to rest in a cool place for 20 minutes before baking. Brush the top with beaten egg and then bake in a very hot oven (475°F. Mark 8) for 10 minutes. Reduce the oven temperature to moderately hot (375°F. Mark 5) for a further 10–15 minutes or until cooked. Meanwhile cut the chicken into bite sized pieces. Prepare the sauce béchamel, add the egg yolk and reheat without boiling. Stir in the chicken and lemon juice. Melt the butter in a small saucepan, add the mushrooms and fry gently for 3–5 minutes. Add the mushrooms to the sauce, reheat, and season with nutmeg, salt and pepper. Remove the centre circle from the vol-au-vent, being careful not to break it. Scoop out the pastry in the centre and spoon in the sauce. Replace the lid.
Serve immediately, on a heated serving dish.

serves 4

note: do not reheat the completed dish or the pastry may become soggy.

Vol-au-vents au volaille et poires
Chicken and pear vol-au-vents

Cut the pâte feuilleté into 4 rounds each 2–2½ inches diameter. Mark and glaze as above, bake in a very hot oven (425°F. Mark 7) for 20–25 minutes. Prepare the chicken filling as above. Peel, core and chop 1 lb. pears and add them to the sauce in place of the mushrooms (add them raw; do not fry them in butter first). Reheat, serve as above.

Canard à la rouennaise
Duck Rouen-style

1 × 4 lb. duck
2 rashers streaky bacon
salt and pepper
1 shallot, chopped
1½ oz. (3T) butter
4 oz. liver pâté
¼ pint (⅝ cup) sauce espagnole (see recipe page 16)
¼ pint (⅝ cup) red wine
fried croûtons for garnish

Rouen is a large town of the North of France in the Normandy area. It is greatly famed for its ducks and, naturally, has its own special recipe for cooking them. Rouen ducks are much more gamey than those we usually buy and the meat is darker in colour. If you buy a good fresh duck, you will still make a delicious dish.

Remove the legs from the duck. Place the duck in a roasting pan with the legs separate. Place the rashers of bacon over the duck and sprinkle with salt and pepper. Roast in a very hot oven (450°F. Mark 7) for about 45 minutes to 1 hour or until the duck is almost cooked but still slightly underdone.
Melt ½ oz. (1T) of the butter in a frying pan and cook the duck liver with the shallot until softened and tender. Mix together thoroughly the shallot, the liver, the remaining butter and the pâté.
Mix the sauce espagnole with red wine, heat until boiling and simmer 2–3 minutes.
Carve the duck. Place the pâté mixture down the centre of a heated serving plate, arranging the carved duck (and the legs) on each side.

serves 4

Pour the sauce over the duck and serve sprinkled with croûtons.

Canard à l'orange Duck with orange

1 × 4 lb. duck
2 oz. (4T) butter
½ pint (1¼ cups) water
¼ pint (⅝ cup) white wine
salt and pepper
1 bay leaf
3 oranges
1 tablespoon (1¼T) arrowroot

Wipe the duck and truss it. Place it on a rack in a roasting pan, prick the skin in 6 or 8 places and rub with butter. Place the water and wine in the base of the pan with a sprinkling of salt and pepper, the bay leaf and the zest of 1 orange (use a potato peeler to peel the zest off in strips). Roast the duck in a moderately hot oven (375°F. Mark 5) for 30 minutes, then reduce the temperature to moderately slow (325°F. Mark 3) for 1¼–1½ hours (allowing 25–30 minutes cooking time for each lb.).

Place the duck on a serving plate and keep hot. Strain the cooking liquor (liquid) into a saucepan and make up to ¾ pint (approx. 2 cups) with water. Add the juice of 2 oranges and the rind of 1 orange cut into matchstick strips. Mix a little of the water with the arrowroot and add to sauce. Bring to the boil, stirring constantly and simmer 3–4 minutes.

Garnish the duck with slices of orange. Pour a little of the sauce over the duck. Serve hot with the remaining sauce in a sauce boat.

note: the giblets can be used to make stock which can then be used instead of water.

If the orange rind is tough, blanche the matchstick strips in boiling water before adding them to the sauce.

serves 4

Chicken with apples and cider (below)

Chicken and pear vol-au-vent (above right)

Duck with orange (below right)

Dinde rôti Roast turkey

1 × 8 lb. turkey
4 oz. (8T) butter
parsley
salt and freshly ground
black pepper
½ tablespoon (1T) melted butter
1 tablespoon plain (all
purpose) flour

Truss the turkey and rub well with 3 oz. (6T) of the butter. Put the remaining butter, with some sprigs of parsley, into the bird. Season the turkey with salt and freshly ground black pepper. Place the turkey in a roasting pan with the giblets (not the liver) and ½ inch depth of water. Roast, covered with greased greaseproof paper or aluminium foil, in a moderately hot oven (375°F. Mark 5) for 2 hours 40 minutes (allowing 20 minutes cooking time for each lb.). It may be necessary to add more water to the pan during the cooking. Remove the paper or foil after 2 hours.
Place the cooked turkey on a serving plate and keep hot. Discard the giblets. Place the melted butter in a frying pan and cook the liver gently until tender. Skim off 1 tablespoon (2T) butter from the turkey and mix it with the flour to make a paste. Return the paste to the gravy, bring to the boil, stirring constantly and simmer 3–4 minutes. Add the liver, sliced thinly.

serves 10 Serve hot with the gravy in a gravy boat.

Oie rôtie à la périgord Roast goose Périgord-style

1 × 8 lb. goose
salt and pepper
3 lb. potatoes, peeled and
quartered
5 hard-boiled eggs
watercress for garnish

Goose is considered a great delicacy in some parts of France. In Strasbourg, as in the Périgord region, geese are fattened for their liver to make pâté de foie gras. The livers can weigh from 1½ to 2½ lb. each. The actual geese, however, tend to be small.

Truss the goose and sprinkle it with salt and pepper. Place it on a rack in a large roasting pan. Cover with greased greaseproof paper or aluminium foil and roast in a moderately slow oven (325°F. Mark 3) for 3–3½ hours (allowing 25 minutes cooking time for each lb.) Remove the paper for the last 30 minutes.
Cook the potatoes in boiling salted water for 5 minutes, drain. When the goose has been cooking for about 1½–2 hours, pour off most of the fat in the roasting pan and add the potatoes.
Cut the eggs into quarters and add them to the roasting pan 10 minutes before cooking time is complete.
Drain the cooked potatoes and eggs. Serve the goose on a heated

serves 10 serving plate surrounded with eggs and potatoes.

Lapin sauté chasseur Fried rabbit hunter-style

1 young rabbit
salt and pepper
flour
1 oz. (2T) butter
2 tablespoons (2½T) oil
2 shallots, chopped
½ tablespoon (¾T) plain (all
purpose) flour
¼ pint (⅝ cup) red wine
¼ pint (⅝ cup) fond blanc (white
stock, see recipe page 30)
1 tomato, skinned, deseeded and
chopped
1 clove garlic, crushed
bouquet garni
4 oz. button mushrooms, sliced
croûtons of fried bread
chopped parsley for garnish
serves 4

Cut the rabbit into joints, wash it in cold salted water, then rinse and dry it. Mix the salt and pepper with flour and coat the rabbit pieces. Heat the butter and oil in a large saucepan, add the rabbit and fry it until it is golden all over. Remove the rabbit and drain. Add the shallots, cook, stirring, until softened. Stir in ½ tablespoon (¾T) flour and cook 2–3 minutes. Add the wine, stock, tomato, garlic, bouquet garni and salt and pepper.
Return the rabbit to the pan, cover and simmer gently for 30 minutes. Add the mushrooms and cook for another 10 minutes or until rabbit is cooked. Remove the bouquet garni.
Serve sprinkled with croûtons and chopped parsley.

Pigeons en cocotte normande
Casseroled pigeons with apples and cider

4 small pigeons
1½ oz. (3T) butter
1 tablespoon (1¼T) oil
1 onion, sliced
4 apples
1 oz. (¼ cup) plain (all purpose) flour
¾ pint (scant 2 cups) water
½ pint (1¼ cups) cider (hard)
salt and pepper
bouquet garni
4 rashers streaky bacon, grilled
chopped parsley for garnish

Pigeons which are young, plump, have supple bones and a rosy red skin are suitable for roasting. Rub each pigeon with butter, season well and roast in a hot oven for 25–35 minutes. Too frequently, however, pigeons are not suitable for roasting. Try cooking them in the following way and they will be both tender and delicious.

Wipe the pigeons. Heat 1 oz. (2T) of the butter and the oil in a large saucepan, add the pigeons and fry until they are browned all over. Remove and drain. Fry the onion, peel and core and slice one apple and add it to the saucepan. Fry the onion and apple until golden, remove and drain. Add the flour to the pan and cook over a low heat, stirring, until cooked and beginning to brown. Add the water and cider, bring to the boil, and simmer 2–3 minutes.
Place the pigeons in an ovenproof casserole, adding the onion, apple, sauce, salt and pepper and bouquet garni. Cover and cook in a moderate oven (350°F. Mark 4) for 1½ hours.
Peel, core and slice the remaining apples into rings, heat the remaining ½ oz. (1T) butter in a frying pan and cook the apple rings until golden.
Remove the cooked pigeons from the casserole. Strain the sauce into a saucepan, bring to the boil and boil rapidly until reduced in quantity and thickening.
Arrange the pigeons on a heated serving dish, pour over the sauce and garnish with the apple rings, crisp bacon and chopped parsley.

Perdrix au chou
Partridge with cabbage

2 large partridges
1 small, firm, green cabbage
6 oz. fat bacon (in one piece)
4 carrots, sliced
2 onions, sliced
4 oz. pork sausage (charcuterie)
salt and pepper
6 juniper berries
2 cloves garlic, crushed
¼ teaspoon ground nutmeg
fond brun (white stock, see recipe page 30)
1 tablespoon (1¼T) arrowroot

This is a classic 'cuisine bourgeoise' recipe. It is an ideal way of cooking two partridges if one is young and tender and the other old.

Wipe the partridges. Cut the cabbage in quarters and blanche in boiling salted water for 3–4 minutes then slice each quarter in thin slices. Slice the bacon thickly, fry a little in a large saucepan, add the partridges and brown all over.
Put a layer of cabbage in the base of a large ovenproof dish, top with the remaining bacon slices, carrots, onions, sausages and the partridges. Season with salt and pepper, add the juniper berries, garlic, nutmeg and enough stock to almost cover the vegetables. Cover with the remaining cabbage.
Cover the dish with greased greaseproof paper and then a tight lid. Cook in a moderately slow oven (325°F. Mark 3) for about 2 hours. The cabbage must be cooked for the whole time but the other ingredients may be cooked sooner. If one partridge is young, remove it from the dish after about 40 minutes; remove the sausages after 30 minutes; remove the bacon after 45 minutes. Return all the ingredients to the dish about 15 minutes before cooking time is completed to allow them to heat through.
Drain all the cooked ingredients, including the cabbage, and carve the partridges. Keep them hot.
Thicken the remaining stock with arrowroot. Mix the arrowroot with a little of the stock, put the remainder in a saucepan, add the arrowroot, bring to the boil and simmer for 2–3 minutes.
Arrange the cabbage and other vegetables on a heated serving plate, putting the carved partridges on top. Pour a little sauce over the
serves 4 cabbage. Serve the remainder separately in a sauce boat.

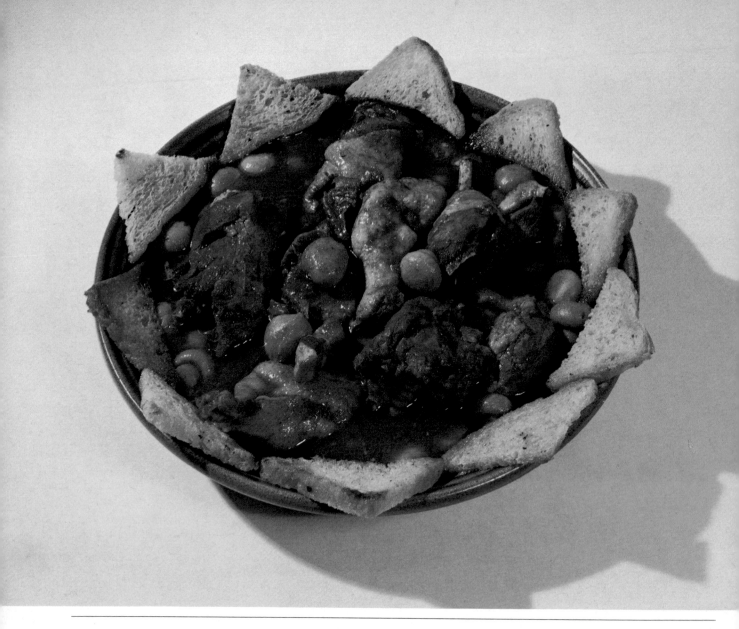

Civet de lièvre landais   Jugged hare Landes-style

1 hare
2 oz. (¼ cup) pork fat
10 shallots, peeled
2 cloves garlic, crushed
4 oz. Bayonne ham, diced
¼ pint (⅝ cup) red wine
½ pint (1¼ cups) water
4 tomatoes, skinned, deseeded
and chopped
1 oz. dried cèpes
salt and freshly ground
black pepper
croûtes of fried bread
for serving

This is a traditional recipe from the Landes department in the South West of France. Bayonne ham should be used, but gammon makes a good substitute. The recipe also includes cèpes which are a type of edible fungus. They are available dried in some shops but, if unavailable, use 2 oz. mushrooms instead.

Cut the hare into serving portions and wash well in cold water. Heat the pork fat in a large saucepan and fry the hare until browned all over. Remove the hare, drain and place it in an ovenproof casserole. Brown the shallots in pork fat and add them to the casserole. Fry the garlic and ham until golden, drain and place in the casserole. Add the remaining ingredients—the wine, water, tomatoes, cèpes and salt and pepper to the casserole.
Cover the casserole tightly and cook in a moderately slow oven (325°F. Mark 3) for 1½–2 hours or until the hare is very tender. Place the hare on a heated serving dish. Strain the sauce into a saucepan, bring to the boil and boil rapidly until it has thickened slightly. Pour the sauce over the hare and serve garnished with croûtes of fried bread around the edge.

note: if you are lucky enough to have some of the hare's blood, add some of it to the sauce to thicken it, just before serving.

serves 6

86   *Jugged hare (above)*   *Stuffed tomatoes and ratatouille (right)*

Vegetables

The French have great respect for their vegetables. Meat, being very expensive, is often replaced by vegetables which can provide almost as much nutritious value. In other cases, carefully prepared vegetables make a very attractive garnish to a meat dish, even giving the dish its name. Fresh spring vegetables, cut into matchstick strips and cooked, give the dish they garnish the name 'julienne'. The same vegetables diced give the name 'brunoise'. A chateaubriand steak has its name because it is always served with a garnish of château potatoes. Always buy first quality vegetables. If fresh are unavailable, use frozen vegetables as these are usually in peak condition. Vegetables, raw or cooked, generally freeze very well, so if you cook too much of one dish, try freezing the remainder for a later date (ratatouille freezes especially well, so make a double or treble quantity).

Except when used as a garnish, vegetables are usually served as a separate course to the meat, either before or after the main course. All the vegetables, however, can also be served with the meat, as we are familiar with this method. Some of these versatile recipes can also be served as hors d'oeuvres.

Pommes château   Château potatoes

1–1½ lbs. potatoes
2 oz. (4T) clarified butter
salt
parsley

serves 4

Peel the potatoes and shape them into small pieces the size and shape of large olives. Cook them in boiling water for 1 minute, drain and dry well.
Melt the butter in a large frying pan, add the potatoes and cook gently, carefully shaking the pan occasionally, until the potatoes are cooked and golden. Drain.
Serve either in a heated dish or as a garnish, sprinkled with salt and finely chopped parsley.

Pommes parisienne   Parisienne potatoes

The potatoes used in the above recipe should be cut into balls about ¼–½ inch in diameter using a ball-cutter. Pommes parisienne are then cooked in exactly the same way as pommes château.

Pommes mousseline   Potato purée

2 lb. potatoes
2 oz. (4T) butter
approximately ¼ pint (⅝ cup) hot milk
salt and pepper

serves 4–6

Wash the potatoes, place in a saucepan of water with enough cold water to cover. Bring to the boil and simmer for about 20 minutes or until tender. Drain thoroughly. Remove the skins.
Add the butter to the potatoes in small pieces and beat well. Gradually add the milk until the potatoes are soft, smooth and creamy. Season with salt and pepper to taste. Reheat gently over a low heat.
Serve as required.

Pommes mousseline provençale

Make pommes mousseline as above. The meat juices from a joint cooked 'à la Provençale' (i.e. with garlic and herbs) are then poured around the edge of the potato on the serving plate.
In France, this dish is sometimes eaten as a separate course before the meat.

Pommes de terre à la savoyarde   Potatoes with cheese

1 lb. potatoes
½ pint (1¼ cups) fond blanc (white stock, see recipe page 30)
1 egg, beaten
salt and pepper
¼ teaspoon grated nutmeg
2 oz. (½ cup) grated gruyère cheese
1 clove garlic
1 oz. (2T) butter

serves 4

Peel and slice the potatoes finely. Put them in a bowl and add the stock with the egg beaten into it. Season with salt, pepper and nutmeg. Add the grated cheese and mix thoroughly.
Grease an ovenproof dish and rub it with a cut clove of garlic. Add the potato mixture and dot with small pieces of butter. Cook in a moderately slow oven (325°F. Mark 3) for 35–40 minutes or until the potato is cooked and the top beginning to brown. Serve in the dish in which it is cooked.

Pommes de terre à la dauphinoise   Potatoes with milk and cheese

Prepare the potatoes as above but substitute milk for the white stock.

Pommes de terre à la lyonnaise
Fried potatoes with onions

1½ lb. potatoes
2 onions
4 oz. (8T) butter
salt
chopped parsley for garnish

serves 4–6

Wash the potatoes and boil them in their skins until tender. Skin them and cut into ¼ inch slices. Peel and slice the onions thinly. Melt 2 oz. (4T) of the butter in a large frying pan and fry the potato slices until golden brown all over, about 15–20 minutes. In a separate frying pan, melt the remaining 2 oz. (4T) butter and fry the onion rings, stirring, until golden, about 10 minutes.
Drain the potatoes and onion thoroughly, sprinkle with salt and mix together gently. Serve in a heated dish, sprinkled with chopped parsley.

Pommes duchesse
Duchess potatoes

1½ lb. potatoes
2 egg yolks
3 tablespoons (¼ cup) milk or single (light) cream
1 oz. (2T) butter
salt and pepper
¼ teaspoon ground nutmeg
beaten egg for glazing

serves 4–6

Wash the potatoes and boil them in their skins until tender. Skin, then press them through a sieve. Return them to a clean saucepan, add the egg yolks, cream, butter, salt, pepper, and nutmeg.
Heat the saucepan very gently and beat the potatoes thoroughly until light and fluffy.
Place the beaten potatoes in a forcing bag with a large star piping tube. Pipe rosettes of potato on to a greased baking tray and brush them lightly with beaten egg.
Bake in a hot oven (425°F. Mark 7) until golden. (The time will vary according to the size of the rosettes.) Serve as required.

Pommes croquettes
Croquette potatoes

½ quantity duchess potatoes (see above)
flour
beaten egg
breadcrumbs (soft or dried – both are suitable)
oil for deep frying

serves 4

Divide the prepared potato into 8 pieces. Shape each piece on a lightly floured board into a cork shape, slightly narrower at one end. Roll the croquettes in flour.
Dip each croquette in beaten egg, then in breadcrumbs. Repeat the process. Deep fry in hot oil (375°F. or until a ¼ inch dice of bread will brown in less than a minute) until crisp and golden.
Drain thoroughly on absorbent kitchen paper. Serve hot.

note: croquettes can be made in practically any shape. Cork-shaped croquettes are traditional.

Carottes vichy
Carrots Vichy

1 lb. carrots
2 oz. (4T) butter
1 teaspoon sugar
pinch of salt
chopped parsley for garnish

serves 4

Peel the carrots and slice thinly. Melt 1 oz. of the butter in a heavy saucepan, add the sugar, salt, carrots and ¾ pint (scant 2 cups) water. Bring to the boil and simmer, uncovered, until the carrots are cooked and the liquid has evaporated. Add the remaining butter and toss the carrots lightly.
Serve in a heated dish sprinkled with chopped parsley.

Choufleur polonaise
Cauliflower polonaise

1 cauliflower
salt
2 oz. (4T) butter
3 tablespoons (¼ cup) dry white breadcrumbs
1 hard boiled egg
chopped parsley for garnish

serves 4

Break the cauliflower into florets and soak in cold salted water for 20 minutes. Cook the cauliflower in a large saucepan of boiling salted water for 15 minutes or until tender. Drain thoroughly.
Place the cauliflower florets in a heated serving dish. Melt the butter in a frying pan and fry the breadcrumbs until golden, then sprinkle them over the cauliflower.
Chop the egg yolk and egg white separately. Sprinkle the yolk on to the cauliflower and place the white at each end.
Serve hot, sprinkled with chopped parsley.

Courgettes aux amandes

Courgettes (zucchini) with almonds

1 lb. courgettes (zucchini) **flour** **salt and pepper** **3 oz. (6T) butter** **2 oz. ($\frac{1}{3}$ cup) almonds, split** **$\frac{1}{4}$ pint ($\frac{5}{8}$ cup) single** **(light) cream**	Wash the courgettes (zucchini) and cut into $\frac{1}{2}$ inch slices. Toss the slices in flour seasoned with salt and pepper. Melt the butter in a frying pan, add the courgettes and fry until golden on both sides. Drain. Arrange the courgettes in a heated serving dish. Fry the almonds in butter until beginning to brown. Drain and sprinkle over the courgettes. Heat the cream gently, season with salt and pepper and pour over
serves 4	the courgettes. Serve as soon as possible.

Onions used in cooking (above)   *Potatoes with cheese (right)*

90

Cassoulet Beanstew

8 oz. haricot beans
4 oz. pickled pork
2 cloves garlic, crushed
4 oz. lamb
2 tablespoons olive oil
1 onion, sliced
bouquet garni
salt and pepper
2 oz. sausage (pork or garlic are both suitable)
2 large tomatoes, skinned, deseeded and chopped
chopped parsley for garnish

serves 4

This dish comes from the Languedoc region of France, although most of the regions have now adapted it for their own. The name cassoulet comes from a small town in Languedoc called Cassol d'Issel where the traditional clay cooking pot for this dish originated.

Soak the beans overnight in water to cover, drain the following day. Place the pork, garlic and lamb in a small saucepan with cold water to cover, bring to the boil and simmer for 5–7 minutes. Drain the meat slice.
Heat the oil in a flameproof casserole, fry the pork and lamb with the onion until golden. Add the beans, bouquet garni, salt and pepper and enough boiling water to almost cover the beans. Cover the casserole tightly and cook in a slow oven (300°F. Mark 2) for 2½–3 hours. Add the sliced sausage and tomatoes 1 hour before the cooking time is completed.
Remove the bouquet garni and serve sprinkled with chopped parsley.

Aubergines farcies provençale

Stuffed aubergines (eggplants) Provençale

2 aubergines (eggplants)
1 oz. (2T) butter
2 onions, chopped
2 tomatoes, skinned, deseeded and chopped
½ teaspoon mixed chopped dried herbs
salt and pepper
3 tablespoons (¼ cup) grated cheese
4 anchovy fillets
olive oil

serves 4

Place the aubergines (eggplants) in a large saucepan of boiling water (to cover). Cook for 10 minutes. Cut in half lengthwise and scoop out the pulp, leaving about a ½ inch wall of skin. Chop the pulp into large pieces.

Melt the butter in a saucepan, add the onions and fry until softened. Add the tomatoes, herbs and salt and pepper. Cover and cook gently for 5 minutes. Add the chopped aubergine and reheat.

Pile the stuffing into the aubergine skin halves, sprinkle each with grated cheese and place an anchovy on top. Brush lightly with a little oil. Place the stuffed aubergines under a hot grill and cook until golden.

Arrange the aubergines on a heated serving dish and serve as soon as possible.

Stuffed aubergines (eggplants) Provençale

Mediterranean vegetable stew

Petits pois à la Française

Peas French-style

1 oz. (2T) butter
6 spring onions, sliced
6 lettuce leaves, shredded finely
¼ teaspoon salt
¼ teaspoon black pepper
1 sprig each parsley and mint
1 teaspoon sugar
1 lb. shelled peas
1 teaspoon plain (all purpose) flour
2 teaspoons butter

serves 4

Melt the butter in a large saucepan, add the spring onions, lettuce, salt, pepper, parsley, mint, sugar and peas. Stir in ¼ pint (⅝ cup) water, bring to the boil, cover and simmer gently for about 20 minutes or until the peas are very tender.

Remove and discard the parsley and mint. Cream the flour and butter together thoroughly and add to the peas in small pieces. Stir gently with a wooden spoon and heat gently until any remaining liquid is thickened.

Serve piping hot.

Haricots verts au beurre
French beans in butter

1 lb. French beans
salt
1 oz. (2T) butter
freshly ground black pepper

serves 4

Tender young French beans are best served in the simplest way. They are easy to prepare, needing only to be topped and tailed.

Prepare the beans and cook them in a saucepan with 1 inch of boiling salted water, for 10–15 minutes. Drain well. Melt the butter in the saucepan, add the beans and toss until coated in butter. Serve in a heated dish and sprinkle generously with black pepper.

Ratatouille
Mediterranean vegetable stew

3 aubergines (eggplants)
3 courgettes (zucchini)
salt
3 red peppers
5 tomatoes
3 onions
¼ pint (⅝ cup) olive oil
2 cloves garlic, crushed
6 coriander seeds, crushed
1 teaspoon chopped dried parsley
½ teaspoon chopped dried basil
freshly ground black pepper
serves 6–8

Slice the aubergines (eggplants) and courgettes (zucchini) into ¼ inch rounds. Place in a colander, in layers, and sprinkle each layer with salt. Cover with a plate and leave for 45 minutes. Drain off excess moisture.

Remove the seeds and membranes from the peppers, cut into thin strips. Skin the tomatoes by immersing them in boiling water for 2 minutes, cool in cold water and peel off the skin. Cut into ½ inch slices. Peel and slice the onions thinly.

Heat the olive oil in a saucepan, add the onion and fry gently until softened but not browned. Add a layer of peppers, then aubergines, courgettes and finally tomatoes with the garlic and coriander seeds. Simmer very gently, covered, for 1–1¼ hours or until the vegetables are soft but not mushy.

Stir in the herbs (taste and add salt and pepper as necessary). Serve in a heated dish.

note: this dish keeps and can be successfully reheated. Mushrooms can also be included in a ratatouille. Add sliced mushrooms to the saucepan about 30 minutes before the cooking time is completed.

Oignons frites
Fried onion rings

1 lb. onions
2 egg whites
flour
salt and pepper
oil for deep frying
serves 4–6

Slice the onions thinly. Whisk the egg whites until frothy. Mix the flour with salt and pepper.

Dip each separate onion ring into egg white then into seasoned flour. Deep fry the rings (adding them individually to prevent them sticking together) in deep hot oil until golden and crisp. (The oil should be 375°F. or a ¼ inch dice of bread will brown in less than a minute.) Drain very thoroughly on absorbent kitchen paper.

Serve as required, piping hot.

Salade verte
Green salad

This salad is often called salade de saison (Seasonal Salad). Which ingredients are used depends on what is available. The following ingredients are all suitable: lettuce; endive; chicory; watercress; dandelion leaves; sorrel; celery; celeriac; cucumber; green pepper. The list is almost endless. Fresh herbs are also frequently included giving a really individual flavour to your salad. Try using one of the following: parsley; chives; lovage; chervil; mint.
Try to obtain vegetables as fresh as possible. Tear green leaves into bite sized pieces and cut other green vegetables into thin slices. Chop the herbs roughly.
Toss the vegetables in just enough sauce vinaigrette (see recipe page 21) to make each individual leaf glisten. Serve your salad as soon as it has been tossed or else it may become soggy.

Salade au chapon

Rub a slice of French bread all over with a cut clove of garlic and sprinkle each side with 1 teaspoon olive oil. Prepare a salad as above and toss the prepared bread into the salad with the dressing. The salad will have a slight but delicious flavour of garlic.

Salade niçoise   Salad from Nice

½ lettuce
½ head curly endive
1 onion, thinly sliced
2 tomatoes, skinned and sliced
¼ cucumber, sliced
1 green pepper, thinly sliced
12 black olives, pitted
4 anchovy fillets
1 × 7 oz. can tuna
1 tablespoon chopped fresh basil
1 clove garlic, crushed
sauce vinaigrette (see recipe page 21)

This salad is served as an hors d'oeuvre in France but is more popular in other countries when served with the main course. Both methods are good. There are many different recipes but each one must include ingredients which are available along the French Mediterranean coast.

Wash, dry and tear the lettuce and endive into bite sized pieces. Prepare the vegetables and olives, cut the anchovy fillet in half lengthwise, drain the tuna and break into large pieces.
Place the vegetables, olives and fish in a salad bowl. Add the basil and garlic to the sauce vinaigrette and sprinkle over the salad. Toss all the ingredients together gently and serve immediately.

note: hard boiled eggs, cut into quarters, are frequently added to this salad to make it more substantial. Cooked French beans or tiny new potatoes make another delicious addition.

Mushroom soufflé (above)   Camembert cream (right)

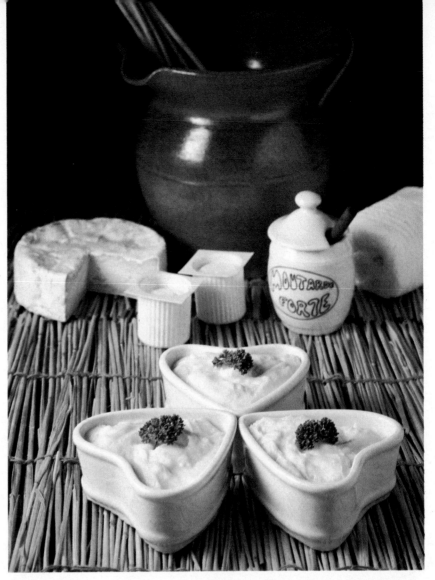

Cheese and savouries

Cheese and savouries play a large part in a French dinner party menu. They are the 'bridge' between the main part of the meal and the sweet or dessert. Normally, cheese is served, but for a more elaborate meal a hot, freshly prepared savoury is delicious.

All the savouries can double as appetizers before a meal or simply with drinks at a cocktail party. They make a very welcome change from the well known canapés and bouchées.

The Cheeses of France

The French make delicious cheeses from both cow's and goat's milk. Some are mild, creamy cheeses while others can be strong and well-ripened.

Cream cheeses These are the very softest kind of cheese. The best known are Petit Suisse, Demi-sel and various herb cheeses (all made from cow's milk) which come from Normandy; Saint-Marcellin comes from Savoie and is made from a mixture of cow's and goat's milk, and Valancay from Touraine is also made from cow's milk.

Soft cheeses The most famous of this kind of cheese is Camembert, which is made from cow's milk, in the Normandy area. Another similar cheese, Livarot, is made in the same area; it is slightly larger in size and stronger in flavour than Camembert. Yet another is Pont-l'Evéque. Brie, again made from cow's milk, is made on the border of Champagne and Ile de France and both provinces claim it for their own. A goat's milk cheese which comes from the village of Sainte-Maure in Touraine and bears the same name as the village, also falls into this category. It does not keep well, though, and is not frequently seen outside France.

Semi-hard cheeses There are more French cheeses of this kind than of any other. The most well-known are St Paulin, Port Salut and Baby Bel from Normandy. Reblochon and Tome de Savoie (that is the one with the grape pip rind) are less well-known and come from the Haute Savoie province. Those cheeses already mentioned are all cow's milk cheeses, but there are also a few goat's milk semi-hard cheeses including Banon and Chèvre, the latter covering a whole range of anonymous goat's milk cheeses which are white, crumbly and mild.

Hard cheeses These are limited in number. One of the most famous is Munster cheese from Alsace; it has a strong flavour and creamy texture. Another is Cantal, a cow's milk cheese from Auvergne. This is similar to a mature cheddar cheese and will keep well.

Blue cheeses Roquefort is the undisputed king of French cheeses. It is crumbly with a green mould and made from ewe's milk, in the midi and sud-oest of France. The true Roquefort is always matured in the caves of Rouergue. Other blue cheeses are Bleu de Bresse and Bleu d'Auvergne, named after their places of origin.

There are of course many, many more French cheeses. Above are mentioned just some of the better known among them.

Always buy cheese with care. If it is wrapped in waxed paper or foil, make sure that the paper is not damaged or the cheese inside may be dry and spoiled. Cream cheeses are best when fresh or slightly mature. Blue cheeses are still at their best when very mature.

Make sure that the cheese you buy has been made in France and avoid imitations manufactured elsewhere. By means of refrigeration, cheese can now be kept fresh for a very long time, so French cheeses are obtainable throughout the world.

Store cheese carefully to keep it in good condition. Cream cheeses can be kept up to 4 days in the refrigerator. Soft cheeses will also keep well in a refrigerator as the cold arrests the ripening process. Outside a refrigerator they will only keep 2–3 days. All other cheeses should be stored in a cool larder or in the warmest part of the refrigerator. Wrap semi-hard cheeses in a damp cloth to keep them moist, and, after cutting, place them in a polythene bag or foil. Blue cheese should be placed in an airtight bag or box.

The French serve the cheese directly after the main course with the bread and butter left over from the meal. The dessert course follows the cheese. Cream cheese can be served straight from the refrigerator but other cheeses must be left at room temperature for at least an hour, or, in the case of Camembert or Brie, two hours. Serve the cheese whole, not cut up in any way, but unwrapped. Petit Suisse is unsalted and can be eaten with either salt or sugar. It is usual to serve a variety of cheeses for the diners to choose from. Make sure that they are not all the same texture but include at least one from each category, from cream to blue cheese.

Crème au camembert   Camembert cream

3×1 oz. portions
Camembert cheese
½ oz. (1T) butter, melted
1×½ oz. portion Petit
Suisse cheese
3 tablespoons (¼ cup) double
(heavy) cream
1 teaspoon French mustard
1 teaspoon finely
chopped parsley
watercress for garnish
serves 4

Cut the rind off the Camembert, mix with the melted butter and beat well until smooth. Add the Petit Suisse and beat well. Lightly whip the cream and add to the cheese mixture with the French mustard and parsley. Mix well.
Pour the mixture into a small mould or serving dish. Chill. Serve unmoulded or in the dish, garnished with watercress.

Diablotine gruyère   Devilled gruyère tarts

4 oz. pâte brisée (shortcrust
pastry, see recipe page 119)
1 oz. (1T) butter
½ oz. (2 tablespoons) cornflour
(cornstarch)
¼ pint (⅝ cup) milk
2 eggs
3 oz. (¾ cup) grated
gruyère cheese
salt and cayenne pepper
1 teaspoon anchovy paste

makes 1–1½ dozen

Make the pâte brisée and roll out thinly on to a lightly floured board. Line 12–18 small patty tins.
Melt the butter in a small saucepan, add the cornflour, then the milk, stirring constantly until the mixture is smooth. Bring to the boil, stirring, simmer 2–3 minutes. Remove the pan from the heat, beat in the egg yolks with 2 oz. (½ cup) of cheese, salt and cayenne pepper. Whisk the egg whites until stiff and fold into the cheese mixture.
Half fill the pastry cases with the egg mixture, put a spot of anchovy paste on top and cover with more egg mixture. Sprinkle with the remaining cheese. Bake the tarts in a moderately hot oven (375°F. Mark 5) for 15–20 minutes or until firm and golden brown. Serve piping hot.

Diables à cheval   Stuffed prunes

8 prunes
8 almonds, toasted
4 rashers streaky bacon
8 small croûtes of fried bread
watercress to garnish

makes 8

Stone the prunes and place a toasted almond in each one. Remove the bacon rind and spread each rasher of bacon with the back of a knife until thin and almost doubled in length, then cut in half.
Wind a piece of bacon around each prune and secure with a wooden cocktail stick. Cook the stuffed prunes under a hot grill until the bacon is golden.
Serve each hot savoury on a croûte of fried bread, garnishing the plate with a sprig of watercress.

note: instead of almonds, try using a rolled up anchovy or a stuffed olive to stuff the prunes.

Aigrettes au fromage   Cheese aigrettes

2 oz. (4T) butter
¼ pint (⅝ cup) water
2½ oz. (good ½ cup) plain (all
purpose) flour
2 eggs, beaten
2 oz. (½ cup) grated
Parmesan cheese
pinch of cayenne pepper
salt
deep oil for frying

Place the butter and water in a saucepan, then heat slowly until the butter is melted and the water is at boiling point. Remove from the heat. Add all the sifted flour and beat well with a wooden spoon until the mixture is smooth and falls away from the sides of the pan. Allow the paste to cool slightly, then add the beaten eggs gradually and mix well. Stir in the cheese and seasoning.
Heat the oil until 375°F. (a ¼ inch dice of bread will brown in less than a minute). Fry teaspoonfuls of the mixture until puffed up, golden and crisp, about 10 minutes. Drain well on absorbent kitchen paper. Sprinkle with salt.
Serve very hot piled on to a plate.

Éclairs savoureux Savoury éclairs

Savoury éclairs are an unusual and delicious hot or cold savoury. They can be made with the same paste used for cheese aigrettes, baked and not fried. Grease a baking tray and pipe 1–1½ inch lengths of the paste (use a ⅜ inch plain round pipe), brush the tops with beaten egg and bake in a hot oven (400°F. Mark 6) for about 25 minutes or until golden and crisp. Serve as soon as possible. Alternatively, omit the cheese from the recipe for cheese aigrettes and make and bake as above. Make a slit in the side of each éclair to let the steam out, then allow to cool. Fill each éclair with a savoury filling just before serving. The filling can be a pâté or even scrambled egg with ham—indeed anything that is available.

Savoury éclairs in preparation

Filling savoury éclairs

Savoury éclairs

Cassolettes chasseur — Prawn butter balls

4 oz. (8T) butter
2 eggs, beaten
soft white breadcrumbs
oil for deep frying
2 oz. (½ cup) chopped prawns (shrimp)
3 tablespoons (¼ cup) sauce béchamel (see recipe page 16)
3 tablespoons (¼ cup) double (heavy) cream
salt and pepper
extra peeled prawns (shrimp)
fried parsley for garnish

makes 8

Cassolettes used to be small batter cases needing a special mould to make them. These butter ball cases are equally light and crisp and need a great deal of care in the making.

Divide the butter into 8 equal pieces and shape each one into a ball. Place the balls in a bowl of iced water or in the refrigerator until they are very hard. Drain the butter balls well, dip them into the beaten egg and then coat in breadcrumbs. Press the crumbs on well. Repeat this process 3 more times. Continue until all the balls are thickly coated.

Heat the oil for deep frying until 375 °F. (a ¼ inch dice of bread will brown in less than a minute). With a small cutter (a plain icing pipe is good) cut a small round in the breadcrumb coating. Deep fry the butter balls until golden brown and crisp. Cool slightly, then remove the round 'lid' with the point of a knife and tip out the melted butter. Drain well on absorbent kitchen paper and keep hot. Mix the chopped prawns (shrimp) with the sauce béchamel and cream, season to taste, reheat gently without boiling.

Spoon the filling into the prepared cases and arrange the extra whole prawns on the top. Serve immediately on a heated serving plate, garnished with fried parsley.

Croustades de merluche fumée — Smoked haddock in crusty cases

1 sandwich loaf
2 eggs, beaten
fresh white breadcrumbs
oil for deep frying
4 oz. (1 cup) flaked cooked smoked haddock
4 anchovies, chopped
1 oz. (2T) butter, melted
cayenne pepper
3 tablespoons (¼ cup) double (heavy) cream

makes 12

Cut the bread into 6 slices, each 1½ inches thick. Cut out 2 rounds from each slice using a biscuit cutter. Dip each round into the beaten egg and then coat in breadcrumbs, pressing them on firmly. Mark another round with a smaller biscuit cutter on the top of each piece of bread.

Heat the oil for deep frying until 375°F. (a ¼ inch dice of bread will brown in less than a minute). Fry the bread rounds until crisp and golden. Carefully remove the smaller round on the top when cooled slightly. Scoop out the soft bread from the centre of the case. Drain on absorbent kitchen paper and keep hot.

Mix the smoked haddock with the anchovies, melted butter, a pinch of cayenne pepper and the cream, in a small saucepan. Reheat without boiling.

Fill the crispy bread cases with the smoked haddock mixture, replacing the lids.
Serve very hot.

Jambon à la diable — Devilled ham

12 rounds cooked ham (2 inches in diameter)
2 teaspoons French mustard
1 teaspoon English mustard
2 teaspoons chutney
salt
lemon juice
olive oil
6 button mushrooms
½ oz. (1T) butter
6 rounds buttered toast (2 inches diameter)
paprika pepper for garnish

makes 6

Cut the rounds of ham carefully. Mix together the mustards and chutney with salt to taste and a few drops of lemon juice to moisten. Sandwich the ham rounds together in pairs. Brush with olive oil and grill until very hot, 2–3 minutes.

Wipe the mushrooms. Heat the butter in a small frying pan and fry the mushrooms until tender.

Place the ham on to the freshly made hot buttered toast rounds, top with a mushroom. Sprinkle with paprika pepper.
Serve piping hot.

Desserts

At one time the dessert course at a French dinner party was divided into two parts: first a rich, usually cream, dessert was served. This was called the 'entremet sucre' and was followed by a lighter course of either fresh fruit or cooked fruit.

Fresh fruit is eaten more frequently today than it used to be, not only because it is very easy to prepare and serve but because, with a shrinking world, a greater variety of fruits are available from other countries. Whether serving local or foreign fruits, always make sure that they are perfect and unblemished. Wash each piece of fruit carefully under running cold water and pat it dry with a clean tea towel or absorbent kitchen paper. Pile the different fruits in one bowl, making an attractive arrangement.

Before any sweet course is served, clear the table of the main course and remove the salt and pepper and bread and butter, leaving only spoons and forks for a prepared dessert and small silver knives and forks for the fresh fruit. Provide small plates.

Sorbet de yaourt à l'orange   Yoghourt orange sorbet

2 × 5 oz. cartons natural yoghourt
1 × 6¼ oz. can concentrated orange juice
grated rind from 2 oranges
sugar to taste
½ oz. (1½ tablespoons) gelatine
2 egg whites
2 oranges
sprigs of mint for decoration
serves 4–6

Although sorbets can be served as a dessert, their place on a French formal dinner menu comes after the relevé (or joint) to clear the palate ready for the roast poultry or game.
Yoghourt is much used in French cookery, especially in the Haute Savoie district where it is made commercially in large amounts.

Turn the refrigerator setting to its lowest point.
Mix the yoghourt, orange juice and grated rind together in a mixing bowl with sugar to taste. Heat 3 tablespoons (¼ cup) water until hot, shower in the gelatine and stir until dissolved. Cool slightly, then add to the yoghourt mixture. Mix well, then put aside until syrupy and beginning to set.
Whisk the egg whites until just stiff, then fold into the yoghourt mixture.
Pour the mixture into a dish or cake tin and freeze until firm.
Peel the oranges, removing all the pith. Slice thinly and remove the pips.
To serve, place layers of orange slices alternately with frozen sorbet. Decorate with sprigs of mint. For a spectacular dessert, try serving the sorbet frozen into half a hollowed out melon.

Yoghourt orange sorbet

Chocolate mousse

Mousse au chocolat   Chocolate mousse

4 oz. plain dark chocolate
4 eggs, separated
double (heavy) cream for decoration

Break the chocolate into small pieces and put into a small heatproof bowl with 4 teaspoons water. Place over hot water until the chocolate has melted, stirring until smooth.
Add the egg yolks to the chocolate, stir well and leave until cool.
Whisk the egg whites until stiff enough to stand in peaks, then fold into the chocolate mixture. Make sure the mixture is perfectly smooth. Pour the mousse into 4 individual serving dishes and leave until set. Decorate with small rosettes of whipped cream.

serves 4

Flan au chocolat   Chocolate flan

6 oz. pâte brisée (see recipe)
page 119)
4 oz. dark plain chocolate
3 eggs, separated
¼ pint (⅝ cup) double
(heavy) cream
extra 1 oz. dark plain chocolate
for decoration

Make the pâté brisée. Roll it out on a lightly floured board until it is a thin round, large enough to line an 8 inch diameter flan ring (standing on a baking tray) or a shallow cake tin. Lift the pastry on to the rolling pin and line the flan ring, trim off the excess pastry. Place a piece of greased greaseproof paper on the pastry, fill with baking beans and bake the flan case 'blind' in a moderately hot oven (375°F. Mark 5) for 15 minutes, then remove the paper and beans and continue baking for a further 10–15 minutes or until cooked. Cool on a wire rack.

Break the chocolate into small pieces, place in a heatproof bowl and melt it over a saucepan of hot water. Stir the chocolate until it is melted, taking care that it doesn't become overheated. Beat in the egg yolks, add the brandy, then allow the mixture to cool. Whisk the egg whites until stiff enough to stand in peaks. Fold the whites gently into the chocolate mixture. Pour into the prepared flan case and leave in a cool place until set.

Whip the cream until thickened and spread it over the chocolate filling. Grate the extra chocolate over the top for decoration. Serve as soon as possible.

serves 6

Chocolate flan

Omelette soufflé   Soufflé omelette

3 oz. (scant ½ cup) castor
(superfine) sugar
3 egg yolks
¼ teaspoon vanilla, almond,
lemon or other essence or
1 tablespoon liqueur
6 egg whites
pinch of salt

Soufflé omelettes are usually cooked in the oven in France although they can also be cooked on the hob (on a warming slate in the fireplace) and the top browned under a hot grill.

Put 2 oz. (good ¼ cup) castor (superfine) sugar in a bowl, add the egg yolks and beat thoroughly with a wooden spoon until creamy. Stir in the chosen flavouring.

Whisk the egg whites with salt until stiff enough to stand in peaks, stir 1 tablespoon into the yolk mixture, then carefully fold in the remainder.

Grease an ovenproof dish and pour in the omelette mixture. Pile the egg high and cut some slashes in the sides to help the middle to cook. Bake in a moderate oven (350°F. Mark 4) for 15–20 minutes. Sprinkle the remaining sugar on the top and brown under a very hot grill. Serve immediately.

serves 6

Apricot soufflé omelette

Omelette soufflée aux abricots
Apricot soufflé omelette

2 eggs, separated
1 tablespoon (1¼T) castor (superfine) sugar
½ oz. (1T) butter
6 oz. hot cooked or canned apricot halves
extra castor sugar

Place the egg yolks in a mixing bowl, add the sugar and 2 teaspoons water. Beat with a wooden spoon until creamy. Whisk the egg whites until stiff enough to stand in peaks. Fold the whites gently into the creamed yolks.

Heat the butter in a 6–7 inch omelette pan until very hot. Add the egg and cook until it is golden brown underneath. Put the pan under a hot grill and lightly brown the top of the omelette. Slide the omelette on to a heated serving plate, place the hot apricots on top of half the omelette. Fold over the other half and dust the top with the extra castor sugar.

serves 1–2   Serve immediately.

Chartreuse de fraises
Strawberry Chartreuse

1 pint (2½ cups) lemon jelly (jello)
24 small strawberries
angelica
¼ pint (⅝ cup) double (heavy) cream

Use freshly made lemon jelly (jello) which is cool but not set. Pour a little (about 2–3 tablespoons (scant ¼ cup)) into the bottom of a 1 pint (2½ cups) capacity deep jelly mould. Rotate the mould until the whole of the inside is covered with a set layer of jelly (jello). It is helpful in setting this layer if the mould is very cold and standing in a bowl of crushed ice.

Pour in more jelly (jello) to ½ inch depth and allow to set. Place 8 small strawberries on the jelly (jello) and use small pieces of angelica to form the 'stalks'. Pour in more jelly (jello) to cover the strawberries well. Allow to set, then add another layer of strawberries and angelia, covering with more jelly (jello). Allow to set, then arrange the remaining strawberries on top. Cover with the remaining jelly (jello) and put aside in a cool place until the entire mould is firmly set.

Turn out of the mould on to a wet serving plate just before serving. Decorate with rosettes of whipped cream. Dry the plate before serving.

note: other fruit—bananas, mandarin orange segments, pineapple
serves 4–6   chunks and so on—can be used in this manner.

Bavaroise à l'orange
Orange cream

¼ pint (⅝ cup) milk
1 egg
1 egg yolk
¼ pint (⅝ cup) orange juice
juice of ½ lemon
½ oz. (1½ tablespoons) gelatine
2 oz. (¼ cup) castor
(superfine) sugar
¼ pint (⅝ cup) double or
heavy cream
extra double (heavy) cream for
decoration

serves 4

Place the milk in a bowl, add the egg and egg yolk and whisk lightly. Place the bowl over a small saucepan of simmering water (don't allow the bowl to touch the water). Cook gently, stirring occasionally with a wooden spoon, until the custard is thick enough to coat the back of the spoon.
Mix orange and lemon juice together.
Dissolve the gelatine in 3 tablespoons (¼ cup) hot water. Add the sugar, the dissolved gelatine and fruit juices to the cooked custard. Strain, then put aside until cold.
Whip the cream until thickened but not stiff. Fold the cream carefully into the gelatine mixture then cool until it begins to thicken.
When the cream is thickened, pour it into an oiled 1 pint (2½ cups) mould to set.
Turn the cream out of the mould on to a serving plate. Decorate with rosettes of stiffly whipped cream.

Bavaroise à l'abricot
Apricot cream

Use ¼ pint (⅝ cup) apricot purée instead of orange juice and only use ¼ oz. (¾ tablespoon) gelatine.

Bavaroise au rhum
Rum cream

Use ¾ pint (⅝ cup) extra milk instead of the orange and lemon juice. Add 1–2 tablespoons rum.

Bavaroise rubané à trois parfums
Ribbon cream

Make the cream as for Bavaroise au Rhum, omitting the rum.
Divide the mixture into three bowls. Add ½ teaspoon coffee essence to one bowl; a few drops of vanilla essence to the second; a few drops of almond essence with a little green colouring, to the third. Pour the first mixture into the oiled mould and allow to set. Pour the second mixture on top and when this is set pour on the third mixture. Unmould when all three layers are well set.

Crème brûlée
Scorched cream

½ pint (1¼ cups) double
(heavy) cream
4 egg yolks, beaten
3 tablespoons (¼ cup) icing
(confectionery) sugar
½ teaspoon vanilla essence
castor (superfine) sugar

serves 4

Pour the cream into the top of a double saucepan (or a small heatproof bowl) and place it over hot water. When hot, pour the cream on to the egg yolks, beating constantly.
Return the mixture to the saucepan, add the icing (confectionery) sugar and vanilla essence and cook over hot water until the mixture thickens, stirring constantly.
Pour custard into a 1 pint (2¼ cups) capacity ovenproof dish. Chill overnight.
Sprinkle the top of the custard liberally with castor (superfine) sugar 2–3 hours before serving. Cook under a hot grill until the sugar has caramelized to a deep golden brown. Chill again before serving.

note: although this is delicious on its own, it can be served with fresh or stewed fruit to make a more substantial dessert.

Charlotte russe — Bavarian cream and jelly with sponge fingers

½ pint (1¼ cups) jelly (jello)
(use lemon or a flavour which
will blend with the cream filling)
about 12 sponge fingers
baverois cream (see recipe
page 105)
double (heavy) cream for
decoration

serves 4

This dessert takes its name from the mould in which it is made. A charlotte mould is round and has slightly sloping plain sides.

Pour the cooled, unset, jelly (jello) into the bottom of a 1 pint (2½ cups) charlotte mould to ½ inch depth.
Cut the sponge fingers to the height of the sides of the mould (less ½ inch) and arrange them around the edge, rounded ends downwards on the jelly (jello). The fingers should fit tightly, leaving as little space as possible between them. Pour the baverois cream into the mould and put in a cool place to set.
Turn the charlotte russe out of the mould on to a wet serving plate (this helps if you have to move the cream into position). The remaining jelly (jello) will now have set, so chop it coarsely with a wet knife and arrange it around the charlotte russe.
Decorate with rosettes of whipped cream. Serve as soon as possible.

Crème caramel — Cream caramel

2 oz. (¼ cup) granulated
(crystal) sugar
3 tablespoons (¼ cup) water
2 eggs
2 egg yolks
¾ pint (approx. 2 cups) milk
1 oz. (2 tablespoons) castor
(superfine) sugar
few drops vanilla essence

serves 4–6

Place the granulated (crystal) sugar in a small saucepan with 2 tablespoons of the water. Heat gently, stirring, until the sugar is dissolved. Boil briskly until the syrup is golden brown (do not stir). Remove from the heat and add the remaining 1 tablespoon of water, stirring until the caramel and water have combined. Pour into a warm, dry 1 pint (2½ cups) capacity heatproof dish. Make sure that the base of the dish is completely covered with the caramel.
Put the eggs, egg yolks, milk and castor (superfine) sugar into a mould. Mix thoroughly but do not let the mixture become frothy. Strain the egg custard into the dish on top of the caramel. Place the mould inside a dish or roasting pan, adding enough water to come halfway up the side of the egg custard mould. Cook in a moderately slow oven (325°F. Mark 3) for about 50 minutes or until firm and set. Allow to cool.
Chill, then turn out of the mould on to a serving plate and serve as soon as possible.

note: this recipe can also be cooked in individual dariole moulds. Divide the caramel and then the custard equally between 6 moulds and cook them for 25–30 minutes.

Cream caramel

Oeufs à la neige Snow eggs

3 eggs, separated
4 oz. (good ½ cup) castor (superfine) sugar
¾ pint (scant 2 cups) milk
½ teaspoon finely grated lemon peel

serves 4

Whisk the egg whites until standing in stiff peaks. Add 3 tablespoons (¼ cup) castor (superfine) sugar and continue whisking until the mixture is firm and glossy.

Place the milk in a large saucepan and heat it until bubbles begin to rise to the surface (do not allow it to boil). Place tablespoonfuls of the mixture into the milk and poach them gently for 5 minutes, turning once. Carefully remove the cooked egg white from the milk with a slotted spoon and drain well on absorbent kitchen paper. When all the egg white has been cooked, strain the milk.

Place the egg yolks in the top of a double saucepan (or in a heatproof bowl) over gently simmering water. Add the milk and beat lightly. Add the remaining sugar and cook, stirring constantly, until the custard thickens and coats the back of the spoon. Add the lemon rind. Pour the custard into a serving bowl and arrange the poached egg whites on top.

Chill before serving.

note: for a more spectacular dessert, pour caramel over the egg whites and scatter flaked almonds on top. To make the caramel, place 3 tablespoons (¼ cup) castor sugar in a small heavy saucepan. Heat very gently until the sugar is melted and golden.

Charlotte russe

Crêpes suzette — Curaçao and tangerine pancakes

8 cooked crêpes (see recipe page 40)
2 lumps sugar
2 tangerines
1 oz. (2T) butter
1 oz. (2 tablespoons) castor (superfine) sugar
1 tablespoon curaçao
3 tablespoons (¼ cup) rum

Prepare the crêpes.
Rub the lumps of sugar all over the unpeeled tangerines until they are saturated in tangerine oil and zest. Crush the lumps of sugar in a mixing bowl and beat in the butter. Add the castor (superfine) sugar, curaçao and 1 tablespoon of juice squeezed from the tangerines. Mix thoroughly.
Reheat the crêpes, covered in aluminium foil, in a moderate oven (350°F. Mark 4) for 15 minutes. Spread the hot crêpes with tangerine butter and fold each in four. Place them in a heated, flameproof serving dish. Heat the rum gently in a small saucepan until warmed, then ignite and pour over the crêpes. Serve immediately.

serves 4

note: use oranges if tangerines are not available.

Riz à l'impératrice — Empress rice

4 oz. (½ cup) round grain rice
1 pint (2½ cups) milk
¼ teaspoon vanilla essence
4 oz. (½ cup) granulated (crystal) sugar
1 oz. (2T) butter
4 oz. glacé (candied) fruits
3 tablespoons (¼ cup) kirsch
½ pint (1¼ cups) double (heavy) cream
4 egg yolks, lightly beaten
2 oz. (¼ cup) granulated (crystal) sugar
extra ½ pint (1¼ cups) milk
½ oz. (1½ tablespoons) gelatine
fruit sauce (see recipe page 22), optional

This dish may be served on its own or it can be decorated with fresh fruit. Try it served with pears, peeled, cored and halved.

Lightly grease a 2½–3 pint (6¼–7½ cups) capacity decorative mould or charlotte tin.
Put the rice in a saucepan and cover with water. Bring to the boil, simmer 2–3 minutes and drain the rice. Return the rice to the saucepan, add the milk and vanilla essence, bring to the boil and simmer, covered, stirring occasionally, until the rice is tender and the milk absorbed. Stir in 2 oz. of the sugar and butter. Allow the rice to cool.
Chop the glacé (candied) fruit into small pieces and soak them in kirsch. Whip the cream until stiff and fold into the rice.
Mix the egg yolks and remaining 2 oz. sugar together in a bowl. Put the extra milk into a saucepan and heat it until bubbles begin to rise to the surface (do not allow it to boil). Pour the milk on to the egg yolks, add the gelatine and stir until the gelatine is dissolved. Cool. Strain the custard on to the rice, add the soaked glacé (candied) fruits and stir together well. Spoon the prepared mixture into the greased mould. Put in a cool place, preferably the refrigerator, until set.
Turn out of the mould on to a chilled serving plate and serve decorated with fruit or with a fruit sauce.

serves 4–6

Coeur à la crème   Cream hearts

8 oz. cottage cheese
½ pint (1¼ cups) double
(heavy) cream
2 level teaspoons (scant ¼ cup)
sifted icing
(confectionery) sugar
8 oz. strawberries, hulled
1 teaspoon lemon juice
2 tablespoons (scant ¼ cup)
castor (superfine) sugar

Coeur à la Crème is a traditional French sweet. It is very rich and delicious when served with soft fruits such as strawberries, raspberries, peaches and fresh currants. It is customary to set the cream in special heart-shaped moulds with perforated bases. It can, however, be made with equal success in a muslin-lined bowl-shaped sieve.

Rub the cottage cheese through a sieve into a mixing bowl. Stir in the cream and icing (confectionery) sugar and beat well. Either press the cottage cheese mixture into 6 individual coeur à la crème moulds or in a muslin lined sieve. Allow to drain overnight.
Turn the cream out of the mould on to a serving plate. Sprinkle the strawberries with lemon juice and castor (superfine) sugar and arrange them around the coeur à la crème.
Serve as soon as possible.

Cream hearts   serves 6   **note:** macaroons (see recipe page 126) are good served with this dish.

Crêpes aux framboises
Raspberry pancakes

8 cooked crêpes (see recipe page 40)
1 × 12 oz. packet frozen or canned raspberries
1 oz. (2 tablespoons) granulated (crystal) sugar
1 tablespoon (1½ tablespoons) cornflour (cornstarch)
red food colouring
double (heavy) cream for serving

serves 4

Prepare the crêpes and keep them hot.
Defrost the frozen raspberries or drain them if canned.
Reserve the liquid and make up to ½ pint (1¼ cups) with water. Place the liquid with the sugar in a saucepan, heat, stirring to boiling point. Blend the cornflour (cornstarch) with a little more water in a bowl and pour the boiling liquid on to it, stirring constantly, then return to the saucepan, bring to the boil and simmer 2–3 minutes until thick.
Add red food colouring if necessary.
Fold each crêpe in half, place some of the raspberry mixture on to the centre of each. Fold the sides of the crêpe in so that the raspberries still show.
Serve as soon as possible with a bowl of whipped cream.

Poires belle Hélène
Pears with ice cream and chocolate sauce

8 oz. (1 cup) granulated (crystal) sugar
3 tablespoons (¼ cup) honey
4 pears
vanilla ice cream
½ pint (1¼ cups) sauce chocolat (see recipe page 22)

serves 4

Place the sugar in a saucepan with ½ pint (1¼ cups) water and heat gently, stirring until the sugar is dissolved. Stir in the honey.
Peel core and halve the pears. Cook the halves gently in the prepared syrup for 15–20 minutes or until tender. Drain and cool.
Place a portion of ice cream in the base of each of 4 individual serving glasses. Arrange the pears on top. Chill the sauce chocolat and pour over the pears. Serve immediately.

Poires bourguignonne
Burgundy pears

4 pears
8 oz. (1 cup) granulated (crystal) sugar
¼ pint (⅝ cup) red Burgundy wine
red food colouring (optional)

serves 4

Peel the pears, without removing the stalks. Place the sugar in a saucepan with ¼ pint (⅝ cup) water.
Bring to the boil, stirring until the sugar has dissolved. Add the pears and simmer, covered, for 15 minutes. Add the Burgundy and continue cooking for a further 15 minutes, uncovered. Add a little red food colouring if liked.
Remove and drain the pears, allowing them to cool. Bring the syrup to the boil again and cook rapidly, stirring, until thick. Pour over the pears, cool and chill.

note: apples can also be prepared in this way. A mixture of both pears and apples can make an interesting dessert.

Pêches au miel
Honeyed peaches

6 fresh peaches
1 lemon
rind of 1 orange
4 oz. (good ¼ cup) honey

serves 6

Skin the peaches by first plunging them into boiling water for 1 minute, then placing them in cold water and peeling off the skin.
Halve the peaches and place each half in lemon juice to prevent discolouration.
Peel the thin zest off the orange and lemon with a potato peeler.
Place these strips in a saucepan with the honey and ¼ pint (⅝ cup) water. Heat the saucepan, gently stirring, until the honey has dissolved, then boil rapidly, uncovered, for 5 minutes.
Remove the rinds and pour the syrup over the peaches. Cool, then chill in the refrigerator. Serve with whipped cream.

Honeyed peaches

Soufflé au citron   Lemon soufflé

3 eggs, separated
3 oz. (scant ½ cup) castor (superfine) sugar
2 lemons
scant ½ oz. (1½ tablespoons) gelatine
¼ pint (⅝ cup) double (heavy) cream
extra double (heavy) cream and chopped nuts for decoration

serves 5–6

Lightly grease a 1 pint (2½ cups) capacity soufflé dish. Cut a double strip of greaseproof paper the height of the dish plus 3 inches and long enough to go around it. Grease the top 3 inches and tie the paper, greased side inside, around the dish.

Place the egg yolks, castor (superfine) sugar, juice and finely grated lemon rind in a heatproof mixing bowl. Put the bowl over a pan of hot water and whisk until the mixture is thickened and creamy. Remove from the heat and whisk until cooled. Dissolve the gelatine in 3 tablespoons (¼ cup) hot water and whisk into the egg mixture. Half whip the cream and fold it into the egg mixture. Cool.

Whisk the egg whites until stiff enough to stand in peaks. When the cream mixture is just about to set, fold in the egg whites. Pour into the prepared soufflé dish and put in a cool place to set firmly. Remove the greaseproof paper from the soufflé, carefully easing it away from soufflé with the back of a knife. Decorate with chopped nuts pressed around the sides and rosettes of whipped cream on top. Serve as soon as possible.

Soufflé aux abricots   Apricot soufflé

Omit the lemon rind and juice from the above recipe. Use instead ¼ pint (⅝ cup) apricot purée and the juice of ½ a lemon. Cook the egg yolks and sugar and, when cooled, add the purée and juice.

Soufflé aux fraises   Strawberry soufflé

Prepare the soufflé as for soufflé aux abricots, substituting strawberry purée for the apricot and omitting the lemon juice.

Lemon soufflé

Pommes en charlotte   Apple charlotte

½ large sandwich loaf,
thick sliced
6 oz. (12T) unsalted butter
6 tablespoons (½ cup) oil
3½ lbs. cooking apples, peeled,
cored and sliced
1 oz. (2T) butter
juice of 1 lemon
¼ teaspoon ground cinnamon
4 oz. (½ cup) granulated
(crystal) sugar
6 tablespoons (½ cup)
apricot jam

Grease a 3 pint (7½ cups) capacity charlotte mould with butter.
Removing the crusts from the slices of bread, cut out 6–8 heart
shaped croûtes with a biscuit cutter. Cut the remaining slices into
'fingers' about ½–¾ inch wide and slightly longer than the depth of
the charlotte mould. Heat the unsalted butter and the oil together
in a large frying pan. Fry the hearts and fingers of bread until
golden. Arrange the hearts, overlapping, in the base of the
charlotte mould. Stand the fingers of bread around the sides, again
overlapping. Prepare the apples. Melt the butter in a large saucepan.
Add the lemon juice, cinnamon and apples. Cover the pan and cook
very gently until the apples are soft and pulpy. Stir in the sugar and
apricot jam until dissolved.
Place the apple pulp in the mould on the fried bread, fill the mould
well, as the filling tends to become absorbed during cooking. Cover
the apple with more fried bread fingers. Bake in a moderately hot
oven (375°F. Mark 5) for 10–15 minutes.
Cool slightly, then turn the apple charlotte out of the mould on to a
heated serving plate.

serves 4–6   **note:** this dish can also be served chilled.

Pommes flambées   Flaming apples

8 dessert apples
lemon juice
6 oz. (1 cup) soft brown sugar
1 teaspoon ground cinnamon
6 tablespoons (½ cup) rum

Peel the apples, without removing the stalks. Dip each apple in lemon juice to prevent discolouration.
Place the sugar and cinnamon in a large saucepan with 2 pints (5 cups) water. Bring to the boil, stirring until the sugar has dissolved. Add the apples and simmer, covered, for 10–15 minutes or until just tender. Drain, place on a heatproof serving dish and keep hot.
Boil the cooking syrup fast, uncovered, until it begins to thicken. Pour the syrup, then the rum, over the apples. Ignite and serve immediately.

serves 4

Tarte aux pommes   Apple flan

6 oz. pâte brisée (see recipe page 119)
2 lbs. cooking apples
¼ pint (⅝ cup) white wine
½ lemon
2 oz. (4T) butter
4 oz. (½ cup) granulated (crystal) sugar
4 crisp eating apples
3 tablespoons (¼ cup) apricot jam
double (heavy) cream for serving

A delicious and easy to prepare dish which can be eaten hot or cold. The recipe originated in the Normandy district of France, which is renowned for its orchards.

Make the pâte brisée. Roll it out on a lightly floured board into a thin round, large enough to line an 8 inch diameter flan ring (standing on a baking tray) or a shallow cake tin. Lift the pastry on a rolling pin, line the flan ring and trim off excess pastry. Peel, core and cut the cooking apples into quarters. Place them in a saucepan with the wine, a strip of lemon rind (peel this off with a potato peeler), butter and 2 oz. (¼ cup) sugar. Cover the pan and simmer gently until the apples are very tender. Remove the lemon rind. Purée the apples by pressing through a sieve or in a blender. Place the apple purée in the unbaked flan case. Peel and core the eating apples, then slice thinly. Arrange the slices, overlapping, on top of the purée. Sprinkle with the remaining sugar and bake in a moderately hot oven (375°F. Mark 5) for 25–30 minutes or until the apples are cooked and the pastry is golden.
Meanwhile, heat the apricot jam in a small saucepan with 1 tablespoon lemon juice. Stir until well blended. Sieve.
Glaze the hot cooked flan with apricot glaze. Serve with a bowl of whipped cream.

serves 6

Tarte aux pommes meringue

Prepare the above recipe but omit the eating apples and the glaze. Whisk 2 eggs until stiff enough to stand in firm peaks. Fold in 4 oz. (good ½ cup) castor (superfine) sugar. Pile the meringue on top of the apple purée in the cooked flan, bringing the meringue down to touch the pastry all round. Bake in a moderate oven (350°F. Mark 4) until the meringue is a pale golden, about 10–15 minutes. Decorate with small marzipan apples.

Tarte aux pommes et oranges

Prepare the above recipe but omit the eating apples and the glaze. Slice thinly 2 thin-skinned oranges. Place 4 oz. (½ cup) granulated (crystal) sugar in a saucepan with ¼ pint (⅝ cup) water, bring to the boil, stirring until the sugar is dissolved. Add the orange rounds and carefully poach them until they are tender. Place cooked orange slices on top of the apple purée in the cooked flan. Boil the remaining syrup very rapidly until it is thickening and beginning to caramelize. Glaze the top of the flan. Serve.

Apple and orange flan

1

2

3

4

5

6

7

Cakes and pastries

French pâtisserie is almost legendary. Anyone who has visited France will know the delicious smell that wafts out of the patisserie shops and will no doubt have sampled their wares. Those who live outside France must make their own. Follow the recipes in this chapter carefully; some are very delicate and tricky to make, but with care you will produce a superb result.

Pâtisserie is served as a dessert with coffee, or, in the case of plainer breads such as croissants or brioches, for breakfast. They are fairly time-consuming to make but the extra effort is well worthwhile, particularly for a special occasion. Serve them as fresh as possible.

St. Honoré cake

Pâte brisée
Short crust pastry

8 oz. (2 cups) plain (all purpose) flour
pinch of salt
4 oz. (8T) butter or margarine
1 egg
3 tablespoons ($\frac{1}{4}$ cup) water

Sift the flour on to a cold surface, make a well in the centre and add the salt, chopped butter, egg and water. Work the butter, egg and water together with the fingertips, gradually blending in the flour. Knead lightly until smooth. Cover with aluminium foil or polythene and put in a cool place for 30 minutes.
Use as required.

Pâte sucrée
Sweet short crust pastry

8 oz. (2 cups) plain (all purpose) flour
4 oz. (8T) butter or margarine
2 oz. (good $\frac{1}{4}$ cup) castor (superfine) sugar
2 egg yolks
$\frac{1}{4}$ teaspoon vanilla essence
3 tablespoons ($\frac{1}{4}$ cup) water

Sift the flour on to a cold surface and make a well in the centre. Add the butter, (cut into pieces), sugar, egg yolks, vanilla essence and water. Work these ingredients together with the fingertips, gradually blending in the flour. Knead lightly until smooth. Cover with aluminium foil or polythene and put in a cool place for 30 minutes.
Use as required.

Pâte à choux
Choux pastry

4 oz. (8T) butter or margarine
$\frac{1}{2}$ pint (1$\frac{1}{4}$ cups) water
5 oz. (1$\frac{1}{4}$ cups) plain (all purpose) flour
4 eggs, beaten

Placing the butter and water in a saucepan, heat slowly until the butter is melted and the water at boiling point. Remove from the heat. Add all the sifted flour and beat well with a wooden spoon until the mixture is smooth and falls from the sides of the pan. Allow the paste to cool slightly, then gradually add the beaten eggs and mix well.
Use as required.

Pâte feuilletée
Puff pastry

8 oz. (2 cups) plain (all purpose) flour
$\frac{1}{2}$ teaspoon salt
8 oz. ($\frac{1}{2}$ lb.) butter or margarine
scant $\frac{1}{4}$ pint ($\frac{1}{2}$ cup) iced water
1 teaspoon lemon juice

Sift the flour and salt on to a cold surface, make a well in the centre and add 1 oz. of butter, the water and the lemon juice. Using the fingertips, work the ingredients together to make a soft dough. Knead very lightly, put on a plate and cover with aluminium foil or polythene. Leave in a cool place for 30 minutes.
Shape the remaining butter into a rectangle block about 4 × 2 × 1 inch. Roll out the dough to a square about $\frac{1}{4}$ inch thick. Place the butter in the centre and wrap it up like a parcel. Roll the parcel of dough and fat into an oblong about 12 × 5 inches. Mark the dough lightly into thirds with a knife. Fold the top third down over the middle third and then fold up the bottom third. Turn the dough a quarter turn to the left (folds are then to right and left), roll and fold as before. Place the dough on a plate, cover with foil or polythene and rest in a cool place again for 30 minutes.
Roll, fold and turn the dough 4 more times. Leave, as before, for 30 minutes. Roll, fold and turn the dough twice more. Leave for 15 minutes, then use as required.

Pâte genoise
Genoise sponge

4 eggs
4 oz. (good $\frac{1}{2}$ cup) castor (superfine) sugar
3 oz. (6T) unsalted butter or margarine, melted and cooled
3 oz. ($\frac{3}{4}$ cup) plain (all purpose) flour

serves 4–6

Place the eggs and castor (superfine) sugar in a large bowl over a saucepan of simmering water. Whisk the eggs and sugar together until the mixture is light in colour and thick enough to leave a trail. Remove the bowl from the heat and whisk for a further 3–4 minutes. Add half the butter then half the sifted flour and fold them into the egg mixture using a metal spoon. Fold in the remaining butter and flour. Mix gently until smooth.
Use as required. (See overleaf for ideas on using pâte genoise.)

Using pâte genoise

Pâte genoise can be cooked in a deep 7 inch diameter cake tin or in two shallow 7 inch diameter tins. For a slab cake, use an 8 by 12 inch rectangular cake tin. Bake in a moderate oven (350°F. Mark 4) for 25–40 minutes, according to the tin used.

Pâte genoise can then be decorated in a variety of ways. Recipes are given for the elaborate gâteaux but an ordinary sponge can be effectively decorated with the minimum of ingredients.

Whipped cream makes an easy and delicious filling for two cakes sandwiched together and it needs only a little more on top, decorated with flaked toasted almonds, for a really luscious gâteau. Try this with pâte genoise au chocolat (below).

Alternatively, bake the entire mixture in a deep cake tin and, when cool, spread the sides with cream and press flaked toasted almonds or toasted desiccated coconut on to the cream with a palate knife. Pipe extra cream on top and your gâteau will have a very professional finish.

Another spectacular idea is to bake the pâte genoise in one 8 inch diameter shallow tin and one 6 inch diameter shallow tin. Sandwich the two cooled cakes together with a little whipped cream and pile fresh seasoned fruit on top. Finish off the gâteau by glazing the fruit with a little syrup thickened with arrowroot and boiled until clear (1 teaspoon arrowroot to $\frac{1}{2}$ tablespoon sugar dissolved in $\frac{1}{4}$ pint ($\frac{5}{8}$ cup) water and cooled). Spread extra whipped cream around the sides and press on chopped almonds. Pipe rosettes of cream around the top.

Pâte genoise au chocolat Chocolate Genoise sponge

Make the recipe as given above but use 2 oz. ($\frac{1}{2}$ cup) plain (all purpose) flour with 1 oz. ($\frac{1}{4}$ cup) cocoa sifted together instead of 3 oz. ($\frac{3}{4}$ cup) plain (all purpose) flour.

Genoise sponge (below)   *Peach cake (right)*

Gâteau aux amandes Almond cake

1 quantity pâte genoise
few drops of almond essence
4 egg whites
6 oz. (scant 1 cup) castor
(superfine) sugar
2 oz. (½ cup) flaked almonds
1 oz. (2 tablespoons) granulated
(crystal) sugar
¼ pint (⅝ cup) double
(heavy) cream

serves 8

Grease and flour two 8 inch diameter sandwich tins, preferably with removable bases. Make the pâte genoise and fold in the almond essence and melted butter. Pour the mixture into the tins, dividing it equally between the two.
Whisk the egg whites until stiff, add half the castor (superfine) sugar and continue whisking until stiff again. Fold in the remaining castor sugar with a metal spoon. Spread the meringue on top of the pâte genoise, dividing it equally between the two tins. Mix the flaked almonds with granulated (crystal) sugar and sprinkle over both meringues. Bake in a moderate oven (350°F. Mark 4) for 40–45 minutes. Allow the cake to cool in the tins before removing. Whip the cream until stiff and sandwich the two cakes together.

Gâteau au chocolat Chocolate cake

1 quantity pâte genoise au
chocolat (see recipe page 120)
3 oz. (⅜ cup) granulated
(crystal) sugar
3 oz. (6T) butter or margarine
3 tablespoons (¼ cup) milk
8 oz. (1¾ cups) sifted icing
(confectionery) sugar
1½ tablespoons cocoa
4 oz. plain dark chocolate

serves 8

Grease and line the bases of two 7 inch diameter sandwich tins with greased greaseproof paper. Make the pâte genoise au chocolat and pour it carefully into the tins, dividing the mixture equally.
Bake in a moderate oven (350°F. Mark 4) for 20–25 minutes or until firm and just cooked. Cool on a wire rack.
Place the granulated (crystal) sugar in a saucepan with butter or margarine and the milk. Heat gently, stirring until the sugar is dissolved and the mixture boiling. Boil for 1 minute. Cool quickly by standing the saucepan in a bowl of cold water. Stir occasionally. Sift the icing (confectionery) sugar and cocoa together and add them to the cooled syrup, beating well until thick and fluffy.
Cut the cold cakes in half and sandwich the layers together again with a quarter of the chocolate icing between each layer. Spread the remaining quarter around the sides.
Break the chocolate into small pieces and melt in a bowl over hot water. Spread half over the top of the cake. Spread the remainder on to a plate or a piece of aluminium foil and allow to harden. Cut this into squares and decorate the sides of the cake.

Gâteau aux pêches Peach cake

1 quantity pâte genoise (see
recipe page 119)
3 tablespoons (¼ cup) peach or
apricot jam
¼ pint (⅝ cup) double
(heavy) cream
13 sponge fingers
4 peaches or 1×15½ oz. can
peach halves
1 teaspoon sugar (optional)
1 teaspoon arrowroot

serves 8

Grease and flour two 7 inch diameter sandwich tins. Make the pâte genoise and pour it carefully into the tins, dividing the mixture equally. Bake in a moderate oven (350°F. Mark 4) for 20–25 minutes or until firm and just cooked. Cool on a wire rack.
Spread one of the cakes with peach or apricot jam and place the other cake on top. Whip the cream until stiff. Cut the sponge fingers in half and arrange the halves around the sandwiched cake, spreading each one with a little whipped cream to make them stick. If fresh peaches are being used, first skin them by plunging them into boiling water for 1 minute, then rinsing them in cold water and peeling off the skin. Cut the peaches in half and remove the stones. Drain canned peach halves, if used, and reserve the syrup. Measure ¼ pint (⅝ cup) peach syrup or measure ¼ pint (⅝ cup) water and add the sugar. Blend a little of the liquid with the arrowroot in a bowl, place the remainder in a saucepan and heat until boiling. Add all the liquid to the arrowroot in the bowl, then return to the pan and bring to the boil, stirring until it clears. Cool.
Arrange the peach halves on top of the gâteau and spoon a little of the arrowroot mixture over them to glaze. When the glaze is completely cold, pipe rosettes of the remaining cream between the peaches. A ribbon can be tied around the biscuits for a very decorative finish.
Serve as soon as possible.

Gâteau surprise
Surprise cake

1 quantity pâte genoise (see recipe page 119)
¼ pint (⅝ cup) double (heavy) cream
6 tablespoons (½ cup) mixed fruit salad
castor sugar
3 oz. (½ cup) icing (confectionery) sugar
apricot jam
2 oz. (½ cup) chopped almonds
glacé (candied) fruits for decoration

serves 8

Grease and flour a 7 inch diameter deep cake tin. Make the pâte genoise, pour gently into the tin and bake in a moderate oven (350°F. Mark 4) for 35–40 minutes or until firm. Cool on a wire rack. Whip the cream until thick, mix with the fruit salad and add castor sugar to taste. Cut out a lid from the sponge, allowing a ½–¾ inch border. Hollow out the centre of the sponge with a spoon. Fill the space with the fruit and cream. Replace the lid.
Mix the sifted icing (confectionery) sugar with enough water to make a thick glacé icing. Warm the apricot jam slightly and brush the edges of the sponge generously, using a palette knife dipped in the jam, then press chopped nuts firmly on to the jam coating. Pour the icing on to the top of the sponge, hiding the joins of the lid. Decorate with glacé (candied) fruits and serve as soon as possible.

Tonille aux ananas
Pineapple nut shortcake

4 oz. (good 1 cup) castor (superfine) sugar
6 oz. (12T) butter
6 oz. (1½ cups) freshly ground toasted hazelnuts
8 oz. (2 cups) plain (all purpose) flour
pinch of salt
½ pint (1¼ cups) double (heavy) cream
2×15½ oz. cans pineapple rings
1 tablespoon icing (confectionery) sugar
extra icing sugar for decoration

serves 6–8

Cream the butter and sugar together in a mixing bowl until soft and fluffy. Add the hazelnuts and mix well. Sift the flour and salt together and work into the butter mixture. Knead lightly. Divide the dough into three pieces and roll two pieces into 8–9 inch diameter rounds, and one 7 inch round on a lightly floured board. Allow to rest in a cool place for 10–20 minutes. Place the rounds on a lightly greased baking tray and bake in a moderately hot oven (375°F. Mark 5) for about 8 minutes. Cool slightly before removing them from the tray. Cut the smaller one into eighths while still warm. Drain the pineapple. Whip the cream until stiff and fold in 1 table-spoon [1¼T] pineapple syrup and the icing (confectionery) sugar. Place a biscuit round on a serving plate, spread it with half of the cream and arrange 4 of the pineapple rings on top. Place another biscuit round on the pineapple and spread with the remaining cream. Arrange the eighths of biscuit like the spokes of a wheel, at an angle, in the cream. Cut the remaining pineapple rings in halves and arrange them between the biscuit wedges.
Serve as soon as possible, dusted with sifted icing sugar.

Chantilly feuilles
Chantilly cream with crisp nut leaves

5 egg whites
2 oz. (½ cup) ground hazelnuts
2 oz. (½ cup) ground walnuts
5 oz. (¾ cup) castor (superfine) sugar
2 oz. (½ cup) plain (all purpose) flour
2 oz. (4T) butter, melted
vanilla essence
1½ oz. dark plain chocolate
½ pint (1¼ cups) double (heavy) cream
1 lb. ripe pears or other fruit (apricots, peaches, strawberries, raspberries etc., as available)
icing sugar

Place 4 of the egg whites in a bowl and whisk until they are stiff enough to stand in peaks. Stir in the hazelnuts, walnuts, castor (superfine) sugar, flour, melted butter and a few drops of vanilla essence, blending gently but thoroughly. Grease 4 baking trays lightly and mark a 6-inch circle on each. Divide the meringue mixture between the 4 circles and spread evenly to form rounds. Bake in a moderate oven (350°F. Mark 4) for about 30 minutes or until the rounds are a pale golden brown in colour. Trim, remove from the baking trays and cool on a wire rack.
Place the chopped chocolate in a heatproof bowl over a saucepan of hot water, until melted. Mix with a palette knife until smooth. Spread the chocolate on waxed paper and allow to set. Cut into rounds 1½ inches in diameter. Cut each round in half to make semi-circles. Whip the cream with a few drops of vanilla essence, until stiff. Whisk the remaining egg white until stiff, then fold into the cream. Prepare the fruit, skin if necessary and remove pips or stones, then chop them and mix into the cream.
Place one layer round on a serving plate, spread it with a quarter of the cream and fruit. Top with another round and continue until all the rounds are sandwiched. Spread the top with cream and decorate with the chocolate. Serve as soon as possible.

Petit fours

1 quantity pâte genoise (see recipe page 119), 1 day old. Make it in a greased and floured 8×12 inch shallow cake tin. Bake it in a moderate oven (350° Mark 4) for 25–30 minutes.
Apricot jam, warmed and sieved.
Almond paste. Make this by mixing 4 oz. (1 cup) ground almonds with 2 oz. ($\frac{2}{3}$ cup) icing (confectionery) sugar (sieved). Mix to a firm paste with a little egg white
Finely chopped almonds.
Glacé icing. Icing (confectionery) sugar, sieved and mixed with enough water to give a good coating consistency. (Cover this icing with a damp cloth).
Butter icing. Use 2 oz. (4T) butter creamed with 4 oz. (1$\frac{1}{3}$ cups) sifted icing (confectionery) sugar.
Food colourings.
Decorations. Crystallized flowers, glacé fruits, mimosa balls, silver dragees.

Pineapple nut shortcake (below)

Chantilly cream with crisp nut leaves (top right)

Fruit pastries (below right)

Petit fours are small, rich fancy cakes served in France for afternoon tea, parties (such as an engagement, wedding, christening etc. . . .), accompanying after dinner coffee or even with ice cream.
They should be very small, two or three mouthfuls at the most, and should be neat, smooth and delicately coloured with an appropriate and, where possible, original decoration.
Petit fours riche are made from pâte genoise (see recipe page 119). It is best if the sponge is made the day before it is needed as it will then be firmer and less likely to crumble.
Before starting to decorate the petit fours, make sure you have everything you will be needing ready mixed and to hand. The accompanying ingredients would make an attractive and varied selection of petit fours riche.

Coat the sponge in a variety of the following ways:
Roll out some almond paste to $\frac{1}{16}$—$\frac{1}{8}$ inch thickness. Cut small rounds or squares of sponge and brush with apricot jam.
Cover completely and evenly with the almond paste. Dip each petit four into white or coloured glacé icing and/or pipe rosettes of butter icing all over with a very small star icing pipe.
Proceed as above but place a small additional almond paste shape on top of the petit fours before dipping into the glacé icing.
Spread the sides of squares of sponge with butter icing and roll in chopped almonds. Spread more butter icing on top and decorate.
Spread the side of ovals and rectangles of sponge with apricot jam. Roll out some almond paste. Spread the almond paste around the sides of the sponge, just coming over the top. Fill the top with glacé icing. Decorate.
Spread sponge shapes with apricot jam and coat with almond paste. Decorate the tops with a different coloured marzipan.
The variety of decoration is endless. Try to make as many shapes as possible, too—ovals, squares, trefoils, rectangles, crescents—but avoid star shapes, as they are too complicated.

Madeleines

1 quantity pâte genoise (see recipe page 119)

This is a classic French dish. Madeleine moulds are small shell-shaped tins.

Grease and flour some madeleine moulds (how many will depend on the size).
Fill the moulds $\frac{2}{3}$ full with the prepared pâte genoise and bake in a moderate oven (350°F. Mark 4) for 7–10 minutes or until risen and golden. Cool on a wire rack.
Store in an airtight tin.

Colettes

6½ oz. plain dark chocolate
1 oz. (2T) butter
2 teaspoons brandy, rum or sherry
4 tablespoons (⅜ cup) double (heavy) cream
flaked almonds for decoration

makes 16

Chop the chocolate coarsely and put 4 oz. in a heatproof bowl or in the top of a double saucepan. Place over hot water and leave until the chocolate has melted. Using a teaspoon handle, smooth the chocolate over the inside of 16 small petit fours cases. Give each case 4 thin coatings. Allow to dry, then peel off the case and put the chocolate case in a fresh paper case.
Melt the remaining 2½ oz. chocolate using the same method as before. Beat the butter, allow to cool, then add the flavouring. Whip the cream lightly and fold in.
Allow the mixture to stand until it is of a piping consistency.
Using a large star icing pipe, pipe a large rosette into each prepared chocolate case. Decorate with flaked almonds.

Macarons
Macaroons

6 oz. (scant 1 cup) castor (superfine) sugar
3 oz. (¾ cup) ground almonds
3 egg whites
split almonds
granulated (crystal) sugar

Macaroons, when made as for petit fours, are the classic accompaniment for ice cream.
Mix the castor (superfine) sugar and ground almonds together.
Whisk the egg whites until frothy, then use enough to bind the sugar and almonds together in a soft dough.
Pipe the mixture on to rice paper on a baking tray, with a plain icing pipe. The size will depend on how you wish to serve the macaroons. Petit fours size—about ¾–1 inch diameter rounds.
Children's tea size 1½–2 inches diameter.
Place a split almond on each macaroon and sprinkle with granulated (crystal) sugar.
Bake in a moderately slow oven (325°F. Mark 3) for 20–40 minutes (according to size) or until pale golden in colour. Cool on a wire rack.

note: petit fours macaroons can be piped with a star icing pipe in fancy shapes, if desired.

Cigarettes russes

2 egg whites
3½ oz. (½ cup) castor (superfine) sugar
1½ oz. (scant ½ cup) plain (all purpose) flour
1½ oz. (3T) butter, melted

These can also be served with ice cream.

Place the egg whites in a bowl and whisk them until they stand in stiff peaks. Add the sugar and sifted flour, mixing lightly, then the butter.
Grease and lightly flour a baking tray. Spread the mixture thinly on to the tray in rectangles about the size of a cigarette paper.
Bake in a hot oven (400°F. Mark 6) for 5–6 minutes.
Remove the rectangles from the baking tray, upside down, and quickly roll them around a pencil. Slide off and cool on a wire rack.
Store in an airtight tin.

note: the ends may be dipped in melted chocolate if desired.

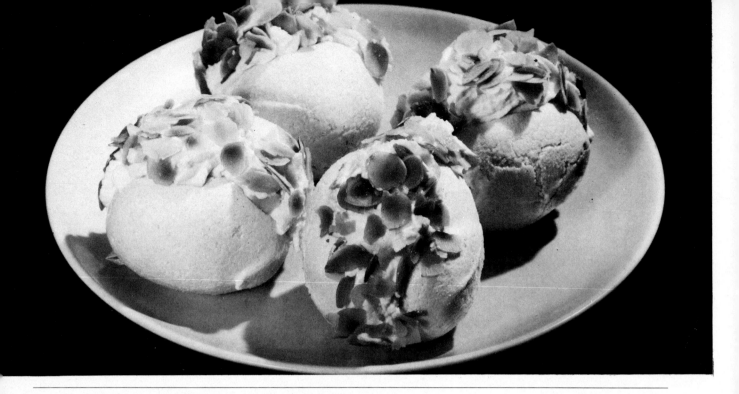

Meringues chantilly
Chantilly meringues

2 egg whites
pinch of salt
4 oz. (good ½ cup) castor (superfine) sugar
icing sugar
¼ pint (⅝ cup) double (heavy) cream
vanilla essence
flaked almonds for decoration (optional)

Place the egg whites and salt in a mixing bowl. Whisk until they are stiff enough to stand in peaks. Add half of the sugar and whisk until thoroughly blended. Fold in the remaining sugar with a metal spoon.
Grease a baking tray lightly, then dust it with a thin layer of flour. Tap the tray gently to spread the flour evenly. Pipe the meringue on to the prepared tray with a plain icing pipe. The size will depend on how the meringues are to be served, from the very small petit fours size to the large dessert size. Sprinkle generously with icing sugar. Bake in a very slow oven (200°F. Mark ¼) for 1–2 hours until firm and crisp but still uncoloured. Cool on a wire rack.
Whip the cream until firm, stir in the vanilla essence. Stick two meringues together with a teaspoon of cream. Serve decorated with flaked almonds if desired.

Gâteau jalousie aux poires et gingembre
Pear and ginger jalousie

8 oz. pâte feuillitée (see recipe page 119)
1 egg, beaten
2 large pears
2 oz. stem ginger (in syrup)

A jalousie can have many fillings, the simplest being jam. This recipe is particularly delicious.

Make the pâte feuillitée. Roll it out on a lightly floured board to form a rectangle 12 × 10 inches and about ¼ inch thick. Cut the pastry in half lengthwise to make two rectangles, each 12 × 5 inches. Trim a ¼ inch strip off each side of one rectangle, brush with egg and place on the top each side of the rectangle from which they were cut to make a rectangular 'flan case'. Place on a wet baking tray. Peel, core and slice the pears. Arrange the slices in the 'flan case'. Chop the ginger and scatter over the pears.
Fold the remaining pastry in half lengthwise. Starting ½ inch in from the end, and leaving a ½ inch border of pastry at the top, make cuts in the pastry along the folded edge at ¼ inch intervals. Open out, without letting the pastry stretch. Brush the 'flan case' edge with beaten egg and place the lid on top. Press the edges firmly together and knock them upwards with the back of a knife. Glaze the top with beaten egg and bake in a hot oven (425°F. Mark 7) for 20–25 minutes or until puffed up, crisp and golden.

serves 6 Serve as soon as possible.

Tuiles
Crisp almond biscuits

2 egg whites
4 oz. (good ½ cup) castor (superfine) sugar
2 oz. (½ cup) plain (all purpose) flour
1 oz. (¼ cup) ground almonds
2 oz. (4T) butter, melted
½ teaspoon vanilla essence

Place the egg whites in a mixing bowl, whisk until frothy, then add the sugar. Continue whisking until the sugar is mixed in. Add the sifted flour, ground almonds, melted butter and vanilla essence, stirring well.

Grease the required number of baking trays and place teaspoons of the mixture on them at well spaced intervals. Bake in a moderately hot oven (375 °F. Mark 5) for 5–6 minutes or until golden brown. Lift off the cooked biscuits and place them on a greased rolling pin to cool. Store in an airtight tin.

note : these biscuits can be served as petit fours or, if larger in size, as tea-time biscuits. The cooking time depends on the size of the biscuits made.

Gâteau pithiviers
Pithiviers cake

8 oz. pâte feuilletée (see recipe page 119)
2 oz. (4T) margarine or butter
2 oz. (good ¼ cup) castor (superfine) sugar
2 oz. (½ cup) ground almonds
1 egg, beaten
¼ teaspoon almond essence
1 teaspoon flour
apricot jam
extra egg for glazing
icing (confectionery) sugar

Pithiviers is a town in the Midi of France. This gâteau is a local speciality.

Roll out the prepared pastry on a lightly floured board to ¼ inch thickness. Cut out 2 × 6–7 inch rounds. Place 1 round on a damp baking tray. Roll the other out into a slightly larger round.
Cream the butter and castor (superfine) sugar together in a mixing bowl, adding the ground almonds, egg, almond essence and flour. Beat the ingredients together thoroughly.
On the baking tray, spread the pastry with a little apricot jam, leaving a ½ inch border all round. Pile the almond mixture on top and make a dome shape. Brush the border with egg and place the second, slightly larger, round on top. Glaze the top with beaten egg, then slash curved cuts into the lid, starting at the centre, like the spokes of a wheel.
Bake in a very hot oven (450°F. Mark 8) for about 30 minutes or until well risen, cooked and golden. Cool on a wire rack.

serves 6 Serve sprinkled with sifted icing (confectionery) sugar.

Palmiers

4 oz. (or scraps) pâte feuilletée
egg white
castor (superfine) sugar

Light crispy pastries which can often be made from left-over scraps of pâte feuilletée.

Roll out the prepared pastry, on a lightly floured board, to a thin oblong 12 inches in length. Trim the narrow ends, then brush with egg white and sprinkle liberally with castor (superfine) sugar.
Mark the centre of the oblong lightly with a knife (across the narrow part). Fold each half into 3, with the folds meeting in the middle.
Fold the pastry in half and cut into ½ inch slices.
Place each pastry on a damp baking tray, leaving room for them to open out a little. Bake in a very hot oven (450°F. Mark 8) for about 10 minutes or until crisp and golden brown. Cool on a wire rack.

Sacristans

The ingredients for sacristans are the same as for palmiers (above) with the addition of a few chopped almonds.
The pastry is rolled thinly, then brushed with egg white and sprinkled with castor (superfine) sugar and chopped nuts. Press the nuts on firmly. Cut the dough into strips ½ inch wide and 3 inches long.
Twist each finger and place on a damp baking tray. Bake as above.

Tartelettes aux fruits Fruit pastries

1 lb. pâte sucrée (see recipe
page 119)
4 pears
juice of 1 lemon
12 black grapes
12 white grapes
6 oz. (¾ cup) apricot jam
glacé (candied) cherries
angelica (candied peel)

Make the pâte sucrée. Using only half of the pastry, roll it out on a lightly floured board and line about 9 or 10 patty tins. Roll out the remaining pastry and cut into thin strips about 10 inches long and ½–¾ inch wide. Dampen each pastry strip with water and wind up around a cream horn tin, wet side outside. Place small rounds of greased greaseproof paper in the patty tins and fill each with some baking beans. Place the cream horns on a baking tray. Bake all the pastry cases and horns in a hot oven (400°F. Mark 6) for about 20 minutes or until cooked and golden. Cool on a wire rack. Peel, core and slice the pears thinly and dip each slice in lemon juice to prevent discolouration. Halve and remove pips from the grapes. Heat the apricot jam in a small saucepan, add the remaining lemon juice, stir until the liquid is blended, then sieve. Fill the cooked pastry cases with the prepared fruits, glaze the tops with apricot glaze. Decorate with glacé (candied) cherries and angelica

makes about 14 (candied peel) and cut into small pieces.

Gâteau st honoré St. Honoré cake

1 quantity pâte à choux
8 oz. fresh strawberries
½ pint (1¼ cups) double
(heavy) cream
4 teaspoons gelatine
castor (superfine) sugar to taste
2 oz. (¼ cup) granulated
(crystal) sugar

Grease a 7 inch diameter ovenproof plate. Prepare the choux paste and, using a large plain icing pipe, pipe circles on the plate from the outside working inwards. Pipe the remaining mixture in small mounds on a greased baking tray. Bake in a moderately hot oven (375°F. Mark 5) allowing 40–45 minutes for the choux case and 20–30 minutes for the choux buns.
Prepare the strawberries, putting aside some of the best for decoration. Press the remaining strawberries through a sieve to make a purée. Mix the purée and the cream together and whip until stiffened. Dissolve the gelatine in about 2 tablespoons hot water and add to the strawberry cream with enough castor (superfine) sugar to sweeten to taste. Leave in a cool place until almost set. Place the granulated (crystal) sugar in a small saucepan with 4 tablespoons (good ¼ cup) water. Heat the saucepan, stirring until the sugar is dissolved, then boil until a light caramel colour. Dip each choux bun into the caramel and press around the rim of the choux case, building up a high wall. Pour any remaining caramel over the buns. Pour the strawberry cream into the middle of the gâteau and leave to set. Decorate the top with the strawberries set aside for the purpose, and serve as soon as possible.

note: the strawberries can be omitted and the buns filled with cream
serves 6–8 before they are built up into a tall cone shape on the choux case.

Choux aux fraises (ou framboises)
Strawberry (or raspberry) cream buns

1 quantity pâte à choux (see recipe page 119)
½ pint (1¼ cups) double (heavy) cream
1 lb. fresh or frozen strawberries (or raspberries)
icing (confectionery) sugar
makes 1 dozen

Put tablespoonsful of the prepared choux paste at intervals on a greased baking tray. Bake in a hot oven (400°F. Mark 6) for 30–35 minutes until well risen and golden brown.
Split each bun down one side and cool on a wire rack.
Whip the cream until stiff. Prepare the fruit. Pipe or spoon the cream into the buns and arrange the fruit on top. Dust each bun heavily with sifted icing (confectionery) sugar. Serve as soon as possible.

Savarin
Rum-soaked yeast cake

8 oz. (2 cups) plain (all purpose) flour
1 oz. fresh yeast or 1 tablespoon (1½T) dried yeast
6 tablespoons (½ cup) milk, warmed
½ teaspoon salt
1 oz. (2T) castor (superfine) sugar
4 eggs, beaten
4 oz. (8T) butter, softened
¼ pint (⅝ cup) fruit syrup or
4 oz. (½ cup granulated (crystal) sugar dissolved in ¼ pint (⅝ cup) water
3 tablespoons (¼ cup) rum or sherry
3 tablespoons (¼ cup) apricot jam

serves 6

Place 2 oz. (½ cup) of flour in a mixing bowl. Stir the yeast into the milk, add to the flour and beat well with a wooden spoon until it becomes a smooth batter. Allow to stand in a warm place until frothy, this will be about 20 minutes for fresh yeast and 30 minutes for dried yeast. Put the remaining 6 oz. (1½ cups) flour in a bowl with the salt, castor (superfine) sugar, eggs and butter. Add the yeast mixture and beat for 3–4 minutes.
Grease an 8 inch diameter ring mould (or two 6 inch diameter moulds) and half fill it with the dough. Cover the mould with a sheet of lightly greased polythene and allow the dough to rise in a warm place until the mould is ⅔ full. Bake in the centre of a hot oven (400°F. Mark 6) for 20 minutes.
Remove the savarin from the mould and place it on a serving plate. Heat the fruit juice with rum, sherry and pour over the savarin to soak it thoroughly. (Prick the savarin well with a skewer first to help the soaking). Cool.
Place the apricot jam in a small saucepan with 2 tablespoons (scant ¼ cup) water. Heat, stirring, until blended. Sieve. Glaze the savarin and fill with fruit as desired.

Savarin à la crème et oranges
Savarin with cream and oranges

Remove the peel and pith from 3 oranges and cut them into sections with a sharp knife, discarding all the skin. Keep on one side all the juice, squeeze the juice from one more orange and mix all the juice with 2 tablespoons rum. Use this syrup instead of fruit syrup to soak the savarin.
Keep aside the best orange segments for decoration, about 16–18. Chop the rest. Halve and remove the pips from 4 oz. grapes, keeping about 8 halves for decoration. Mix the chopped orange and the remaining grapes with ¼ pint (⅝ cup) whipped cream. Pile this mixture into the centre of the savarin. Decorate the top of the savarin with the fruit put on one side and about ¼ pint (⅝ cup) extra whipped cream, piped in rosettes.

Savarin aux pommes et caramel
Savarin with apples and caramel

Place 6 oz. (¾ cup) granulated (crystal) sugar in a small heavy pan and heat it gently until the sugar has caramelized into a rich golden brown. Meanwhile, halve and remove the pips of 4 oz. black grapes, remove the skin and pith from 2 small oranges and cut into segments, discarding all the skin. Core and chop 2 red-skinned dessert apples and dip in lemon juice to prevent discolouration. Mix the fruit together and pile into the centre of the fruit syrup and rum-soaked savarin. Dip small clusters of grapes into the caramel for decoration. Pour the remaining caramel over the savarin and arrange the caramel-dipped grape clusters around the edge.

Babas au rhum Rum babas

1 oz. fresh yeast or 1 tablespoon (1½T) dried yeast
6 tablespoons (½ cup) milk, warmed
8 oz. (2 cups) plain (all purpose) flour
½ teaspoon salt
1 oz. (2T) castor sugar
4 eggs, beaten
4 oz. (8T) butter, softened
4 oz. (about ⅔ cup) currants
4 tablespoons (good ¼ cup) honey
rum to taste
3 tablespoons (¼ cup) apricot jam
double (heavy) cream for serving
makes 16–17

Stir the yeast into the milk. Place 2 oz. (½ cup) flour into a mixing bowl, add the milk and yeast and beat well with a wooden spoon to a smooth batter. Allow to stand in a warm place until frothy. This will be about 20 minutes for fresh yeast and 30 minutes for dried. Put the remaining 6 oz. (1½ cups) flour into a bowl with the salt, sugar, eggs, butter and currants. Add the yeast mixture.
Mix and beat well for 3–4 minutes.
Grease some dariole moulds (about 16 or 17 medium sized ones). Half fill the moulds with the yeast mixture, cover with a sheet of lightly greased polythene and allow to rise in a warm place until the moulds are ⅔ full.
Bake at the top of a hot oven (400 °F. Mark 6) for 15–20 minutes. Cool for a few minutes and then turn out on to a wire rack with a tray underneath.
Place the honey in a small saucepan with 4 tablespoons (good ¼ cup) water and rum to taste. Heat until blended and syrupy, stirring constantly. Pour the syrup over the warm babas, soaking them thoroughly.
Place the apricot jam in a small saucepan with 2 tablespoons (just ¼ cup) water.
Heat gently, stirring. Sieve. Brush the glaze generously over the babas.

Rum baba decorated with fruit   Cool, transfer to a serving plate and top with whipped cream.

Croissants

1 lb. (4 cups) plain (all
purpose) flour
2 teaspoons salt
1 oz. (⅛ cup) lard
1 egg, beaten
1 oz. (good ¼ cup) fresh yeast or
1 tablespoon dried yeast plus 1
teaspoon castor sugar
6 oz. (12T) butter or margarine
extra egg for glazing
extra ½ teaspoon castor
(superfine) sugar

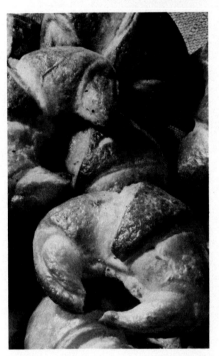

Mix the flour and salt, rub in the lard and stir in the egg. Blend
the fresh yeast into 7 fluid oz. (⅞ cup) water or mix the dried yeast
with 7 fluid oz. (⅞ cup) water plus 1 teaspoon castor (superfine)
sugar. Leave either for 10 minutes or until frothy. Add the yeast
mixture to the rubbed-in mixture. Mix well, then place on a lightly
floured board and knead the dough until smooth, 10–15 minutes.
Roll the dough out to a strip ¼ inch thick, 20 inches long and 8
inches wide, keeping the sides straight and the corners square.
Soften the butter with a knife, then divide into 3. Mark the dough
lightly into thirds, then dot the two-thirds with a third of the butter.
Fold the plain lower third up over the middle third and then fold the
top third down. Turn the dough a quarter turn to the left so that
the folds are to right and left. Press the edges lightly with a rolling
pin to seal them.
Roll out the dough again very gently by pressing the dough at
intervals with the rolling pin. Incorporate the other portions of
butter, separately, as before. Place the dough in a lightly greased
polythene bag and place in a cool place, preferably the refrigerator,
for 30 minutes. Roll out, as before, and repeat rolling and folding
3 more times. Leave in the refrigerator for a further 1 hour.
Roll out the dough into a rectangle about 23 inches long and 14
inches wide. Cover with lightly greased polythene and leave for
10 minutes. Trim with a knife to 21 inches and 12 inches wide.
Divide the dough in half lengthwise, then cut each strip into 6
triangles each 6 inches high with a 6 inch wide base.
Mix the extra egg with a little water and the extra pinch of sugar.
Brush the egg wash over each triangle and roll up, loosely finishing
at the point. Place the point underneath and curve the roll into a
crescent.
Place the shaped croissants on to an ungreased baking tray and
brush the tops with some egg wash. Place in a lightly greased
polythene bag and leave in a warm place for 20–30 minutes or until
puffed up. Brush with egg wash once more and bake in the centre
of a hot oven (425°F. Mark 7) for 20 minutes.
Serve warm.

makes 12

Brioche

½ oz. fresh yeast or 2 teaspoons
dried yeast plus ½ teaspoon
castor (superfine) sugar
8 oz. (2 cups) plain (all
purpose) flour
½ teaspoon salt
½ teaspoon castor
(superfine) sugar
2 eggs, beaten
2 oz. (4T) butter, melted and
cooled
extra egg for glazing
extra pinch of sugar

Stir the yeast into ½ tablespoon cold water; or, if dried yeast is
being used, mix the yeast and sugar together and sprinkle with
1½ tablespoons water.
Using either method leave for 10 minutes in a warm place until
frothy. Sift the flour, salt and castor (superfine) sugar together. Add
the yeast liquid, eggs and butter and mix to a soft dough. Place on a
lightly floured board and knead well for about 5 minutes. Place the
dough in a lightly greased polythene bag and allow to rise in a warm
place for about 1–1½ hours.
Grease twelve 3 inch diameter brioche tins or deep bun tins. Divide
the dough into 12 equal pieces. Shape ¾ of each piece into a ball and
put into the tins. Press a hole firmly in the centre, then roll the
remaining ¼ of dough into a small ball and place it in the centre.
Put the filled tins on a baking tray. Put inside a large lightly
greased polythene bag and leave to rise until doubled in size, about
1 hour, in a warm place.
Mix an extra egg with pinch of salt and 1 tablespoon water. Brush
over the brioche and bake in the centre of a very hot oven (450°F.
Mark 8) for 10 minutes.

makes 12   Serve warm, with butter if desired.

Entertaining

The French people are hospitable and love to entertain. Whether it is a completely formal dinner party or merely a light luncheon on the beach, you can be sure that it will be beautifully prepared and served.

Further on in this chapter you will find some menu suggestions suitable for dinner parties. It is difficult, however, to go into menus for other occasions in such detail, since the dishes will rely so much on the occasion and the climate – whether the meal is to be eaten indoors or outside, and which foods are available at the time of year in your part of the world. After all, there is no such thing as a typical French menu; for instance, a Provençale menu would only very vaguely resemble a Breton menu or a Savoyard menu.

So select the recipes in this book which you feel would take in the above points but would also look attractive together when served according to variations in colour, texture and the main ingredients. It would be wrong to serve more than one cream dish or to present eggs or fish more than once. Serve a crisp light dish with a rich creamy one, checking that the finished dishes are not all of the same colour.

Serve French bread and butter as a matter of course, throughout the meal. If you are going to be very French, don't have side plates for the bread; your guests will just tear the bread into bite sized pieces on the table to their left. Always serve wine. The French are avid wine drinkers and it is the usual drink with everyday meals. Even the little children drink it, albeit with a little water added. Vin ordinaire is the everyday wine. The more important the occasion, the finer the wine to be served. Whether the wine is red or white, dry or sweet, will depend largely on yours or your guests' tastes. There are certain conventions which can be followed if in doubt (you will find these later on in the chapter) but the main thing is to enjoy the wine.

The wines of France

French wines are considered among the best, if not the best, in the world. Wherever vines are grown outside Europe, it is frequently French vines that are used and the wine produced is as near to its French counterpart as the vigneron can make it. Even wines made as far from France as Australia and America are still called Burgundys, Sauternes, Chablis and so on. It is impossible, though, to produce an exact imitation, because each year's grapes are slightly different and the taste and quality of a wine is affected by the weather and other natural factors such as the soil, local vegetation and the situation of the vineyard. On some wine labels you will now find the words 'appellation d'origine'. This ensures that the wine in that bottle actually came from the region after which it is named, e.g. Médoc.

You will find vines all over France with the exception of the extreme north. The most northerly vineyards are those in Champagne which produce grapes to make the inimitable sparkling wine of the same name. It is the fermentation process which makes the Champagne and, according to the amount of sugar added, the wine can be dry or sweet.

Bordeaux wines are among the best in France. The old vineyards produce a wine which has a good clear colour, a delicate bouquet and is smooth with a fine subtle flavour. The wines produced here are some of the most famous names such as

Red	White
Médoc, Margaux, Moulis, Listrac, Saint-Julien, Pauillac, Saint-Estèphe, Les Graves rouge, Saint-Emilion, Pomerol, Blayais, Canon et Côtes de Fronsac, Bourgeais, Côtes de Castillon.	Graves, Entre-Deux-Mers, Saint-Macaire, Haut-Benauge, Saint-Foy, Blaye et Bourg, Sauternes, Barsac, Cérons, Loupiac, St-Croix-du-Mont.

The Sud-Ouest and Bearn districts produce wines of mixed qualities. White, red, rose and sparkling wines are all made here. Some of the most famous are:

Red	Sparkling wines
Bergerac, Côtes de Duras, Pecharmant, Madiran	Gaillac, Rosé-Rosé de Bearn

White

Montravel, Bergerac, Rosette, Monbazillac, Jurançon

Burgundy is perhaps the most well-known wine growing area. Here they produce both red and white wines. The north of Burgundy makes fine dry white wine which is known as Chablis. Just south of this is the Côte de Nuits, which makes smooth velvety wines and is the home of the famous Nuits-St-George, Chambertin, Musigny, Clos de Vougeot, and so on. Again southwards, to the Côte de Beaune and such glowing wines as Corton, Pommard, Volnay and many more. The vineyards still stretch southwards through the Côte de Chalonnaise, Mâconnais and Beaujolais, producing, among many others, Pouilly-Fuissés, Montagny, and Chardonnay. In Beaujolais there are so many vineyards that each village has its own label. These wines are delicate and light with a rich bouquet. Some are very rough and need to be laid down to mature for some time before drinking.

Rhône wines have earned themselves an enviable reputation but those from the north are completely different from their southern counterparts. The white wines from the north are few but have an individual character. The better known wines are Condrieu, Chateau-Grillet, Hermitage and Saint Péray. The southern wines are varied in quality but the best are fine with a certain elegance. If drunk young, these wines are perfect when drunk with freshly

A typical pruned Grenach vine in the top terraces of Châteauneuf-du-Pape.

caught Mediterranean fish. The most famous are Laudun, Lirac and white Châteauneuf-du-Pape. Red Rhône wines again vary from north to south. The northern reds are full-bodied and robust with a high alcohol content. Red-Hermitage and Crozes-Hermitage are both rich red in colour, mellow and elegant. To the south, the red wines are lighter and more delicate although some have a powerful aroma and bouquet. The most famed is Châteauneuf-du-Pape, which is traditionally served with game, especially venison. Rosé wines are also produced in this area, the best of which come from Chusclan, Lirac and Tulan. A few fruity dessert wines also come from the Rhône valley.

Provence produces a variety of wines white, red and rose. The vineyards stretch along the Mediterranean coast and inland as far as Aix-en-Provence. Although some are exported, such as Cassis, Bandol, Bellet de Nice and Palatte d'Aix, the majority of wines are drunk locally as they are the perfect partner to Provençale food.

Alsace. The character of Alsace wines has made them famous throughout the world. Mainly white wines are produced and they are rich in bouquet. Who does not know these familiar names, Riesling, Traminer, Gewurztraminer, Tokay and Muscatel?

Jura and **Savoy** wines are not too well-known outside of France. Jura wines can be white or rosé and are well-balanced, fruity but delicate. They are at their best when laid down or placed in barrels to mature for a long time. Savoy wines are fresh and light. They are at their best when served with lake or river trout in the Savoy. White, red and rosé wines are all produced here.

The **Loire** Valley is noted for its vineyards which stretch for miles either side of the river. The sweet white wines of Anjou are famous

The vineyards of Gigondas (Department Vaucluse) which produce one of the appellation controlée Côtes-du-Rhone-Villages wines.

for their smoothness and fruitiness. Coteaux de Layon, Aubance, Bonnezeaux and Savennières are just a few of the better known. Vouvray, Montlouis, Saumer and Touraine are the names of just a few of the sparkling and semi-sparkling wines produced in the Loire valley. Muscadet is a well-known local dry white wine. This area is also just becoming recognised for its rosé wines, especially those from Anjou and Touraine. Red wines are in the minority here although some very good ones are made such as the light red Chinon and Bourgeuil.

Languedoc Roussillon in the south of France is the home of the simple table wines. Vin ordinaire, which every household in France drinks, mainly comes from here as this wine can be drunk very young and does not have to be pampered. Dry white wines such as Languedoc 'Clairettes' and Bellegarde, red wines such as Corbières, Minervois, Fitou and St George d'Orques and sparkling wine such as Blanquette de Limoux are famous throughout France although not so well-known outside the country. Many of the sweet natural dessert wines such as Muscatel and some fortified wines are also from this area.

Choosing and serving wines

Generally, the more you pay for a bottle of wine, the superior the quality—but this is not always so. It would be an advantage if you could find out the quality of the vintage year in which the wine was made. Sometimes a poor vintage year produces only a limited crop of grapes and therefore only a limited number of bottles of wine. On the other hand a good vintage year, producing a really superb wine, may also coincide with a good crop and therefore more than enough bottles which can be sold at a reasonable price. Whatever its quality, the wine must be cool to touch, sealed (preferably with a cork) and a good clear colour.

It is as well to know what food is to be eaten with the wine. You may have your own ideas as to which wines you prefer—and why not, as this is definitely a matter of personal taste and the main idea is to enjoy your wine? If, however, you are giving a dinner party and would like to serve the correct wines with each course, you may find the following suggestions helpful:

Hors d'oeuvres	Dry or medium dry white wines.
Fish and shellfish	Dry white wines; dry white sparkling wines.
Poultry	White or red dry and rich in bouquet but not too full-bodied.
Meat	Red wine, dry and not too fullbodied.
Game	A full-bodied, rich and generous red wine.
Cheeses	Serve a full-bodied good vintage red wine with strong cheeses. A lighter dry white wine should be served with mild and soft cheeses.
Desserts and fresh fruit	Champagne; sweet sparkling and still wines; sweet dessert wines.

Champagne is the only wine that can correctly be served throughout a meal. At some time before it is to be drunk, make sure that the wine will be the correct temperature at the time of serving. White and rosé wines should be served chilled but not iced. Sweet white wines should be even cooler. Place the bottle in the refrigerator for at least 1 hour or until the wine is sufficiently cool. Sparkling wines should be served slightly chilled; if possible the bottle should be placed in a bucket of ice for a while before serving. Red wines should be served at room temperature and the bottle should be opened about half an hour before the wine is to be drunk. Never try to alter the temperature of wine quickly; it should be a slow, gradual process so as not to spoil the wine.

To my mind, wine tastes good out of any glass, but if you have gone out of your way to obtain a good quality (and probably expensive) wine, it is well worthwhile serving it in the correctly shaped glass. Only use uncoloured glasses which will show off the colour and clearness of the wine. Generally speaking, only half fill a wine glass, as this will enable the full bouquet of the wine to rise and be appreciated before the actual wine is sampled. This is especially true of red wines which are generally served in rounded glasses to stop the bouquet from escaping. For a full dinner party you will probably need four glasses on the table for each person: one for dry white wine, one for red, one for sweet white and the last for sparkling wines or Champagne. They will also be placed on the table in that order, since light and white wines are generally served before full-bodied and red wines—excepting, of course, the wines served with the dessert and fruit.

Dinner parties in the French manner

When the French entertain, they can produce anything from a full eight course dinner party (for very special occasions) to the simplest of cold picnics. Either way, care is lavished on each dish and great attention is paid to the serving.

A complete dinner for a special occasion can still be the same elaborate type of banquet which was frequently given in the last century. The various courses would be as follows:

Hors d'oeuvres	Appetizers.
Potage	Soup.
Poisson	Fish
Entrée	Meat dish made in an elaborate manner.
Relevé	Joint of meat.
Rôti	Roast game or poultry.
Entremet	This is a vegetable, a sweet, and an after dinner savoury or cheese.
Dessert	Fresh fruit, petit fours or small ice cream.
Café	Coffee.

A suitable menu for such a splendid dinner (if you feel that you could cope) might be:

Pamplemousse au Gingembre	medium dry or sweet white wine
Crème de Concombre	dry or medium dry white wine
Sole à la Colbert	dry white wine
Tournados au Poivre	dry red wine
Rôti de Porc	dry red wine
Poulet Rôti au Beurre	dry red wine
Choufleur Polonaise	dry red wine
Diables à Cheval	dry red wine
Mousse au Chocolat	sweet white wine
Poires Bourguignonne	sweet white wine
Café	liqueurs

The flavour of Italy

The flavour of Italy is abundant freshness and, because this country is blessed with an enviable climate, one is warmly welcomed by a profusion of aromatic basil, sage, rosemary, marjoram, thyme, mint, parsley and bay. Sweet, sun-ripened tomatoes which drip with juice. Delicate, champagne-gold olive oil. Garlic and salami and Mortadella and heady wines. Crusty bread and pungent cheeses. Parma ham and ripe figs. Artichokes, honey-sweet melons and myriads of olives in green, black, purple and brown. Fleshy apricots, peaches, pears and cherries with grapes that taste like nectar. Wood strawberries and multi-coloured pimentos. Sweet-scented oranges and lemons. Exotic fish from sea and lakes. Saffron and white truffles and such a lavish array of fresh vegetables that every Italian street market looks like an Aladdin's cave.

What emerges from a study of Italian cuisine is the fact that it does not depend for its success on elaborate and rich sauces, on expensive and impressive additions and on ornate decorations and garnishes. Rather it is totally unpretentious, relatively uncomplicated, traditional, individual and, like the Italian people themselves, charming and utterly captivating. The food—be it a simple bowl of pasta shimmering with melted butter or a glass of warm zabaione—is always a pleasure and a joy to eat. The simplicity of style and presentation, coupled with the freshness and quality of the ingredients used, place it, without question, in the haute cuisine class. But looking back in time, this should come as no surprise, for the splendours of the early Roman banquets made history and, ever since, the Italians—who make no secret of their love of good food—have eaten and drunk handsomely and heartily and enjoyed every minute of it!

Now that Italian ingredients are more readily available everywhere, there is no reason why the rest of us should not share, with the Italian people, some of their own distinctive cooking. This book, containing a reasonable sprinkling of the kind of everyday dishes eaten in the average Italian home, should serve as a useful introduction to a style of food which, as early as the 16th century, was brought to the French Court by Catherine de Medici, the Italian wife of King Henry II of France.

140   *Preparing the meal*

Antipasti

Fanciful starters figure very little in the repertoire of Italian cookery. Instead it is more customary to have a small bowl of freshly cooked pasta crowned with Parmesan cheese or a traditional sauce. Or gnocchi, pizza or risotto. Mortadella sausage (a Bolognese speciality) with a dish of olives to go with it. Beef and chicken broth with pastini. Minestrone or the simple but unique stracciatella. Huge tomatoes grilled with tuna. A plate of bean salad. Raw mushrooms and anchovies tossed with the simplest of dressings. Mild ham and salami in all its varieties. Freshly fried sardines or local scampi. Bagna cauda with fresh vegetables. Ravioli. Nothing, you might say, particularly elaborate; nothing especially impressive —just eminently appetizing, which is surely what a good starter ought to be.

Antipasto misto — Mixed antipasto

4 oz. Italian salami, finely sliced
12 each, black and green olives
4 hard boiled eggs
1 small can anchovies in oil
2 oz. (⅝ cup) raw button
mushrooms, sliced
1 canned red pimento
3 oz. (1 cup) cooked green beans
(French or snap)
2 tablespoons (2½T) olive oil
1 tablespoon (1¼T) lemon juice
seasoning to taste
serves 4

A colourful mixed hors d'oeuvre which makes an appetizing and fairly substantial starter to a light meal.

Arrange the salami and olives on a long platter. Cut the eggs into wedges and stand on top of the salami. Drape the drained anchovies over the eggs.
Put the mushrooms into a bowl. Chop the pimento and add to the bowl with the green beans. Beat the oil, lemon juice and seasoning well together. Add to the mushroom mixture and toss well. Arrange in small heaps round the edge of the platter.

Antipasto di peperoni e pomodori — Pimento and tomato antipasto

4 pickled red and
yellow pimentos
4 large tomatoes, skinned and
sliced
2 tablespoons (2½T) olive oil
1 tablespoon (1¼T) lemon juice
seasoning to taste
1 small onion, chopped
1 heaped tablespoon (1½T) finely
chopped parsley
serves 4

A gay and flavourful hot weather starter.

Cut the pimentos into strips and arrange on a platter, then top with tomato slices.
Beat the oil, lemon juice and seasoning well together and pour over the pimentos and tomatoes. Sprinkle with onion and parsley.

Melanzane ripiene — Stuffed aubergines (eggplants) with egg

2 medium aubergines (eggplant)
salt and pepper
olive oil
4 oz. (2 cups) fresh white
breadcrumbs
2 large hard boiled
eggs, chopped
8 green olives, stoned and
sliced
1 small garlic clove, crushed
8 anchovy fillets, chopped
squeeze of lemon juice
1 heaped tablespoon (1½T)
chopped parsley
1 level teaspoon marjoram

The aubergine—or eggplant—established itself in Italy many centuries ago but despite its familiarity to the people of the country, it is used much less in Italian cuisine than other vegetables of lesser worth. Consequently recipes for it are scarce and those that do exist are surprisingly unimaginative. This version of Stuffed Aubergines is more interesting than most and is a tasty dish with anchovies, garlic, olives and egg adding the flavour interest. It may be eaten either hot or cold but in my opinion is best straight from the oven with crusty bread and red wine.

Preheat the oven to moderate (350°F, Mark 4). Wash and dry the aubergines (eggplant) and cut them in half lengthwise. Make gashes in the flesh with a knife then stand, cut sides uppermost, on an oiled baking tray.
Sprinkle with salt and pepper then brush fairly heavily with oil.
Cook in the centre of the oven for 30 minutes. Remove from the oven and cool off slightly.
Carefully cut out the flesh (leaving ¼-inch thick aubergine (eggplant) shells), chop finely and put into a bowl. Add all the remaining ingredients then season well to taste, but watch the salt as the anchovies will doubtless contribute their own share.
Return the mixture to the aubergine (eggplant) shells and sprinkle lightly with oil. Cook in the centre of the oven for a further

serves 4   30 minutes.

Mixed antipasto

143

*Mixed salads with mortadella
and salami (left)*

Cauliflower salad (below)

Raw mushroom salad (right)

*Asparagus on artichoke hearts
(below right)*

Insalata di fagioli Dressed beans

¾ lb. (2 cups) shelled broad,
lima or haricot beans
1 cut clove garlic
3 oz. (½ cup) lean ham,
finely chopped
3 tablespoons (3¾T) olive oil
3 dessertspoons (3T) lemon
juice or mild vinegar
seasoning to taste
½ level teaspoon dried or 1 level
teaspoon fresh basil

serves 4

A simple hors d'oeuvre for summer eating.

Cook the beans in boiling salted water until just tender and still crisp.

Meanwhile, rub the cut clove of garlic round the inside of a salad bowl. Add the drained beans and ham.

Beat the olive oil and lemon juice or vinegar well together with the seasonings. Add to the beans in the bowl and toss thoroughly to mix.

Chill thoroughly and sprinkle with basil just before serving.

Alternatively, top the beans with a little mayonnaise, then garnish with anchovy fillets, rolled round black olives, and tomato slices.

Dressed beans

Crostini di provatura Hot cheese antipasto

These are filling mouthfuls, simply made from fried bread and Bel Paese cheese. They must be served piping hot and are a pleasurable experience on bleak winter days.

Allowing 3 or 4 per person, cut de-crusted slices of white bread into small rounds or squares and fry in a mixture of hot olive oil and butter until crisp and golden on both sides.

Top each round or square with a slice of Bel Paese cheese then stand under a preheated hot grill. Leave until cheese just begins to melt then serve straight away.

Anchovies—so beloved by the Italians—are the traditional garnish but the antipasti are just as good without anything at all.

Insalata di riso   Rice salad

8 oz. (1¼ cups) long grain rice
2–3 tablespoons (2½–3¾T)
mild vinegar
2–3 dessertspoons (2–3T)
olive oil
seasoning to taste
nutmeg (optional)
1 level dessertspoon (1T) finely
chopped parsley
1 oz. (⅛ cup) flaked almonds or
pine nuts
2 oz. (½ cup) prawns
(shrimp), chopped
1 small red or green pimento,
de-seeded and chopped
1 medium celery stalk,
finely chopped
1 small onion, grated
green olives, or ham and
watercress for garnishing
serves 4

An easily prepared dish which may be livened up with any manner of additions, depending on what is in the refrigerator or store cupboard. Chicken may be substituted for prawns [shrimp], chopped cucumber for green pepper, walnuts for almonds and leek for onion. Capers may be added as well and so may lightly cooked green peas, cooked mussels, finely chopped ham and a hint of finely chopped fresh mint.

Cook the rice in about 1 pint (2½ cups) boiling salted water until tender; 12–15 minutes. Drain thoroughly. Add vinegar and olive oil and mix well with a fork. Season to taste with salt and pepper and, if liked, a grinding or two of nutmeg.
Stir in all the remaining ingredients (except the olives), then transfer the rice mixture to a lettuce-lined serving dish.
Garnish with olives or with rolls of ham and watercress.

Ham, tuna and fennel appetizer (left)

Parma ham with melon (below)

Raw vegetables with hot garlic sauce (right)

Carciofi   Globe artichokes

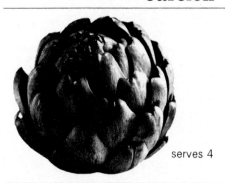

Cut the stems off the artichokes and remove the first two rows of leaves. Cut the tips off the remaining leaves with scissors. Soak the artichokes for 30 minutes in cold, salted water. Drain thoroughly. Stand the artichokes upright in a saucepan and add about 4 inches of boiling water and one level teaspoon of salt. Bring to the boil, lower the heat and cover the pan. Simmer gently for 30 to 40 minutes or until the leaves pull out easily. Drain very thoroughly by turning the artichokes upside down on to paper towels.

serves 4   Serve hot with melted butter or cold with mayonnaise (see opposite) or salad dressing.

Carciofi alla maionese   Artichokes with mayonnaise

Medium-sized, fresh and tender artichokes which, ideally, should be used for this dish are prolific in Italy but not so readily available elsewhere. Consequently one has to compromise and use either freshly boiled globe artichokes (see above)—the large leafy variety —or canned artichoke hearts instead.

If using the latter, allow 2 per person. Drain well on paper towels and stand on lettuce-lined plates. Coat thickly with mayonnaise then sprinkle with chopped hard-boiled eggs and the merest suspicion of freshly chopped basil or mint.

Artichokes with mayonnaise

Maionese Mayonnaise

2 or 3 egg yolks (from large eggs)
½ level teaspoon salt
¼ level teaspoon white pepper
2 tablespoons (2½T) fresh lemon juice
½ pint (1¼ cups) olive oil

In Italy mayonnaise is widely used for all manner of dishes and in its simplest form is a mixture of the best possible olive oil—the finest is said to come from Lucca in Tuscany—egg yolks, lemon juice, salt and white pepper to taste. Occasionally a sparing amount of chopped garlic is added as well, as are finely chopped parsley and freshly chopped basil. For most general purposes, though, the mayonnaise is used without any additions at all.

Put the egg yolks, salt, pepper and 1 dessertspoon (1T) of lemon juice into a basin. Beat thoroughly. Gradually add half the oil, drop by drop, beating hard all the time.
When the mayonnaise is thick and glistening, add a further dessertspoon (1T) of lemon juice. Add half the remaining oil in a slow, steady stream, beating all the time. Beat in the rest of the lemon juice and oil.
Adjust seasoning to taste, adding a dash of wine vinegar if the mayonnaise seems on the bland side. To stop separation, stir in a dessertspoon of boiling water at the very end.
The mayonnaise may be stored in a lightly closed container in the least cold part of the refrigerator or pantry for up to one week.
Curdled mayonnaise is the result of adding the oil too quickly in the early stages. Should this happen—and not even expert cooks are immune—break a fresh egg yolk into a basin and very gradually beat the curdled mayonnaise into it.

Preparing mayonnaise
(a) The egg yolks, salt, pepper and lemon juice are beaten together thoroughly.
(b) Oil is added to the egg mixture drop by drop, beating hard all the time.
(c) Curdled mayonnaise can be rescued by breaking an extra yolk into a bowl and very gradually beating the curdled mayonnaise into it.

a

b

c

Fondi di carciofi all'olio e aglio   Garlic dressed artichoke hearts

Make a dressing by beating 6 dessertspoons (6T) olive oil with 2 dessertspoons (2T) lemon juice and 1 dessertspoon (1T) wine vinegar. Season to taste with salt and pepper, then pour into a screw-topped jar. Add 1 large cut clove of garlic, cover and leave overnight.
Allow 2 or 3 canned artichoke hearts per person. Just before serving, stand them on a lettuce-lined plate. Shake the dressing thoroughly then pour over the artichokes. Sprinkle with chopped ham and serve straight away.

Fondi di carciofi con asparagi   Asparagus on artichoke hearts

4 artichoke hearts
4 eggs
2 lb. asparagus
Hollandaise sauce

Poach the artichoke hearts, then leave them to cool. Hardboil the eggs. Wash and scrape the asparagus and discard the tough part of the stalks. Tie in bundles and cook in boiling, unsalted water for 15 to 20 minutes.
Chop the eggs, mix with some of the asparagus tips and place on the artichoke hearts. Place the remaining asparagus tips on top and pour over Hollandaise sauce.

serves 4

Antipasto di pomodori e gamberi

Tomato prawn antipasto

4 large tomatoes
1 small onion, very
finely chopped
1 oz. (2T) butter
4 oz. (1 cup) shrimps or
prawns, finely chopped
½ oz. (¼ cup) fresh
white breadcrumbs
4 anchovy fillets, finely chopped
1 level tablespoon (1¼T) finely
chopped parsley
pepper to taste

serves 4

Preheat the oven to moderately hot (375°F, or Mark 5).
Cut the tops off the tomatoes, then scoop out the inside fibres and
seeds and reserve these. Stand the tomatoes upside down to drain on
soft kitchen paper.
Fry the onion gently in the butter until pale gold. Stir in the shrimps
or prawns, crumbs, anchovies, parsley and salt and pepper to taste.
Stir in sufficient tomato pulp to moisten the mixture. (Keep
remainder for soup and stews.)
Return the mixture to the tomato cases. Cook just above the centre
of the oven for 20 minutes.

Pomodori ripieni di acciughe
Anchovy stuffed tomatoes

4 very large tomatoes
8 anchovy fillets
1 oz. (½ cup) fresh white breadcrumbs
1 garlic clove
1 tablespoon (1¼T) olive oil
salt and pepper to taste
a little beaten egg
4 stoned green olives

serves 4

Preheat the oven to moderately hot (375°F, or Mark 5).
Cut the tops off the tomatoes, then scoop out the inside fibres and seeds and reserve these. Stand the tomatoes upside down to drain on soft kitchen paper.
Finely chop the anchovy fillets and put them into a basin with the crumbs. Crush the garlic and add to the basin then stir in the olive oil. Season well to taste with salt and pepper then bind with a little tomato pulp (keep the remainder for soup and stews) and a little beaten egg.
Return to the tomato cases then top each with an olive or with the tomato tops. Cook just above the centre of the oven for 20 minutes. Garnish with parsley.

153

Pomodori ripieni di tonno e capperi
Tuna stuffed tomatoes with capers

Prepare the tomato cases exactly as in the previous recipe.
To make the filling, combine 6 heaped tablespoons (8T) mashed tuna with 1 level dessertspoon (1T) finely chopped capers.
Stir in sufficient mayonnaise both to moisten and bind the mixture.
Season to taste with salt and pepper, then return to the tomato cases.

serves 4 — Sprinkle with finely chopped parsley and serve very cold.

Prosciutto con tonno e finocchio
Ham, tuna and fennel appetizer

4 slices lean ham
1 can (approximately 7 oz.) tuna
¼ pint (⅝ cup) mayonnaise
3 level tablespoons (3¾T) grated fennel
12 black olives
1 small red pimento, de-seeded and cut into strips

serves 4

Tuna, with its meaty texture and superb yet subtle flavour, combines admirably with most other ingredients and, when teamed with aniseed flavoured fennel and mild, lean ham, makes an intriguing starter to a hot or cold meal.

Arrange the ham on a serving platter.
Drain the tuna and break the flesh into smallish chunks. Stand in a line on top of the ham.
Combine the mayonnaise and fennel well together. Spoon over the tuna then stud with olives and decorate with a criss-cross of pepper strips.

Uova tonnate
Egg and tuna mayonnaise

lettuce
½ can (approximately 3½ oz. tuna
¼ pint (⅝ cup) mayonnaise
4 hard boiled eggs
8 anchovy fillets
serves 4

Arrange the lettuce leaves on 4 individual plates.
Drain the tuna thoroughly. Mash it finely then stir it into the mayonnaise.
Cut the hard boiled eggs in half and stand 2 halves, cut sides down, on each plate. Coat them with the tuna mixture, then garnish each with anchovy fillets.

Antipasto di patate con tonno e peperoni
Potato antipasto with tuna and pimento

6 medium potatoes
3 tablespoons (3¾T) olive oil
3 dessertspoons (3T) lemon juice
salt and pepper to taste
1 can (7 oz.) tuna
¼ pint (⅝ cup) mayonnaise
1 medium onion, finely chopped
1 medium green pimento

serves 4–6

Wash and scrub the potatoes and boil in their skins until tender.
Drain and leave until cool enough to handle, then peel and cut them into dice. Toss with oil and lemon juice and sufficient salt and pepper to taste.
Drain the tuna and mash finely. Combine it with the mayonnaise and onion. Add the potatoes and toss gently but thoroughly with a spoon.
Cut the stem off the green pimento, then remove the inside fibres and seeds. Cut the pimento itself into rings and arrange on top of the potatoes.

Tonno con faglioli
Florentine tuna and bean antipasto

1 cut garlic clove
1 can (7 oz.) tuna
3 dessertspoons (3T) lemon juice
1 teacup (½ cup) haricot beans, soaked overnight and freshly cooked until tender
salt and pepper to taste
serves 4

Rub the salad bowl with the cut clove of garlic.
Drain the tuna and beat the tuna oil with lemon juice. Pour into the salad bowl and add French or snap beans and drained haricot beans. Toss thoroughly and season well to taste with salt and freshly milled pepper.
Flake the tuna and arrange in a mound on top of the beans.

Insalata di funghi   Raw mushroom salad

12 oz. (3¼ cups) button mushrooms
1 clove garlic
½ level teaspoon finely grated lemon peel
3 tablespoons (3¾T) olive oil
3 dessertspoons (3T) lemon juice
pinch of ground nutmeg
salt and pepper to taste
4 anchovy fillets, or parsley

serves 4

Morning-fresh button mushrooms are essential for the success of this starter, as only these have the delicacy of flavour so esteemed by epicures.
Wipe the mushrooms clean, then cut into thin slices.
Cut the garlic clove in half and rub it round the inside of a wooden or glass salad bowl. Add the lemon peel, oil, lemon juice, nutmeg and salt and pepper to taste. Beat thoroughly to mix.
Add the mushrooms and toss gently with a spoon until all the slices are coated with oil/lemon juice mixture. Cover and leave to stand at room temperature for 15 minutes.
Transfer to 4 individual plates and sprinkle the tops of each with thin slivers of anchovies or with chopped parsley.

Bagna cauda con crudita   Bagna cauda with raw vegetables

3 oz. (⅜ cup) unsalted butter
5 tablespoons (6¼T) olive oil
1 small can anchovies in oil, drained and chopped
2–6 garlic cloves, chopped
to serve
4 celery stalks, cut into 2-inch lengths
1 red pimento, cut into fairly wide strips
1 green pimento
4 small carrots, peeled and cut lengthwise into sticks
¼ small white cabbage, cut into fairly wide strips

serves 6–8

A sophisticated but essentially simple starter from the Piedmont region. Basically bagna cauda is a buttery, garlic-flavoured hot sauce into which pieces of crunchy raw vegetables are dipped and then eaten. For those who can stomach rich, strong foods without suffering any after-effects, this Northern speciality is a worthwhile experience; however, those with more delicate digestions are advised to settle for something less potent!

Put the butter, olive oil, anchovies (plus their oil) and the garlic cloves into a saucepan and cook gently for 15 minutes.
Transfer to a heatproof dish standing on a spirit stove or electric plate warmer and serve the hot sauce accompanied by the raw vegetables.

Bagna cauda con panna

Bagna cauda with cream

A more mellow-tasting version, but infinitely richer.
Make the bagna cauda as directed in the previous recipe. When it has cooked for 15 minutes, blend in ¼ pint plus 4 tablespoons (1 cup) double (heavy) cream, heated until hot.
Transfer to a heatproof dish and serve straight away.

Bagna cauda con panna e tartufi

Bagna cauda with cream and truffles

Simultaneously with the cream, add 1 or 2 very thinly sliced canned white truffles.

note: bagna cauda may also be served as an appetizer with drinks.

Crostini di acciughe
Hot anchovy antipasto

8 slices French bread, each between ¼ and ½-inch thick
2 oz. (¼ cup) butter
2 tablespoons (2½T) olive oil
1 tablespoon (1¼T) melted butter
1 level tablespoon (1¼T) flour
¼ pint (⅝ cup) milk
1 oz. (¼ cup) grated Parmesan cheese
salt and pepper to taste
8 anchovy fillets
2 extra level tablespoons (2½T) grated Parmesan cheese
about 1 oz. (2T) butter
serves 4

A rich and satisfying starter with a memorable flavour.
Fry the bread in the hot butter and olive oil until crisp and golden on both sides. Drain on soft kitchen paper then stand in the grill pan. Heat the melted butter in a saucepan. Stir in the flour and cook for 2 minutes without boiling. Gradually blend in the milk. Cook, stirring, until the sauce comes to the boil and thickens. Simmer for 2 minutes. Stir in 1 oz. (¼ cup) Parmesan cheese then season well to taste with salt and pepper.
Spoon equal amounts over the fried bread in the grill pan then top each with an anchovy fillet. Sprinkle the rest of the Parmesan cheese over each, then dot with flakes of butter. Brown quickly under a hot grill and serve straight away.

Salame con le olive
Olive and salami antipasto

4 oz. Italian salami, very thinly sliced
4 oz. (1 cup) Bel Paese or Provolone cheese, cubed
4 large tomatoes, skinned and sliced
2 dozen small black olives
1 red pimento
2 level tablespoons (2½T) finely chopped parsley
1 tablespoon (1¼T) olive oil
1 dessertspoon (1T) lemon juice
salt and pepper to taste
serves 4

Cover a serving platter with salami then arrange cheese, tomatoes and olives attractively on top.
De-seed the red pimento and cut it into thin strips. Put them into a bowl with the parsley. Add oil, lemon juice and salt and pepper to taste and toss ingredients well to mix.
Place, in mounds, on top of the antipasto and serve with bread sticks and a robust red wine.

Prosciutto di parma con melone
Parma ham with melon

A classic and famous dish from Parma, beloved by connoisseurs all over the world. Parma ham, with its mild, delicate flavour and colouring, owes its distinctive and unique qualities to curing methods and climate and when combined with cool, honey-sweet melon or fresh ripe figs, it makes one of the most superb starters ever created. Like all good things, Parma ham is now very expensive so one must be grateful that it is always served in paper thin slices and in fairly sparing quantities!
There are two ways of serving Parma ham with melon.
One: cut a melon (sweet, ripe and preferably chilled) into 2–3-inch thick slices and remove the skin and seeds. Allow one slice per person and stand on a plate. Cover with 1 or 2 slices of Parma ham and serve straight away.
Two: cut slices of melon into reasonably large cubes and wrap pieces of ham round each. Secure with cocktail sticks (cocktail picks) then transfer to a serving platter. Allow 4 to 5 per person.

Prosciutto di parma con fichi
Parma ham with figs

Try this when fresh figs (purple skinned and red hearted) are available. Simply cover plates with 2 or 3 thin slices ham per person then stand 2 fresh figs on top. Eat both together.

Parma ham with melon

Soups

There are two main kinds of soup in Italy. The first are thick, minestrone-type affairs with pasta or rice and a miscellany of vegetables. The second are clear and thin beef or chicken broths, usually served with baby pasta or ravioli. In addition, one finds simple versions of tomato, mushroom, pea and spinach soups, certain regional specialities and unusually delicious zuppe di pesce or fish soups. No Italian soup is arduous to make. No soup is so rich that it is an effort afterwards to eat the main course. Maybe this is the reason why, in almost all Italian homes, soup is part of the daily pattern of life and enjoyed through all four seasons of the year.

Visitors to Italy in summer may be astonished, when they sit down to lunch in a hotel or restaurant, at being presented with large plates of steaming soup when all they want is something iced and fruity. It may seem like a touch of madness, but just as soup alleviates the cold of winter, so does it reduce the overbearing heat of summer. In fact, soup acts as a perfect insulation and for this reason it is worth going along with this old Italian custom.

Minestrone — Minestrone

If Italy is famous for one dish—apart from spaghetti—then surely it must be minestrone, the hearty vegetable and pasta (or rice) soup which is a speciality from the Northern regions, including Lombardy and Liguria. As with all traditional dishes, recipes for minestrone vary from family to family and even in cook books, few versions are identical. Therefore to give an exact recipe is a hard task, although I have attempted to keep the following three as authentic as possible. Italian housewives—for reasons of economy—make minestrone with almost any vegetables in season and if there is a glut of artichokes or aubergines (eggplant), then in it goes!

Minestrone Milanese — Minestrone Milanese

1 ham bone
1 large onion, chopped
2 medium carrots, diced
3 medium celery stalks, coarsely chopped
½ small head (3 cups) cabbage shredded
1 large leek, trimmed and chopped (optional)
3 pints (7½ cups) beef broth
2 oz. (approximately ¼ cup) dried haricot beans, soaked overnight
salt and pepper to taste
1 small marrow or squash, diced
4 oz. (⅝ cup) long grain rice
1 large potato, diced
1 garlic clove, finely chopped
1 level teaspoon fresh chopped basil or ½ level teaspoon dried
1 level tablespoon (1¼T) chopped parsley
grated Parmesan cheese

serves 6

Put the ham bone into a large saucepan with the onion, carrots, celery, cabbage, leek and beef broth.
Drain the haricot beans, then add to the pan with salt and pepper to taste. Bring the soup to the boil and remove any scum that rises to the surface. Cover the pan, lower the heat and simmer gently for 2¾ hours or until the beans are tender, adding a little extra water if the soup thickens too much.
Add the marrow or squash, rice, potatoes and garlic and continue to simmer for a further 20 minutes. Stir in the basil and parsley and serve very hot.
Accompany with cheese.

Minestrone Genovese — Genoese minestrone

1 breakfast cup (1 cup) loosely packed parsley
2 garlic cloves, chopped
a good shake of salt
1½ oz. (approximately ¼ cup) shelled walnut halves, chopped
2 oz. (½ cup) grated Parmesan cheese
3 tablespoons (3¾T) olive oil

This is minestrone soup with the addition of pesto, a green coloured flavouring with the consistency of butter. Italians make pesto themselves, often laboriously in a pestle and mortar, and add it not only to soup but also to pasta. Alas, in other countries, the essential ingredients may not be so easy to find and therefore we would advise either buying pots of pesto from Italian food shops or making a sort of substitute pesto with more familiar ingredients. The previous recipe for Minestrone soup will serve admirably and here is an adaptation of pesto.

Remove the parsley from the stalks and put into a large mortar. Add garlic, salt, walnuts and cheese.
Pound with a pestle until the mixture thickens to a paste-like consistency. Gradually work in oil, a drop at a time, and continue stirring until mixture is like soft butter. Stir about 2 tablespoons (2½T) (or more to taste) into the Minestrone.
Any left-over pesto should be put into a jar, covered with foil and stored in the least cold part of the refrigerator.

True Pesto
To make this, use leaves of fresh basil instead of the parsley, and pine nuts instead of the walnuts.

serves 6

Minestrone with shell pasta

159

Minestrone   Minestrone

2 tablespoons (2½T) olive oil
1 large onion, finely chopped
4 rashers lean bacon, chopped
(bacon strips)
1 small head (approximately
6 cups) white
cabbage, shredded
4 celery stalks, chopped
3 pints (7½ cups) beef stock
2 oz. (¼ cup) dried haricot
beans, soaked overnight
salt and pepper to taste
4 large tomatoes, skinned and
chopped
2 level tablespoons (2½T)
tomato concentrate
1 garlic clove, finely chopped
6 oz. (1 cup) any other
vegetables in season, such as
diced marrow, diced aubergines
or eggplant, cauliflower florets,
diced turnips, diced parsnips,
diced swedes, shelled peas or
sliced green or snap beans
2 oz. (½ cup) broken macaroni
1 level teaspoon dried basil
or thyme
grated Parmesan cheese
serves 6

Heat the oil in a large saucepan. Add the onion and fry very gently, with a lid on the pan, until soft but still white. Add the bacon and fry for a further 3 minutes.

Add the cabbage, celery, beef broth and drained haricot beans. Bring to the boil and season well to taste with salt and pepper. Lower the heat and cover the pan. Simmer gently for 2¾ hours or until the beans are tender.

Add all the remaining ingredients and continue to simmer for a further 15 to 20 minutes or until the macaroni is just tender.

Serve very hot and accompany with the Parmesan cheese.

Minestrone

Zuppa di pomodori   Tomato soup

12 ripe tomatoes, skinned
1 garlic clove, chopped
2 tablespoons (2½T) olive oil
2 level tablespoons (2½T)
tomato concentrate
¾ pint (2 cups) chicken stock
3 level tablespoons (3¾T) finely
chopped parsley
1 level teaspoon sugar
salt and pepper to taste
2 level tablespoons (2½T)
cornflour (cornstarch)
4 tablespoons (5T) cold water
serves 4—6

Chop the tomatoes and put them into a saucepan with the garlic, oil, tomato concentrate and stock. Bring to the boil, lower the heat and cover the pan. Simmer gently for 15 minutes. Stir in the parsley, sugar and salt and pepper to taste.

Mix the cornflour (cornstarch) to a smooth cream with the cold water. Add an equal quantity of hot soup then stir well and return to the saucepan. Cook, stirring, until the soup comes to the boil and thickens. Simmer for 5 minutes, adjust the seasoning to taste then serve straight away.

note: if fresh basil is available, chop a few of the leaves and sprinkle them over each portion of soup.

Pea soup

Minestra di fagioli   Haricot bean soup

2 tablespoons (2½T) olive oil
1–2 garlic cloves, chopped
6 oz. (¾ cup) haricot beans,
soaked overnight
1 medium onion, grated
1 medium carrot, grated
2½ pints (6¼ cups) chicken stock
or broth
salt and pepper to taste
4 level tablespoons (5T)
chopped parsley
serves 4–6

A speciality from the province of Tuscany.

Put the oil and garlic into a saucepan and heat until hot. Add the drained beans, onion, carrot, half the stock or broth and salt and pepper to taste. Bring to the boil, lower the heat and cover the pan. Simmer gently until the beans are tender: 2½ to 3 hours.
Either rub the soup through a sieve or blend until smooth in an electric blender. Return to a clean saucepan, add the rest of the stock or broth and heat slowly until hot, stirring.
Adjust the seasoning to taste, stir in the parsley, then serve straight away.

Zuppa di piselli   Pea soup

1 small onion, chopped
2 medium celery stalks, chopped
1 level dessertspoon (1T) each,
melted butter and olive oil
2 lb. fresh peas (approximately
2 cups when shelled)
1 small ham bone
¾ pint (2 cups) chicken stock
or water
1 level tablespoon (1¼T)
cornflour (cornstarch)
½ pint (1¼ cups) cold milk
salt and pepper to taste

serves 4

A soup which demands fresh peas; canned or frozen ones will not do at all.

Fry the onion and celery very gently in the butter and oil until soft but not brown. Add the peas and cook gently, stirring frequently, for a further 5 minutes.
Add the ham bone and stock or water. Bring to the boil, lower the heat and cover the pan. Simmer gently, stirring occasionally, until the peas are very soft; 30 to 40 minutes.
Remove the ham bone, then either rub the soup through a sieve or blend until smooth in an electric blender. Return to a clean saucepan.
Mix the cornflour to a smooth liquid with the cold milk. Add to the soup. Cook, stirring continuously, until the soup comes to the boil and thickens. Simmer for 5 minutes. Season to taste with salt and pepper and serve straight away.

Zuppa di funghi Mushroom soup

2 oz. (¼ cup) butter
1–2 garlic cloves, chopped
12 oz. (3¾ cups)
sliced mushrooms
3 level tablespoons (3¾T) flour
¾ pint (2 cups) warm chicken
stock or broth
¾ pint (2 cups) milk
salt and pepper to taste
½ breakfast cup (½ cup)
chopped parsley
grated nutmeg
serves 4–6

Heat the butter in a saucepan. Add the garlic and mushrooms and fry gently for 5 minutes, turning all the time.
Stir in the flour, then gradually blend in the warm stock or broth, followed by the milk. Bring to the boil, stirring. Simmer for 5 minutes, then season to taste with salt and pepper and stir in the parsley.
Serve straight away and sprinkle the top of each with nutmeg.

Zuppa di spinaci Spinach soup

2 oz. (¼ cup) butter
1 garlic clove, chopped
2 level tablespoons (2½T) flour
½ pint (1¼ cups) spinach purée
1½ pints (3¾ cups) chicken stock
or water
¼ pint (⅝ cup) single cream
(coffee cream)
salt and pepper to taste
serves 4–6

Spinach is a well-loved vegetable in Italy and one of its favourite uses is in this delicious soup, which comes from the North East.

Melt the butter in a saucepan. Add the garlic and fry gently for 5 minutes.
Stir in the flour. Gradually blend in the spinach purée, stock or water and the cream.
Cook, stirring continuously, until the soup comes to the boil and thickens. Simmer for 10 minutes then serve straight away.

Zuppa di lentecchie Lentil soup

½ lb. (1 cup) lentils,
soaked overnight
1 medium onion, chopped
2 medium celery
stalks, chopped
2 tablespoons (2½T) olive oil
2 level tablespoons (2½T)
tomato concentrate
1 to 2 garlic cloves,
finely chopped
2 pints (5 cups) chicken stock
or water
salt and pepper to taste
2 level tablespoons (2½T)
chopped parsley
2 oz. (approximately ½ cup)
pastini (small pasta in the
shape of stars, alphabets,
rice etc.)
grilled bacon rashers, cut into
strips (optional)
serves 4

Drain the lentils. Fry the onion and celery in the oil until soft but not brown.
Add the lentils, tomato concentrate, garlic, stock or water and salt and pepper to taste. Bring to the boil, lower the heat and cover the pan. Simmer gently, stirring occasionally, for approximately 1 hour or until lentils are soft.
Add the parsley and the pastini and continue to simmer for a further 10 minutes. Serve very hot, adding grilled bacon rashers (strips) if liked.

Lentil soup

Zuppa di patate · Potato soup

1 large onion, chopped
2 tablespoons (2½T) olive oil
4 large potatoes
1 small ham bone
2 pints (5 cups) chicken stock
or broth
salt and pepper to taste
3 tablespoons (3¾T) single
(coffee) cream
grated nutmeg
serves 4

A quickly and easily-made soup for winter eating.

Fry the onion gently in the oil until soft but not brown.
Coarsely grate the potatoes and add to the pan with the ham bone, stock or broth and salt and pepper to taste. Bring to the boil, cover the pan and simmer slowly for about 20 minutes.
Stir in the cream and sprinkle the top of each portion very lightly with nutmeg.

Potato soup

Zuppa di pesce *Fish soup*

2 tablespoons (2½T) olive oil
2 garlic cloves, chopped
8 large tomatoes, skinned and chopped
4 level tablespoons (5T) finely chopped parsley
2 level tablespoons (2½T) tomato concentrate
1 small onion, chopped
1 celery stalk, finely chopped
¼ pint (⅝ cup) dry white wine
¼ pint (⅝ cup) water
1 level teaspoon sugar
salt and pepper to taste
1 lb. smoked cod fillet
½ lb. firm white fish fillet
1 teacup (¾ cup) peeled prawns, shrimp or pieces of lobster or crab
4–6 anchovy fillets, chopped
serves 4

Quite obviously, exact replicas of the superb fish soups (which, in fact, are more like stews) found along the coastlines of Italy cannot be made because the exotic fish common to those waters are hard to find elsewhere. Nevertheless, with a few modifications, highly successful substitutes are possible and below are two fish soup recipes which we have always enjoyed and taken pleasure in making.

Heat the oil in a saucepan. Add garlic and fry gently for 5 minutes. Stir in the tomatoes, parsley, tomato concentrate, onion, celery, wine, water, sugar and salt and pepper to taste. (Not too much salt, though, as the smoked fish and anchovies contribute some of their own.) Bring to the boil and cover. Lower the heat and simmer for 15 minutes.
Meanwhile, skin the fish and cut the flesh into large chunks.
Add to the soup and cook for 5 minutes.
Add the prawns etc. and anchovies and cook for a further 3 minutes.
Serve in large plates and accompany with crusty French bread.

Zuppa di cozze *Mussel soup*

¼ pint (⅝ cup) olive oil
4 garlic cloves, halved
1 small onion, chopped
4 level tablespoons (5T) finely chopped parsley
¼ pint (⅝ cup) dry white wine
¼ pint (⅝ cup) water
2 level tablespoons (2½T) tomato concentrate
6 large tomatoes, skinned and chopped
1 medium celery stalk, chopped
salt and pepper to taste
4 pints (10 cups) mussels
serves 4

A feast for mussel lovers.

Heat the oil in a large frying pan. Add the garlic and onion and fry gently until pale gold.
Stir in the parsley, wine, water, tomato concentrate, tomatoes, celery and salt and pepper to taste. Cook slowly, uncovered, until the liquid is reduced by about a third.
Meanwhile, prepare the mussels. Cut off the beards with kitchen scissors. Transfer the mussels to a colander and wash under cold running water, shaking the colander all the time to prevent the mussels from opening.
Add the mussels to the hot tomato soup and cook fairly briskly for approximately 10 minutes or until all the mussels have opened.
Serve in deep plates and accompany with freshly made toast.

Brodo di manzo *Beef broth*

2 lb. boiling beef
1 lb. soup bones
4 pints (10 cups) water
2 large onions
2 medium carrots
3 medium celery stalks, each broken into 4
1 small turnip
½ breakfast cup (½ cup) parsley
3 to 4 level teaspoons salt

serves 8–10

This is a relatively uncomplicated beef broth usually served with the same pastini as given in the recipe for zuppa di lentecchie. It is a clear, light soup and may be found in most parts of Italy.

Put the beef (in one piece), the bones, water, onions, carrots, celery stalks, turnip and parsley into a large saucepan. Add salt. Bring to the boil then remove the scum as it rises to the surface. Lower the heat, cover the pan and simmer gently for 4 hours with the heat as low as possible.
Strain into a clean bowl and refrigerate when cold.
Before serving, remove the hard layer of fat from the top and re-heat as much soup as is required. Add pastini to each serving.

Brodo misto *Beef and chicken broth*

serves 8–10

This is a combination of chicken and beef broth which, like the previous recipe, forms the basis of a number of soups.
To make it, simply follow the recipe for brodo di manzo but use 1 lb. boiling fowl or chicken giblets instead of the soup bones.

Brodo con farfallo
Beef broth with farfalle pasta

Take the beef stock exactly as directed in the recipe for brodo di manzo (page 164), then add bow-shaped pasta (farfalle) to each serving.

Zuppa pavese
Pavese soup

A nourishing soup meal which makes an excellent lunch or supper dish.
Prepare brodo di manzo or brodo misto as directed.
For 4 servings, fry 4 slices of bread in olive oil until crisp and golden on both sides.
Transfer to 4 individual soup bowls and top each with a lightly poached egg.
Fill the bowls with hot broth, sprinkle with grated Parmesan cheese and serve straight away.

Stracciatella
Egg-laced broth

1–1¼ pints (2½–3 cups) brodo di manzo or brodo misto
2 eggs
1 level tablespoon (1¼T) semolina (cream of wheat)
3 level tablespoons (3¾T) grated Parmesan cheese

serves 4

A popular soup all over Italy, although stracciatella—or egg drop soup—comes from Rome.

Put the brodo di manzo or brodo misto on to heat.
Meanwhile, fork-beat the eggs with the semolina (cream of wheat), grated Parmesan cheese and ½ a cup of the hot broth.
Pour back into the hot soup and bring just up to the boil, whisking continuously. As the egg cooks, it will separate out into shreds and give the soup its characteristic—ragged—appearance.

Brodo di manzo e prosciutto
Beef and ham broth

Make exactly as brodo di manzo, adding 1 large ham bone instead of the soup bones. Include also 2 tablespoons (2½T) tomato concentrate. Serve each portion with freshly cooked rice instead of pastini and sprinkle with grated Parmesan cheese.

Pasta in brodo
Tomato and beef broth with macaroni

Make up brodo di manzo as directed but include 2 level tablespoons (2½T) tomato concentrate and 4 large skinned and chopped tomatoes. Serve each portion with freshly cooked elbow macaroni and a little skinned and chopped fresh tomato. Accompany with grated Parmesan cheese.

Zuppa crema di pollo
Cream of chicken soup

2 level tablespoons (2½T) cornflour (cornstarch)
1 pint (2½ cups) cold brodo misto
salt and pepper to taste
½ breakfast cup (½ cup) cooked chicken, cut into strips
¼ pint (⅝ cup) double (heavy) cream
2 egg yolks
grated nutmeg

serves 4–5

A handsome, creamy soup for elegant eating.

Mix the cornflour (cornstarch) to a smooth liquid with a little brodo misto. Add the rest of the brodo misto and cook, stirring continuously, until the soup comes to the boil and thickens.
Season to taste with salt and pepper then add the chicken.
Simmer for 7 minutes.
Beat the cream and egg yolks well together. Pour into the soup and re-heat gently without boiling. Serve each portion lightly sprinkled with nutmeg.

Milanese

*Pizza
Pasta
Rice
and Gnocchi*

These days, **pizza** is so well known that it requires no description, except to say that it should be eaten while still warm and fragrantly fresh. Probably **pasta** requires no description either, for in every big city, supermarket shelves are laden with boxes of macaroni, noodles, spaghetti, lasagne and cannelloni—to name but a few— and cookery books and magazines are equally laden with recipes on how to use them. All we would ask you is to try, just once, the following recipe for pasta. It is good— and when turned into noodles and served with melted butter and grated Parmesan cheese, superb! It needs time, as you will see, but—Rome wasn't built in a day either!

Risotto is almost as well known as pizza and pasta, but outside Italy it rarely tastes or looks authentic and one is all too often confronted with a kind of nondescript pilaff, which is supposed to be risotto but bears little or no resemblance to it whatsoever! A pity. The real thing is so much better and very easy to make, if one is prepared to use the right ingredients. It needs Italian rice above all else or, if this is completely impossible to find, old-fashioned round grain pudding rice. Long grain rice, good though it is, fails with risotto and should be avoided.

Gnocchi can be made from semolina, polenta or potatoes and is a deliciously satisfying dish which deserves to be better known and cooked more frequently than it is. The following recipes for it have been made over and over again with success. The nicest, in our view, is the semolina gnocchi, tastefully flavoured with Parmesan cheese and served, golden brown and sizzling, straight from the oven. With creamy spinach purée and fried or baked tomatoes, it makes a luxurious meal at little cost and is just right for a mid-week lunch or supper dish.

Less difficult to prepare than one would imagine, pasta is a great therapeutic occupation, for it is both fun to make and immensely satisfying. But it requires space, patience and time and if none of these is available, then one is well advised to settle for the packet pastas which are good and in abundant variety.

The varied forms of raw pasta

Pasta alla casalinga   Home made pasta

**8 oz. (1½ cups) plain (all
purpose) flour
1 level teaspoon salt
1 egg
1 dessertspoon (1T) olive oil
4 tablespoons (5T) hot water**

Sift the flour and salt into a bowl and make a well in the centre.
Break in the egg, then add the oil and water. Work to a dough
with the fingertips.

Turn out on to a floured surface and knead until the dough no longer
sticks to the fingers—about 10 to 15 minutes, which is the
lengthiest part of the whole operation. Divide the dough into
2 equal-sized pieces.

Cover a working surface with a brightly patterned table cloth or
tea towel and flour heavily. Stand one portion of the dough on top.
Roll out as thinly as possible then stretch and pull gently with the
fingers until the dough is so thin that the pattern from the cloth
shows through. The dough is very elastic and therefore stretches
fairly easily.

Roll up the piece of dough loosely then cut it into slices, about
¼-inch in thickness. Open out each slice (one noodle) and drape over
the back of a chair, first covered with a tea towel.

Repeat with second piece of dough and leave the noodles to dry out
for about ½ an hour.

Cook in plenty of boiling salted water for 5 to 7 minutes.

Drain and use as required.

Spaghetti

note: home made pasta takes less time to cook than packet varieties.

Cooking packet pasta

Cooking spaghetti as it is cooked in Italy is an art, but fortunately an art readily mastered if one obeys the basic rules.

First and foremost, pasta must always be al dente; soft without being soggy, and chewy without being hard. Thus cooking time must be watched carefully and between 10 and 12 minutes should be quite long enough for large pasta such as spaghetti and macaroni, while no longer than 5 to 7 minutes should be allowed for small pasta (pastini).

The amount of pasta per person depends on appetite and the kind of meal. Quite obviously, less pasta is needed for a meal starter than for a main course and the amount, therefore, can vary from 2 oz. per person to 4 oz. ($\frac{1}{2}$ to 1 cup).

All pasta should be cooked in plenty of boiling salted water—about $\frac{3}{4}$ pint (2 cups) to each oz. ($\frac{1}{4}$ cup) pasta—drained thoroughly, transferred to a warm dish and served immediately.

note: a little oil added to the cooking water helps to keep the pasta separate.

Ingredients for home made pasta
Cutting macaroni with a rotary
blade cutter

Spaghetti al burro   Spaghetti with butter

Cook the spaghetti following the directions for cooking packet pasta.
To make eating easier, it may be broken up first, but strictly
speaking, the spaghetti should be left whole and cooked whole.
To do this, hold one end of the spaghetti strands in the hand and
stand the other end in the saucepan of boiling water. As the spaghetti
softens, it will curl round in the pan and may then be pushed
downwards gradually until it is completely covered with the water.
After cooking, drain thoroughly, put into a large warm dish
containing plenty of butter or olive oil and toss gently with two forks
until each spaghetti strand is coated. Serve straight away with
grated Parmesan cheese.

to vary: cook any different pasta shapes as above, and toss with
butter.
Garnish with fried onions and serve with grated Parmesan cheese.

Spaghetti with butter

172

Spaghetti alla Bolognese
Spaghetti Bolognese

2 tablespoons (2½T) olive oil
1 medium onion, finely chopped
2 garlic cloves, finely chopped
3 rashers unsmoked bacon (bacon strips)
1 medium celery stalk, finely chopped
1 medium carrot, grated
4 oz. (1¼ cups) sliced mushrooms
8 oz. raw minced (ground) beef
4 level tablespoons (5T) tomato concentrate
1 wine glass dry white or red wine
4 medium tomatoes, skinned and chopped
½ pint (1¼ cups) beef stock
2 level teaspoons brown sugar
pinch of ground nutmeg
freshly cooked spaghetti (see page 171)
grated Parmesan cheese
serves 4

Perhaps the best known and best loved of all the pasta dishes.

Heat the oil in a saucepan. Add the onion, garlic, chopped bacon, celery, carrot and mushrooms. Fry slowly for 7 minutes.
Add the beef and fry for a further 5 minutes, breaking it up with a fork all the time. Add all the remaining ingredients and bring to the boil, stirring. Lower the heat, cover the pan and simmer very gently for 45 minutes, stirring occasionally.
Add to the well-drained spaghetti and toss thoroughly.
Serve with grated Parmesan cheese.

Spaghetti bolognese

Tagliatelle alla Bolognese
Tagliatelle Bolognese

Make exactly as spaghetti Bolognese but use flat ribbon noodles (known as tagliatelle or fettuccine) instead of the spaghetti.

Spaghetti alla carbonara
Spaghetti with ham and eggs

spaghetti (see page 171)
8 bacon rashers (strips)
a little olive oil
2 eggs
2 tablespoons (2½T) single (coffee) cream
grated Parmesan cheese

This simple but delicious combination comes from Rome and is equally good as a starter or as a main course.

Cook the spaghetti as directed. Five minutes before it is ready, chop the bacon rashers (strips) into small pieces and fry gently in a little olive oil for 3 minutes. Beat 2 eggs with 2 tablespoons (2½T) single (coffee) cream. Drain the spaghetti thoroughly and transfer to a warm dish. Add the fried bacon (and any left-over oil or fat from pan), the egg mixture and 2 or 3 level tablespoons (2½–3¾T) grated Parmesan cheese. Toss with two forks until the eggs thicken and scramble with the heat from the pasta. Accompany with extra
serves 4   Parmesan cheese.

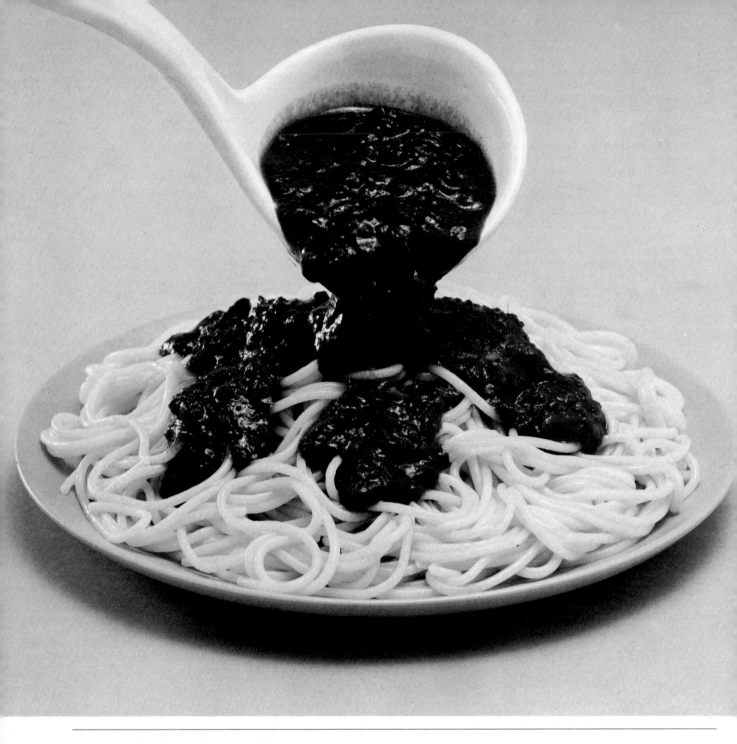

Spaghetti alla matriciana

Spaghetti with salt pork and tomato

1 tablespoon (1¼T) bacon dripping
1 medium onion, chopped
4 bacon rashers (strips), or equivalent weight of salt pork, cut into thin strips
8 large tomatoes, skinned and chopped
salt and pepper to taste
freshly cooked spaghetti
clove of garlic
1 tablespoon (1¼T) olive oil
grated Pecorino or Parmesan cheese
serves 4

A speciality from the Abruzzo e Molise region, which is noted for its excellent but unsophisticated cuisine.

Heat the dripping in a saucepan. Add the onion and bacon rashers and fry gently for 5 minutes. Add the tomatoes and salt and pepper to taste, then simmer for 5 minutes.
Drain the spaghetti thoroughly and put into a warm serving dish, rubbed first with a cut clove of garlic.
Add the olive oil and toss the spaghetti thoroughly. Pour the sauce on top and accompany with grated Pecorino cheese (if available) or grated Parmesan.

Lasagne

Spaghetti alla marinara

Spaghetti with fresh tomato and basil sauce

2 tablespoons (2½T) olive oil
2–4 garlic cloves, chopped
8 large tomatoes, skinned and chopped
6–8 anchovy fillets, chopped (optional)
2 level teaspoons mint, finely chopped
or 1 level tablespoon (1¼T) parsley, chopped
or 1 level tablespoon (1¼T) fresh basil, chopped
salt and pepper to taste
freshly cooked spaghetti (see page 171)
butter
grated Parmesan cheese

A typically Neapolitan dish, marinara meaning 'sailor-style'.

Make a sauce by heating the olive oil with the chopped garlic cloves. Add the tomatoes and chopped anchovy fillets, if liked. Cook for 5 minutes then add the herbs and season well to taste with salt and pepper. Pour on top of freshly cooked spaghetti, first tossed with butter.
Accompany with grated Parmesan cheese.

Spaghetti al tonno

Spaghetti with tuna

1 oz. (2T) butter
1 tablespoon (1¼T) olive oil
1 can (7 oz.) tuna
¼ pint (⅝ cup) chicken stock
2 level tablespoons (2½T) chopped parsley
salt and pepper to taste
freshly cooked spaghetti

Heat the butter and oil in a saucepan. Break up the tuna and add, with its oil, to the saucepan. Cook gently for 3 minutes.
Add the stock and simmer for a further 5 minutes. Add the parsley and salt and pepper to taste.
Drain the spaghetti thoroughly and put into a warm dish.
Add the tuna sauce, toss well and serve straight away.

Spaghetti Napoletana

Spaghetti Neapolitan

10 very ripe tomatoes, skinned and chopped
1 oz. (2T) butter
1 tablespoon (1¼T) olive oil
1 medium celery stalk, chopped
1 small onion, chopped
2 garlic cloves, chopped
1 level teaspoon sugar
¼ pint (⅝ cup) water
salt and pepper to taste
1 level teaspoon dried basil (or use double the amount of fresh chopped basil if available)
2 level tablespoons (2½T) chopped parsley
freshly cooked spaghetti
grated Parmesan cheese

Put the tomatoes into a pan with the butter, oil, celery, onion, garlic, sugar, water and salt and pepper to taste. Bring to the boil, stirring, then lower the heat and simmer the sauce, uncovered, for 15 minutes. Add the basil and parsley and continue to simmer for a further 20 to 30 minutes until the sauce is thick and purée-like.
Drain the spaghetti thoroughly and put into a warm dish. Add the sauce, toss well and accompany with grated Parmesan cheese.

Spaghetti all'olio e aglio

Spaghetti with garlic sauce

freshly cooked spaghetti
5 tablespoons (6¼T) olive oil
4–6 garlic cloves, finely chopped
2 heaped tablespoons (2¾T) parsley, finely chopped
½ level teaspoon dried basil
salt and pepper to taste

Bliss for garlic lovers but possibly a bit overwhelming for those who like milder, gentler food with less aftertaste!

5 minutes before the spaghetti is cooked, heat the olive oil with the garlic cloves. Keep the heat low to avoid frying the garlic. Add the parsley and basil. Drain the spaghetti thoroughly and transfer to a warm dish. Add the oil mixture, season with salt and freshly ground pepper and toss gently. Serve straight away.

Maccheroni al gratin
Macaroni with cheese

8 oz. (2 cups) elbow macaroni
2 oz. (¼ cup) butter
3 level tablespoons (3¾T) flour
¾ pint (2 cups) milk and
macaroni water mixed in
equal proportions
4 oz. (1 cup) grated
Parmesan cheese
salt and pepper to taste
1 oz. (2T) extra butter

serves 4–6

Preheat the oven to moderate (350 F, or Mark 4).
Cook the macaroni in boiling salted water as directed for spaghetti (see page 171). Drain and reserve 1½ gills (1 cup) macaroni water.
Melt the butter in a saucepan. Stir in the flour and cook for 2 minutes without browning. Gradually blend in the macaroni water followed by the milk. Cook, stirring, until the sauce comes to the boil and thickens. Simmer for 2 minutes. Stir in ¾ of the cheese then season well to taste with salt and pepper.
Transfer to a buttered heatproof dish. Sprinkle the rest of the cheese on top then dot with flakes of butter. Reheat in the centre of the oven for 30 minutes.

Maccheroni alla pizzaiola
Macaroni with tomato, garlic and herbs

12 medium sized ripe tomatoes,
skinned and chopped
2 tablespoons (2½T) olive oil
2 garlic cloves, chopped
1 heaped tablespoon (1½T)
parsley, coarsely chopped
½ level teaspoon oregano
1 level teaspoon
granulated sugar
salt and pepper to taste
freshly cooked macaroni
grated Parmesan or
Pecorino cheese

serves 4

Put the tomatoes into a saucepan with the oil, garlic, parsley, oregano, sugar and salt and pepper to taste. Bring to the boil, lower the heat and simmer, uncovered, for 15 minutes.
Drain the macaroni thoroughly and transfer to a warm dish.
Add the tomato sauce and toss.
Accompany with grated Parmesan cheese or Pecorino cheese.

Macaroni with cheese and bacon pieces

Meat balls and tomato sauce
with spaghetti (below)

Risotto (right)

Pizza Neapolitan (far right)

Tagliatelle with liver sauce (below
far right)

Maccheroni con piselli
Macaroni with peas

2 tablespoons (2½T) olive oil
4 oz. (1 cup) cubed ham, very finely chopped
1 small onion, chopped
1 garlic clove, chopped
2 medium celery stalks, chopped
6 large tomatoes, skinned and chopped
½ pint (1¼ cups) chicken stock
2 level tablespoons (2½T) tomato concentrate
1 heaped tablespoon (1½T) parsley, chopped
6 oz. (1 cup) fresh peas, shelled
salt and pepper to taste
freshly cooked macaroni (see page 171)
fresh basil or mint

serves 4

Heat the oil in a saucepan. Add the ham, onion, garlic and celery. Fry gently for 7 minutes. Add the tomatoes, stock, tomato concentrate, parsley, peas and salt and pepper to taste. Bring to the boil, lower the heat and simmer gently for 30 minutes.

Drain the macaroni and transfer to a warm dish. Add the sauce and toss thoroughly.

Serve straight away and dust each portion with a little finely chopped fresh basil or mint.

Lasagne
Lasagne

6 oz. lasagne
1 recipe Bolognese sauce (see page 173)
1 recipe cheese sauce (see page 177)
nutmeg
grated Parmesan cheese
butter

serves 4

Cook the leaves of lasagne in plenty of boiling salted water for 10 to 15 minutes. Drain thoroughly, then stand each piece on paper towelling to absorb surplus moisture. Butter a fairly deep heatproof dish well. Cover the base with the Bolognese sauce. Add a layer of cheese sauce to which a dash of ground nutmeg has been added. Top with lasagne leaves.

Repeat, finishing with a layer of cheese sauce topped with a little Bolognese sauce. Sprinkle thickly with Parmesan cheese then dot with flakes of butter. Re-heat for 30 minutes in the centre of a moderate oven (350°F, Mark 4).

Serve straight away with a green salad.

Lasagne verdi
Lasagne with spinach

Make exactly as above but use lasagne verdi which, during manufacture, is coloured green through the addition of spinach.

Tagliatelle con fegatini di pollo
Tagliatelle with liver sauce

8 oz. (1 cup) chicken livers
2 level tablespoons (2½T) flour
1 oz. (2T) butter
1 tablespoon (1¼T) olive oil
1 small onion, finely chopped
1 small garlic clove, chopped
4 oz. (1¼ cups) mushrooms, sliced
¼ pint (⅝ cup) chicken stock
¼ pint (⅝ cup) dry white wine
salt and pepper to taste
freshly cooked tagliatelle (see page 171)

A substantial dish which may be made with spaghetti or macaroni as well as with tagliatelle.

Cut the livers into small pieces and coat with flour.

Heat the butter and oil in a saucepan. Add the onion and garlic and fry gently until pale gold. Add the liver and mushrooms. Fry more briskly for 3 to 4 minutes, stirring all the time.

Add the stock and wine, then season well to taste with salt and pepper. Bring to the boil, stirring, then lower the heat and cover the pan. Simmer gently for 15 minutes.

Transfer the tagliatelle to a warm dish. Add the sauce, toss well and serve straight away.

Tagliatelle alle acciughe
Tagliatelle with anchovy sauce

1 tablespoon (1¼T) olive oil
2 oz. (¼ cup) butter
2 garlic cloves, finely chopped
1 small can anchovy fillets
½ teacup (⅜ cup) parsley, finely chopped
½ level teaspoon oregano
pepper to taste
freshly cooked tagliatelle (see page 171)

A potent brew which oils and flavours the pasta in hearty fashion.

Heat the oil and butter in a saucepan. Add the garlic and heat very slowly for 5 minutes.

Open the anchovies and drain the oil into the saucepan. Chop the anchovies and add to the pan with parsley and oregano. Heat through for 5 minutes then season to taste with freshly milled pepper. Drain the tagliatelle and transfer to a warm dish. Add the anchovy mixture and toss well. Serve straight away.

Cannelloni with cheese sauce

Cannelloni   Cannelloni

8 oz. cannelloni
1 breakfast cup (1 cup) cubes of
stewed beef
1½ oz. (¾ cup) fresh white
breadcrumbs
2 oz. (½ cup) grated
Parmesan cheese
1 beaten egg
¼ level teaspoon ground nutmeg
a little gravy from the
stewed beef
salt and pepper to taste
1 oz. (2T) butter
¼ pint (⅝ cup) chicken stock
serves 4

Cook the cannelloni in boiling salted water for 8 to 10 minutes. Drain thoroughly. When cool enough to handle, split each one lengthwise and open out.

To make the stuffing, mince the stewed beef finely and combine with the breadcrumbs, half the cheese, egg and nutmeg. Bind with a little gravy then season well to taste with salt and pepper.

Put equal amounts of the stuffing on to each cannelloni, then roll up like fat sausages. Place side by side in a shallow buttered heatproof dish. Dot with flakes of butter then sprinkle with the rest of the cheese. Pour the stock into the dish then re-heat in the centre of a moderate oven (350°F, Mark 4) for 25 to 30 minutes.

Home made Cannelloni

Artichoke omelette

Prepare the dough as directed for basic pasta (see page 170). Roll out thinly and cut into squares measuring 3 × 4 inches. Cook in plenty of boiling salted water, to which 1 or 2 teaspoons of oil have been added, for about 5 minutes. Drain thoroughly, then fill and roll as above.

Ravioli verdi Ravioli with spinach

dough (see page 170)
filling
3 oz. (⅜ cup) spinach purée
2 oz. (¼ cup) Italian Ricotta
cheese or curd cheese
1 oz. (¼ cup) grated
Parmesan cheese
½ a beaten egg
1½ level dessertspoons
(1¼T) flour
1 teaspoon melted butter
salt, pepper and ground nutmeg
to taste

serves 4

Divide the dough into 2 equal-sized portions and roll both out very
thinly, making one slightly larger than the other.
To make the filling, combine all the ingredients well together and
beat until smooth.
Stand the smaller piece of rolled dough on to a floured surface.
Brush with water and cover with small heaps of filling, leaving
plenty of space round each.
Cover with the second piece of dough, allowing it to lie loosely over
the first piece. Stamp out the ravioli with a fluted biscuit cutter,
cutting round the dough and avoiding the filling.
Place in a single layer, on a floured board or plate, dust with flour
and cover with a tea towel. Leave in a cool place until required.
To cook, drop gently into plenty of boiling salted water and simmer
for about 5 minutes or until the ravioli float to the top. Lift out of the
saucepan with a perforated spoon and serve with plenty of butter
and grated Parmesan cheese.

a

b

Preparing ravioli
(a) Filling ravioli cases
(b) Stamping out the ravioli with
a fluted biscuit cutter

Ravioli Meat ravioli

**4 oz. (½ cup) finely minced
(ground) stewed beef
½ oz. (¼ cup) fresh
white breadcrumbs
¼ level teaspoon dried thyme
salt and pepper to taste**
serves 4

Make exactly as the spinach/cheese ravioli given in the previous recipe, but fill with a mixture of beef, breadcrumbs and seasoning.

Raviolo con Sugo di Pomodoro Meat ravioli with tomato sauce.

Prepare the ravioli as above.
Heat the ravioli in any of the tomato sauces suggested for pasta.
Sprinkle with grated Parmesan cheese and serve hot.

Meat ravioli

Risotto in cagnon Risotto

1 oz. (2T) butter
2 teaspoons olive oil
1 small onion, finely chopped
12 oz. (2 cups) Italian rice
1 wine glass dry white wine
2 pints (5 cups) hot water
salt and pepper to taste
1 extra oz. (2T) butter
4 level tablespoons (5T)
Parmesan cheese

Risotto is a classic dish of the North—the most famous version being risotto Milanese—and, when properly cooked, is one of the delights of Italian cuisine. Risotto is almost always eaten as a dish by itself and rarely accompanies anything other than osso buco (see page 211) the equally well-known and robust veal stew from Milan.

Heat the butter and oil in a large saucepan. Add the onion and fry very gently, covered, for 5 minutes or until the onion is soft but still white.

Add the rice and cook gently for 3 minutes, turning all the time until each rice grain is coated with butter and oil. Add the wine and cook over a moderate heat until it evaporates. Blend in the stock, gradually adding more as each amount becomes absorbed by the rice. Stir frequently with a fork and allow 20 to 30 minutes cooking time, when the rice should be creamy but still firm.

Using a fork, stir in extra butter and the Parmesan cheese and serve straight away. Pass extra butter and Parmesan cheese separately.

Risotto alla Milanese Risotto Milanese

Follow the recipe for plain risotto but after frying the onion and before adding the rice, add 1 oz. raw beef marrow taken from a marrow bone. Use chicken stock instead of water and when the rice has absorbed all the liquid, stir in a large pinch of powdered saffron with the extra butter and Parmesan cheese.

Risotto con prosciutto Ham risotto

Another version of risotto which comes from Verona in the region of Venice.

Make a plain risotto as directed but stir in 4 oz. (1 cup) cubed ham with the extra butter and Parmesan cheese.

Risotto alla finanziera Risotto with sweetbreads

Make a plain risotto as directed.
While it is cooking, fry 1 small chopped onion and 1 breakfast cup (1 cup) chicken livers in 2 oz. ($\frac{1}{4}$ cup) butter for 10 minutes.
Add $\frac{1}{2}$ wine glass Marsala and cook a little more briskly until Marsala evaporates.
Stir the livers etc. into the cooked risotto, just before the extra butter and Parmesan cheese.

serves 4

Risotto alla sbirraglia Chicken risotto

Make a plain risotto as directed but use chicken stock instead of water.
When the rice is half cooked, add 1 breakfast cup (1 cup) freshly boiled diced chicken.
Stir in extra butter and Parmesan cheese at the end and serve straight away.

serves 4

Risotto di frutta di mare   Seafood risotto

Make exactly as risotto alla Milanese but omit the beef marrow.
5 minutes before the risotto has finished cooking, fry 8 oz. (2 cups)
shelled seafood (lobster, shrimp or scampi) in a little butter for 2 or
3 minutes. Add half a wine glass Marsala and cook briskly until the
Marsala evaporates. Add to the risotto just before stirring in extra
butter and Parmesan cheese.

note: the flavour of this risotto is improved if made with half water
and half fish stock.
To make a reasonable fish stock, simmer for approximately 30
minutes, 1 lb. fish trimmings, 1 sliced onion, 1 celery stalk, 1 carrot,
$\frac{1}{2}$ bay leaf, and 2 level teaspoons salt in 1 pint (2$\frac{1}{2}$ cups) water. Strain
and use as required.

serves 4

Risotto di peoci   Risotto with mussels

Another speciality from Venice.

Prepare a plain risotto as directed.
Meanwhile wash and scrub 4 pints (10 cups) mussels. Heat 4
tablespoons (5T) olive oil and 1 oz. (2T) butter in a large saucepan.
Add 2 finely chopped garlic cloves and 2 heaped tablespoons chopped
parsley.
Add the mussels and leave over a medium heat until they open.
When cool enough to handle, take the mussels out of their shells and
add to the risotto with mussel liquor, followed by extra butter and
Parmesan cheese.

serves 4

Risotto with mussels

Risotto con agnello   Lamb risotto

8 oz. lamb fillet, cut from top
of leg
2 oz. (¼ cup) butter
1 medium onion, finely chopped
4 medium tomatoes, skinned
and chopped
12 oz. (2 cups) Italian rice
1 wine glass dry white wine
2 pints (5 cups) chicken stock
salt and pepper to taste
4 level tablespoons (5T) grated
Parmesan cheese
serves 4

A more unusual risotto from Venice.

Cut the raw lamb fillet into tiny cubes. Heat the butter in a sauce-pan. Add the onion and fry slowly until pale gold. Add the lamb and fry a little more briskly until the pieces are well sealed and golden. Add the tomatoes and rice and cook for 2 minutes, stirring frequently. Add the wine and cook over a low heat until it evaporates. Blend in the stock gradually, adding more as each amount becomes absorbed by the rice.

Stir frequently with a fork and allow 20 to 30 minutes cooking time, when the rice should be creamy but still firm. Stir in the Parmesan cheese and serve straight away.

Risi e bisi   Venetian risotto with green peas

2 rashers streaky bacon
(bacon strips)
2 oz. (¼ cup) butter
1 small onion, finely chopped
12 oz. (2 cups) shelled peas
3 pints (7½ cups) hot chicken
or beef stock
12 oz. (2 cups) Italian rice
2 heaped tablespoons (2¾T)
parsley, finely chopped
salt and pepper to taste
3 oz. (¾ cup) grated
Parmesan cheese
serves 4

Also from Venice comes this rice and green pea risotto-style dish, which is now world famous. It is more liquidy than the standard risotto and therefore is usually eaten with a spoon.

Chop the bacon finely. Heat the butter in a large pan. Add the bacon and onion and fry gently until pale gold.

Add the peas and 4 teacups (3 cups) of the stock. Cover and simmer for 10 minutes. Add the rice, then very gradually blend in the rest of the stock, adding more as each amount becomes absorbed by the rice. Stir frequently with a wooden fork and allow about 20 to 25 minutes cooking time, when the rice should be soft and most of the liquid absorbed.

Stir in the parsley, salt and pepper to taste and the cheese. Serve straight away.

La polenta   Polenta

1¼ pints (3 cups) boiling water
2 level teaspoons salt
7 oz. (1 cup) polenta

Polenta is a warm, golden-yellow flour—rather like semolina in appearance—made from maize. It is very much favoured in Northern Italy where it is cooked in water and then eaten with butter and cheese or with tomato or Bolognese sauce. Polenta is traditional, comforting and very typically Italian and makes a satisfying substitute for potatoes, pasta or rice. It is also used to accompany small roast game birds such as pigeons and quails.

Pour the boiling water into a saucepan and add salt. Tip in all the polenta then bring slowly to the boil, stirring continuously. At once lower the heat and simmer very slowly, stirring frequently, for 20 minutes or until the polenta is very thick.

Serve each portion liberally topped with flakes of butter and grated Parmesan cheese or coat with the sauces suggested above and then sprinkle with grated cheese.

serves 4–6

Chicken breasts with shell pasta,
chicken pilaff and varied raw
pasta

La pizza Napoletana Pizza Neapolitan

dough base
¼ level teaspoon sugar
**¼ pint (⅝ cu) warm
water (110°F)**
1 level teaspoon dried yeast
**8 oz. (1½ cups) plain
(all-purpose) flour**
1 level teaspoon salt
1 dessertspoon (1T) butter

filling
olive oil
**6 medium tomatoes, skinned and
sliced**
1 garlic clove, chopped
12 anchovy fillets
**4 oz. Mozzarella cheese,
thinly sliced**
6 large black olives, stoned
oregano
pepper
serves 2

To make the dough, dissolve the sugar in the warm water and
sprinkle the dried yeast on top. Leave in a warmish place for 10 to 16
minutes or until frothy.
Meanwhile, sift the flour and salt into a bowl and rub in the
butter. Mix to a dough with the yeast liquid, adding a little extra
flour if the dough is sticky. Knead for a good 10 minutes or until the
dough is smooth and elastic, then put into an oiled bowl. Cover with
oiled paper and leave to rise until the dough doubles in size.
Turn out on to a floured surface then knead lightly until smooth.
Roll out into a ¼-inch thick circle and stand on an oiled baking tray.
Brush with olive oil then cover with slices of tomato. Sprinkle with
garlic. Top with anchovy fillets, slices of cheese and the olives.
Sprinkle with the oregano and pepper then bake near the top of a
hot oven (450°F, Mark 8) for 25 to 30 minutes.
Serve while still warm.

Pizza neapolitan

Pizza al prosciutto — Ham pizza

Make exactly as pizza alla Neapolitana but use 2 oz. ($\frac{1}{2}$ cup) coarsely chopped ham instead of the anchovies.

Pizza con funghi e olivi — Pizza with mushrooms and olives

Make the dough exactly as given for pizza alla Neapolitana. Cover with 4 skinned and sliced tomatoes, 1 small chopped garlic clove, 4 oz. (1$\frac{1}{4}$ cups) sliced mushrooms (first fried in a little butter) and 12 sliced pimento-stuffed olives.

Pizza al salame — Pizza with salami

Make exactly as pizza alla Neapolitana but omit the anchovy fillets. Use 6 to 8 thin slices of Italian salami instead.

Pizzette — Small pizza

Roll the dough out into 4 equal sized rounds. Stand on an oiled baking tray and cover as directed for any of the other pizza. Bake for 15 to 20 minutes.

Gnocchi alla Romana — Semolina gnocchi

1 pint (2$\frac{1}{2}$ cups) milk
5 oz. ($\frac{3}{4}$ cup) coarse semolina (cream of wheat)
1 level teaspoon salt
shake of pepper
2 oz. ($\frac{1}{4}$ cup) butter
3 oz. ($\frac{3}{4}$ cup) grated Parmesan cheese
$\frac{1}{4}$ level teaspoon ground nutmeg
1 large egg, beaten
1 extra oz. (2T) butter

serves 4

Pour the milk into a saucepan. Add the semolina, salt, pepper and butter. Stir continuously over a low heat until the mixture comes to the boil and thickens. Continue to simmer until the mixture is very thick; anything from 5 to 7 minutes. Stir frequently to prevent sticking.
Remove from the heat then beat in 2 oz. ($\frac{1}{2}$ cup) cheese, nutmeg and egg. Beat until well mixed then turn out on to a flat dish or tin, spreading the mixture to $\frac{1}{4}$-inch thick. Leave in the cool for several hours or until firm, then cut into 1$\frac{1}{2}$-inch squares or rounds with a knife or cutter dipped in cold water.
Butter a shallow heatproof dish well, then fill with layers of the gnocchi squares or rounds and arrange in overlapping circles. Sprinkle with the rest of the cheese then top with flakes of extra butter. Re-heat and brown towards the top of a hot oven (425°F, Mark 7) for 15 minutes.

Gnocchi di prosciutto — Ham gnocchi

serves 4

Make as the previous recipe, but add 4 level tablespoons (5T) very finely chopped ham with the cheese. 1 or 2 level tablespoons (1$\frac{1}{4}$–2$\frac{1}{2}$T) parsley may also be included, as may 1 or 2 level teaspoons very finely grated onion.

Gnocchi di polenta — Polenta gnocchi

Make exactly as semolina gnocchi, using polenta instead of semolina.

Gnocchi di patate   Potato gnocchi

1 lb. potatoes (before peeling)
4 oz. (½ cup) plain
(all-purpose) flour
1 teaspoon butter
1 beaten egg
plenty of salt and pepper
to taste
butter
grated Parmesan cheese

serves 4

A substantial form of gnocchi which is suitable either as a starter or as a main course.

Cook the potatoes in boiling salted water until tender. Drain thoroughly. Stand the pan of potatoes on the lowest possible heat and mash finely with a fork or masher. Alternatively—and this is the best method—rub the potatoes through a sieve.
Transfer to a bowl, then work in the flour, butter, beaten egg and salt and pepper to taste. Knead until the mixture is smooth then, with damp hands, shape pieces of the mixture into small balls. Drop into a saucepan of boiling salted water and cook until the gnocchi float to the top. Lift out of the pan with a perforated spoon and transfer to a warm dish. Top with pieces of butter then sprinkle with Parmesan cheese and serve straight away.

Gnocchi con salsa di fegatini   Potato gnocchi with liver sauce

Cook the potato gnocchi as directed then serve with liver sauce, see tagiatelle with liver sauce, page 180.

Polenta gnocchi

Eggs

Italian egg dishes are similar to those found anywhere else. Familiarity in this instance is both endearing and surprising when one finds, under a blue Mediterranean sky, the frittata—or omelette—packed with all sorts of fillings, or scrambled eggs with Parmesan cheese or salami, sophisticated baked eggs or the famous egg and spinach combination known as egg Florentine.

Uova alla Fiorentina — Eggs Florentine

½ pint (1¼ cups) spinach purée
1 dessertspoon (1T) butter
1 tablespoon (1¼T) double (heavy) cream
pinch of ground nutmeg
1 oz. (2T) butter
2 level tablespoons (2½T) flour
½ pint (1¼ cups) milk
3 oz. (¾ cup) grated Parmesan cheese
salt and pepper to taste
4 eggs
1 level tablespoon (1¼T) fine white breadcrumbs
serves 4

A classic luncheon or supper dish.

Heat the spinach purée with the butter and cream. Remove from the heat and add the nutmeg. Arrange in a buttered heatproof dish and keep warm.

Melt the butter in a pan. Stir in the flour and cook for 2 minutes without browning. Gradually blend in the milk. Cook, stirring continuously until the sauce comes to the boil and thickens. Simmer for 2 minutes. Add 2 oz. (½ cup) cheese and stir until melted. Season to taste with salt and pepper.

Poach the eggs lightly and arrange on top of the spinach. Pour over the sauce, coat with the remaining cheese and crumbs and brown under a hot grill. Serve straight away.

Uova in tazzine — Baked eggs

4 level tablespoons (5T) grated Parmesan cheese
4 level tablespoons (5T) Italian ham or salami, finely chopped
4 tablespoons (5T) double (heavy) cream
4 eggs
salt and pepper
1 dessertspoon (1T) melted butter
serves 4

Preheat the oven to moderate (350°F, Mark 4).
Butter 4 individual heatproof dishes well.
Sprinkle the base of each dish with the cheese and ham or salami, then pour in a tablespoon of cream. Break an egg into each and sprinkle with salt and pepper. Spoon the butter over the tops then stand in a roasting pan containing ½-inch cold water.
Cook in the centre of the oven for approximately 8 minutes or until the whites are set and the yokes still creamy. Serve straight away.

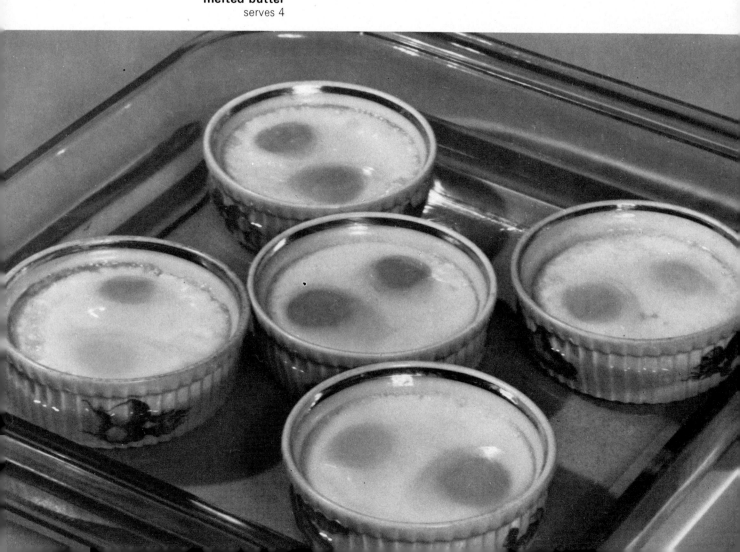

Scrambled eggs with cheese, surrounded by (left to right) bacon rolls, mushrooms, braised pimentos and tomatoes, croutons, mussels and kidneys

Uova strapazzate al formaggio
Scrambled eggs with cheese

1 oz. (2T) butter
4 tablespoons (5T) single (coffee) cream
8 eggs, beaten
salt and pepper to taste
4 level tablespoons (5T) grated Parmesan cheese
1 level teaspoon very finely chopped fresh basil or 2 level teaspoons finely chopped parsley
serves 4

Heat the butter and cream in a saucepan. Add the eggs, salt and pepper to taste and 2 tablespoons $(2\frac{1}{2}T)$ of the cheese. Scramble over a low heat until the eggs are just set.
Transfer to a warm dish. Sprinkle with the rest of the cheese and basil or parsley.

Uova strapazzate con salame
Scrambled eggs with salami

Make exactly as scrambled eggs with cheese but include 8 thin slices of Italian salami, cut into thin strips. Add to the pan with the beaten eggs.

Baked eggs

195

Frittata di carciofi   Artichoke omelette

**2 canned or fresh
artichoke hearts
1 oz. (2T) butter
3 eggs
3 teaspoons water
salt and pepper to taste
1 level tablespoon (1¼T) grated
Parmesan cheese**

serves 1

Cut the artichoke hearts into quarters and fry gently in half the butter while preparing the omelette.

Beat the eggs lightly with water and salt and pepper to taste. Heat the rest of the butter to sizzling point in an 8-inch omelette pan, keeping the heat fairly high. Pour in the egg mixture, then draw the edges towards the centre with a knife, at the same time tilting the pan in all directions so that the uncooked egg flows back to the edges and gets cooked (about 1 minute).

Arrange the artichoke hearts on one half of the omelette, sprinkle with cheese then fold the omelette over. Slide out on to a warm plate and serve straight away.

Frittata Genovese   Spinach omelette

serves 1

Prepare the omelette exactly as directed for frittata al carciofi but fill with 4 or 5 tablespoons (5 or 6¼T) spinach purée heated with 1 dessertspoon (1T) each, melted butter and cream and a dash of ground nutmeg. While still in the pan, cover half the omelette with spinach, fold over and slide on to a warm plate. Sprinkle with 1 level tablespoon (1¼T) grated Parmesan cheese and serve straight away.

Frittata di patate   Potato omelette

serves 1

Prepare the omelette exactly as described in the recipe for frittata al carciofi.

While still in the pan, cover one half with 4 tablespoons (5T) very creamy mashed potato combined with 1 level dessertspoon (1T) lightly fried onion. Slide out on to a warm plate, sprinkle with 1 level tablespoon (1¼T) grated Parmesan cheese and serve straight away.

Frittata di formaggio   Cheese omelette

serves 1

Prepare the omelette exactly as described in the recipe for frittata al carciofi but add 2 level tablespoons (2½T) grated Parmesan cheese to the beaten eggs.

While still in the pan, sprinkle with a little extra Parmesan cheese. Fold over and slide out on to a warm plate. Serve straight away.

Frittata di cipolla   Onion omelette

serves 1

Fry slowly 1 medium sliced onion in 1 dessertspoon (1T) oil and 1 dessertspoon (1T) melted butter, until soft but not brown.

Prepare an omelette exactly as described in the recipe for frittata al carciofi. While still in the pan, cover one half with the fried onion, fold over and slide out on to a warm plate.

Sprinkle with 1 level tablespoon (1¼T) grated Parmesan cheese and a very light dusting of ground nutmeg. Serve straight away.

Frittata di funghi   Mushroom omelette

serves 1

Prepare the omelette exactly as directed in the previous recipe but first add a good pinch of ground nutmeg to the beaten eggs.

While still in the omelette pan, fill with 2 oz. (⅝ cup) sliced mushrooms, first fried in a little butter. Fold the omelette over, slide on to a warm plate and sprinkle with 1 level tablespoon (1¼T) grated Parmesan cheese. Serve straight away.

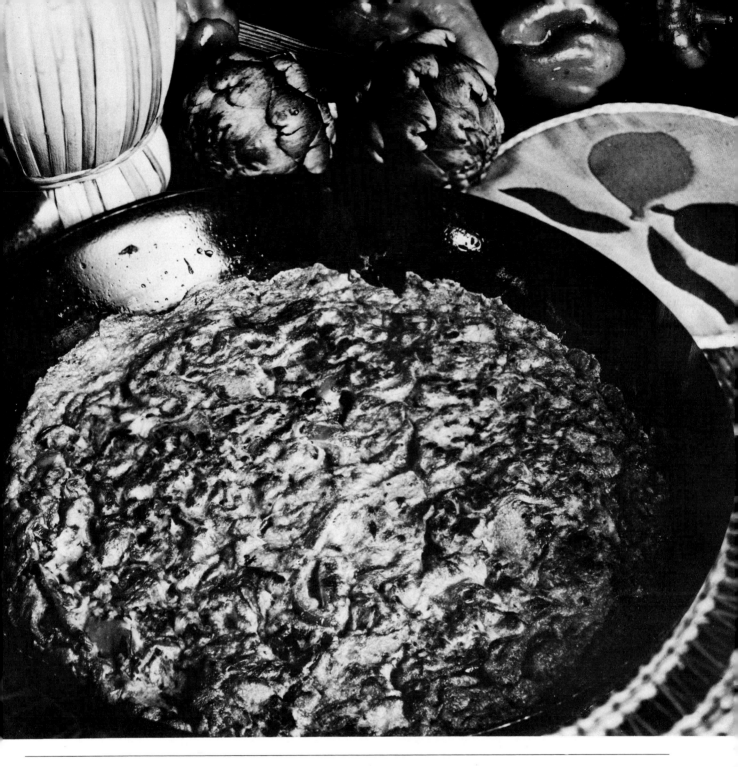

Frittatine imbottite   Meat stuffed pancakes

**4 oz. (½ cup) plain
(all-purpose) flour
1 level teaspoon salt
1 egg
1 dessertspoon (1T) olive oil
½ pint (1¼ cups) milk
olive oil
filling as given for cannelloni
(see page 183)
4 level tablespoons (5T) grated
Parmesan cheese
1 oz. (2T) butter
¼ pint (⅝ cup) chicken
or beef stock**

serves 4

Sift the flour and salt into a bowl. Add the unbeaten egg, oil and half
the milk. Beat briskly until smooth and creamy. Stir in the rest of the
milk, then cover the batter and leave to stand for 15 minutes.
Brush a heavy frying pan with oil and heat until hot. Pour in
sufficient batter to cover the base of the pan thinly. Fry until the
underside is golden then turn over and fry the other side. Repeat,
using the rest of the batter (8 pancakes).
Fill the pancakes with the meat mixture, roll up and place in a
well-buttered heatproof dish. Sprinkle with cheese, dot with flakes
of butter then pour the stock into the dish. Cook, uncovered, in the
centre of a moderately hot oven (400°F, Mark 6) for about 15 minutes.
Serve straight away.

197

Crespolini Spinach and cheese pancakes

4 oz. (½ cup) plain
(all-purpose) flour
1 level teaspoon salt
1 egg
1 dessertspoon (1T) olive oil
½ pint (1¼ cups) milk
olive oil
⅔ teacup (½ cup) thick
spinach purée
⅔ teacup (½ cup) Ricotta cheese
(or cottage cheese)
1 egg
2–3 chicken livers, finely chopped
butter
salt and pepper to taste
nutmeg
1 oz. (2T) butter
2 level tablespoons (2½T) flour
½ pint milk
3–6 level tablespoons (3¾–5T)
grated Parmesan cheese
Mozzarella cheese
butter
serves 4

These are pancakes stuffed handsomely with a combination of cheese, chicken liver and spinach, then coated with sauce. Extremely rich but, at the same time, extremely good.

Cook the pancakes as directed in the previous recipe and stack, one on top of the other, in a tea towel while preparing the filling and sauce.

Combine the purée with the Ricotta cheese (or cottage cheese rubbed through a sieve), egg and butter-fried chicken livers. Season well to taste with salt and pepper and a dash of nutmeg.

Put equal amounts of filling on to each pancake, roll up and cut each into 3 triangles. Arrange in 4 well-buttered individual heatproof dishes.

Make a well-flavoured white sauce with ½ pint (1¼ cups) milk. Add the grated Parmesan cheese and stir until melted.

Pour equal amounts over pancakes in dishes, cover with thin slices of Mozzarella cheese and flakes of butter then re-heat in centre of hot oven (425°F, Mark 7) for 15 to 20 minutes. Serve straight away.

Spinach omelette

198

Fish

Fish in Italy is treated simply and with respect and is either fried, grilled, poached or stewed. Lemon is well liked as an accompaniment, but involved and creamy sauces—so important to the French—are not, although occasionally fish is served with garlic or tomato sauce or with salsa verda (green sauce) consisting of a basic oil and lemon juice dressing with additions of garlic, anchovies, parsley and capers.

Grilled trout

Fritto misto di mare Mixed fried fish

¾ lb. white fish (sole, halibut, turbot or plaice)
¾ lb. shellfish (mussels, prawns, lobster, pre-cooked ink-fish, oysters etc.)
1–2 courgettes (zucchine)
4 artichoke hearts, halved
8 mushrooms
4 oz. (½ cup) plain (all-purpose) flour
1 egg
1 tablespoon (1¼T) olive oil
¼ pint (⅝ cup) milk
salt and pepper to taste
oil
lemon wedges
serves 4

There are many varieties of fritto misto in Italy which consist, in the main, of small pieces of food dipped in coating batter and then deep fried in hot oil. Fritto misto mare is basically a fish version. Again, it is difficult to be strictly authentic with the recipe because of the unavailability of Mediterranean and Adriatic fish but this adaptation gives a reasonable result and is worth trying.

Cut the fish into fairly small pieces. Slice the courgettes (zucchini) and halve the artichoke hearts.
Prepare a fritter batter by beating together until smooth the sifted flour, 1 egg, olive oil, milk and salt and pepper to taste.
Coat the prepared food with batter then fry in deep hot oil until crisp and golden. Drain carefully on paper towels then serve hot with wedges of lemon.

Scampi fritti Fried scampi

Allow at least 1 lb. scampi or Dublin Bay prawns for 4 people (shelled weight).
Prepare a batter as directed for fritto misto mare. Coat the prawns with the batter then fry and serve hot with wedges of lemon.

Scampi fritti e impanati Egg and crumbed fried scampi

Dust the scampi lightly with well-seasoned flour then coat with beaten egg and fine breadcrumbs. Fry and serve as above.

Fried scampi

Anguilla alla Fiorentina
Eels Florentine

1½ lb. fresh eel
2 oz. (1 cup) fresh white breadcrumbs
¼ level teaspoon dried sage or double quantity of fresh sage
salt and pepper to taste
6 tablespoons (7½T) olive oil
3 garlic cloves, finely chopped
2 bay leaves
¼ pint (⅝ cup) dry white wine

serves 4

Wash the eels and cut into 2-inch pieces. Dry on paper towels. Combine the breadcrumbs with sage and plenty of freshly ground pepper and salt to taste. Coat the pieces of eel very thoroughly with the crumbs.
Heat the oil in a large frying pan. Add the garlic and bay leaves and cook very gently for 3 minutes. Add the pieces of eel and fry a little more briskly until crisp.
Remove to a heatproof baking dish. Coat with the oil and garlic from the frying pan but discard the bay leaves. Pour the wine into the dish then cook, uncovered, in the centre of a moderate oven (350°F, Mark 4) for 35 to 40 minutes, turning the eels over once. Serve with crusty bread.

Anguilla coi piselli
Braised eel

Prepare exactly as previous recipe but add 6 oz. (1 cup) shelled peas to the pan with the tomato concentrate, water and wine.

Anguilla in umido al vino bianco
Eels in white wine

1½ lb. fresh eels
4 tablespoons (5T) olive oil
1 small onion, finely chopped
1 garlic clove, finely chopped
1×2-inch strip of lemon peel
1 level teaspoon chopped fresh sage or ¼ level teaspoon dried sage
1 level tablespoon (1¼T) tomato concentrate
4 tablespoons (5T) warm water
1 wineglass dry white wine
salt and pepper to taste

serves 4

Clean the eels then cut into 2-inch pieces. Dry on paper towels. Heat the oil in a saucepan. Add the onion and garlic and fry very gently until the palest gold. Add the eel and fry until golden all over. Add the lemon peel and sage, then put in the tomato concentrate blended with the water and wine. Season to taste with salt and pepper then simmer gently, uncovered, for approximately 20 minutes or until the fish is tender and most of the liquid has evaporated.

Pesce marinato alla griglia
Marinated grilled fish

4 fish steaks
6 tablespoons (7½T) olive oil
1 finely chopped garlic clove
juice of 1 lemon
2 level teaspoons chopped fresh herbs such as basil, mint, thyme, parsley or sage
salt and pepper to taste

serves 4

Wipe the fish steaks dry with paper towels.
To make the marinade, beat together all the remaining ingredients and put into an enamel or glass dish. Add the fish and turn in the marinade so that both sides are well coated. Cover and leave at room temperature for 1 hour, turning once.
Place fish steaks in an oiled and preheated grill pan and grill for 6 to 8 minutes, brushing frequently with the marinade. Turn over and grill for a further 5 to 6 minutes, brushing with the marinade. Serve hot with wedges of lemon.

Sogliola alla griglia   Grilled sole

Allow 4 whole soles per person and have them skinned on both sides. Place them, 2 at a time, in the preheated grill pan heavily brushed with melted butter. Brush the soles with more butter, sprinkle with salt and pepper and grill for 5 to 6 minutes. Turn over, brush with more butter, and grill for a further 5 to 6 minutes, depending on thickness. Serve straight away with wedges of lemon and savoury butter pats.

Sogliole al marsala   Sole with marsala

8 sole fillets
4 level tablespoons (5T) flour,
well-seasoned with salt
and pepper
2 oz. (¼ cup) butter
1 dessertspoon (1T) olive oil
4 tablespoons (5T) Marsala
4 tablespoons (5T) double
(heavy) cream
1 level tablespoon (1¼T) parsley
serves 4

Dust the sole fillets with the flour. Put the butter into a large frying pan with the oil and heat until both are hot. Add the sole and fry for about 5 to 6 minutes, turning once. Transfer to a warm platter and keep hot.

Add the Marsala, cream and parsley to the pan and shake gently until the sauce is well blended and hot. Pour over the fish and serve straight away.

Filleting fish

Sogliole alla Parmigiana
Sole Parmesan

Prepare 8 fillets of sole as above and fry briskly until golden brown on both sides.
Shake some grated Parmesan cheese over the soles then add 2 tablespoons (2½T) cream and 4 tablespoons (5T) chicken stock (beaten together) to the pan. Cover and simmer for a further 5 minutes. Sprinkle lightly with parsley and serve straight away.

serves 4

Pesce all'agliata
Fish steaks with garlic sauce

1 oz. (½ cup) breadcrumbs
2–3 garlic cloves
1–2 dessertspoons (1–2T) lemon juice
salt and pepper
olive oil
4 fish steaks
flour

serves 4

Put the breadcrumbs into a bowl with the crushed garlic cloves, lemon juice and salt and pepper to taste. Beat with a wooden spoon until smooth, then very gradually beat in olive oil until the sauce is creamy in texture.
Dust the fish steaks with flour and grill or fry until cooked through and golden on both sides. Drain on paper towels and serve straight away with the garlic sauce.

Pesce bollito con salsa verde
Boiled fish with garlic sauce

Because the garlic sauce tends to be rich, we prefer poached fish steaks to fried.
Simply boil, for 15 minutes, 1 whole onion and 1 sliced carrot in a frying pan containing salted water, a few tablespoons dry white wine, a scraping of nutmeg, a short strip of lemon peel and freshly ground pepper. Add the fish then reduce the heat so that water bubbles gently. Cover and simmer for 7 to 10 minutes, depending on the thickness of the fish steaks.
Remove from the pan with a perforated fish slice and serve straight away with the sauce.

serves 4

Tonno alla livornese
Tuna in tomato sauce

Alas, fresh tuna or tunny does not grace our shores and therefore we must settle for the canned variety which—excellent in texture and flavour though it is—doesn't quite match up to the delicacy of freshly caught and freshly cooked tuna. Be that as it may, a couple of cans of middle cut tuna, combined with tomato sauce and served with a dish of buttered pasta is relatively easy to prepare and makes an ample and tasty meal for four, a useful recipe to have up one's sleeve if time is short or if one is suddenly confronted with unexpected guests.
Make up the Neapolitan sauce as given in the recipe for spaghetti neapolitan, page 176.
After it has simmered for the required amount of time, add to it 2 cans of tuna—broken up into largish chunks—and the oil from the cans. Heat through for about 7 to 10 minutes but no longer, or the fish will collapse. Serve over portions of freshly cooked pasta, coated with butter.

Grilled trout

Trote   Trout

One of my happiest moments in Italy was being presented, late one afternoon, with four outsize trout caught by my husband and son on one of their lone pilgrimages to the lakes. The locals advised us to boil them quickly in salted water, smother them with butter and eat them straight away. No more ceremony than that and no other adornments other than some mellow white wine as an accompanying drink. Of course the trout were memorable and how often since have I longed for those same, delicate fish with their unrivalled flavour and soft creamy texture. Poaching is not always the best method of cooking trout and even the Italians tend to grill or fry them if the fish are smaller than average and from yesterday's catch.

Trote alla griglia   Grilled trout

Allow 1 trout per person. To grill, have them cleaned but see that the heads are left on.
Wash them thoroughly then dry on paper towels. Place in a well-buttered preheated grill pan and brush with melted butter. Grill for 6 to 8 minutes, depending on thickness. Turn over, brush with more butter and grill for a further 6 to 8 minutes.
Serve straight away and accompany either with extra melted butter or with salsa verde (green sauce) dressing.

Trote fritte   Fried trout

Allow 1 trout per person. Prepare as in previous recipe then dust the trouts with well-seasoned flour.
Fry in about 1-inch of melted butter and olive oil mixed, allowing 8 to 10 minutes and turning once. Drain on paper towels and serve with wedges of lemon and salsa verde.

Salsa verde   Green garlic sauce

4 tablespoons (5T) olive oil
2 tablespoons (2½T) lemon juice
1 small garlic clove, finely chopped
3 fillets of anchovy, very finely chopped
2 level dessertspoons (2T) capers, drained and chopped
freshly ground pepper to taste

Combine all the ingredients and beat until the dressing thickens slightly and forms an emulsion.

Green garlic sauce

205

Meat and Poultry

All meat and poultry dishes are noteworthy and while the Italians specialize in, or are most well known for, the way they handle veal, they are just as successful with other meats. Their roast lamb with garlic and rosemary, their Florentine steaks, beef stuffato, chicken cacciatore and duckling elegantly roasted with sage and garlic, are just a few of the specialities which are outstanding and absolutely delicious.

Scaloppine di vitello al Marsala

Veal escalopes with Marsala

1 lb. veal escalopes
flour, well-seasoned with salt
and pepper
3 oz. (⅜ cup) butter
1 dessertspoon (1T) olive oil
1 wineglass Marsala

serves 4

A simple but exceedingly good veal dish.

Cut the veal into very thin slices, then beat each until paper thin. Coat with flour.
Heat the butter and oil in a large pan and add the slices of veal. Brown quickly on both sides. Add the Marsala then simmer, uncovered, for 3 minutes.
Serve immediately and accompany with broccoli and baby potatoes tossed in butter.

Scaloppine di vitello con sugo di pomodoro

Veal escalopes with tomato sauce

Prepare a tomato sauce as for spaghetti Neapolitan (see page 176). Fry the veal as directed in the previous recipe but omit the Marsala. Transfer the veal to 4 individual plates then coat with the sauce. Serve straight away.

Costelette di vitello alla Milanese

Veal cutlets Milanese

4 best quality veal cutlets
1 egg, beaten
fine white breadcrumbs
4 oz. (½ cup) clarified butter
1 tablespoon (1¼T) olive oil
wedges of lemon for serving

serves 4

These are made from veal cutlets—or veal chops—comprising both meat and bone. The cutlets should be large, cut fairly thinly and cooked in clarified butter or olive oil. Although it sounds simple, the dish can be disastrous if the meat is tough, if coarse crumbs are used for coating and if anything other than butter and oil is used for frying. Instructions for clarifying butter are given after the veal recipe.

Beat the cutlets until as thin as possible. Coat them with the egg then toss in the crumbs.
Heat the butter and oil in a large frying pan. Add the cutlets, 2 at a time, and fry briskly on both sides until crisp and golden. Lower the heat and fry a little more slowly for about 7 minutes or until the cutlets are cooked through.
Remove from the pan and serve straight away with wedges of lemon.

to clarify butter: melt 4 oz. (½ cup) butter slowly in a saucepan. Leave to stand for 5 minutes.
Gently pour the butter into a clean bowl, leaving the sediment behind in the saucepan. Alternatively, strain the butter through muslin into a clean bowl.

Scaloppe Milanese

Veal escalopes Milanese

Make exactly as directed in the previous recipe but use 4 escalopes of veal instead of cutlets.
Make sure the escalopes are beaten until wafer thin, then snip round the edge of each with kitchen scissors to prevent them from curling as they cook.

Scaloppine fredde

Cold veal escalopes

Cook as above, drain thoroughly on paper towels and leave until cold. Serve with salad.

Costolette bolognese   Veal escalopes bolognese

A rich and gratifying combination from Bologna.
Fry the veal escalopes as directed, but for 5 minutes only then return all four to the pan.
Cover each with a slice of the mildest lean ham available, then sprinkle with grated Parmesan cheese. Top with flakes of butter, cover the pan and cook for 3 to 4 minutes or until the cheese melts. Serve straight away.

Scaloppine di vitello Torinese   Veal escalopes Torinese

A variation on the basic veal escalope theme which is said to come from Turin.
Coat 4 veal escalopes (see veal escalopes Milanese, page 208) with beaten egg, then toss in a mixture of breadcrumbs and grated Parmesan cheese.
Fry as directed then top each with anchovy fillets and fresh tomato slices.

Scaloppine al Marsala con panna   Veal with Marsala and cream

1 lb. veal escalopes
flour, well-seasoned with salt and pepper
3 oz. (⅜ cup) butter
1 tablespoon (1¼T) olive oil
4 oz. (1¼ cups) sliced mushrooms
1 wine glass Marsala
¼ pint (⅝ cup) double (heavy) cream
salt and pepper to taste
serves 4

Cut the veal into very thin slices then beat each until paper thin. Coat with flour.
Heat the butter and oil in a large frying pan. Add the mushrooms and fry fairly briskly for 2 to 3 minutes. Move to one side of pan.
Add the slices of veal and brown quickly on both sides. Add the Marsala then simmer, uncovered, for 3 minutes. Transfer to a warm serving dish and keep hot.
Add the cream to the remaining oil in the pan and heat through without boiling. Pour on to the veal and serve straight away.

Spezzatino di vitello   Veal stew

1–1½ lb. stewing veal
1 oz. (2T) butter
1 tablespoon (1¼T) olive oil
1 garlic clove, finely chopped
1 medium onion, finely chopped
4 tomatoes, skinned and chopped
¼ pint (⅝ cup) dry white wine
1 level dessertspoon (1T) tomato concentrate
1 teacup (¾ cup) finely chopped parsley
1 level teaspoon chopped fresh basil or half the amount, dried
1 red or green pimento, de-seeded and chopped
2 medium celery stalks, chopped
salt and pepper to taste
serves 4

Cut the veal into cubes.
Heat the butter and oil in a saucepan. Add the garlic and onion and fry over a low heat until soft but not brown. Add the veal cubes and fry a little more briskly until well sealed and brown.
Add the tomatoes, wine, tomato concentrate, parsley, basil, red or green pimento, celery, and salt and pepper to taste. Bring to the boil, lower the heat and cover the pan. Simmer for 1½ to 2 hours or until the veal is very tender.
Serve with noodles tossed in butter and either a salad or green vegetables.

Braciolette ripiene Anchovy stuffed veal rolls

4 veal escalopes
Mozzarella cheese
4 anchovy fillets
pepper
2 oz. (¼ cup) butter
¼ pint (⅝ cup) dry white wine
2 level tablespoons (2½T)
chopped parsley

serves 4

Beat the veal escalopes until very thin. Cover each with thin slices of cheese then place the anchovy fillets on top. Sprinkle with pepper. Roll up (cheese side inside), and hold in place by tying with fine string or thick thread.

Heat the butter in a fairly shallow pan. Add the veal rolls and fry briskly until golden brown all over. Pour the wine into the pan, cover and simmer for 10 minutes.

Transfer the veal rolls to a warm dish and remove the string or thread. Coat with juices from the pan then sprinkle with parsley.

Maiale alla Napoletana
Pork Neapolitan

Neapolitan sauce, (see
spaghetti Neapolitan, page 176)
4 pork chops
1 cut clove garlic
flour
2 tablespoons (2½T) olive oil
½ level teaspoon dried sage or
1 level teaspoon fresh
chopped sage
salt and pepper to taste

Arrange the sauce over the base of a heatproof dish.
Rub the chops with the cut clove of garlic, then coat with flour. Fry
briskly in the hot olive oil until crisp and golden on both sides.
Place in the dish on top of the sauce, then sprinkle with sage and salt
and pepper to taste. Cover and cook in the centre of a preheated
moderate oven (350°F, Mark 4) for 30 minutes.

Fritto misto Milanese
Mixed fried meat Milanese

Make as fritto misto mare (page 200) but instead of fish, use
1 lb. escalopes of veal and ½ lb. (1 cup) chicken livers, both cut into
fairly small pieces. Also include florets of cooked cauliflower.

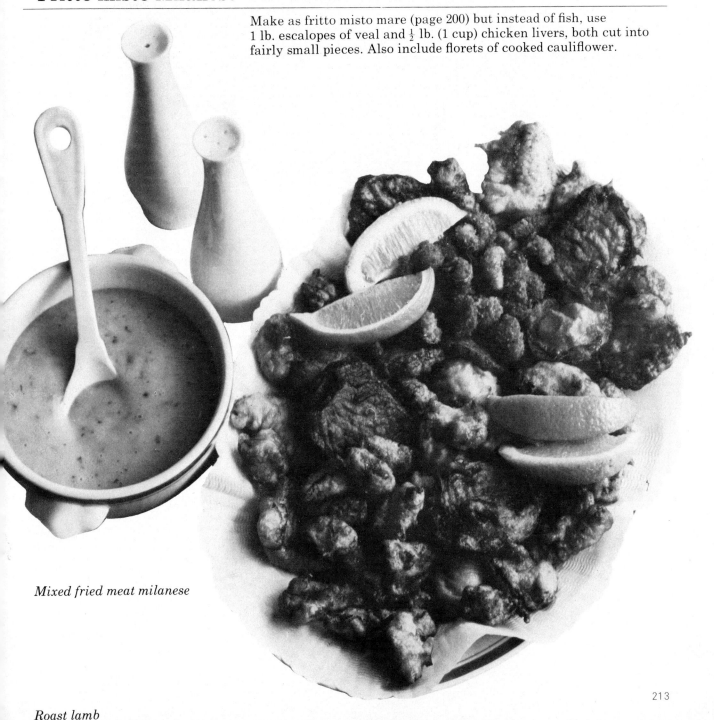

Mixed fried meat milanese

Roast lamb

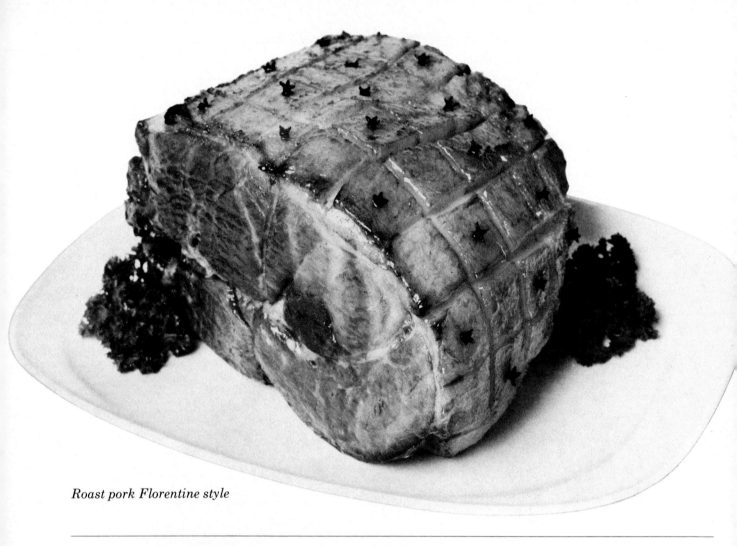

Roast pork Florentine style

Arrosto di maiale alla Fiorentina
Roast pork Florentine style

3 to 4 lb. loin of pork
2 garlic cloves, cut into slivers
1 level teaspoon fresh or ½ level
teaspoon dried rosemary
4 cloves
5 tablespoons (6¼T) water
5 tablespoons (6¼T) red wine
salt and pepper

serves 4–6

Usually roasted in a tin containing water, the flavour of the pork is greatly improved if a little red wine is used in addition.

Ask your butcher to score the skin by cutting into lines about ⅛-inch apart.

Make incisions in the flesh of the joint, then insert slivers of garlic and rosemary into each. Press the cloves into the meat then place the joint in a roasting tin containing the water and wine.
Sprinkle heavily with salt and lightly with pepper. Roast in a moderate oven (350°F, Mark 4) for 2 to 2½ hours or until the meat is very tender but still moist. Baste occasionally.

Bistecca alla Fiorentina
Steak Florentine

I remember buying my first Florentine steaks in a supermarket in Viareggio and being staggered by their immense size—and price! They were mammoth affairs—closely resembling the American T-bone rib steaks—moist, tender and succulent and perhaps the finest tasting beef I have ever eaten. Being a speciality from Tuscany, the cut is obviously hard to find elsewhere but T-bone steaks, rubbed with a cut clove of garlic, brushed with oil and grilled, make an admirable substitute.

Bistecca alla pizzaiola
Beefsteak Neapolitan

Prepare pizzaiola sauce (see macaroni alla pizzaiola, page 177). Grill 4 rump steaks according to taste (rare, medium or well cooked). Arrange on warm plates then top with the sauce. Serve straight away.

Stufato di manzo
Beef stew

2½ to 3 lb. lean stewing beef
1 level teaspoon salt
good shake pepper
1 small bay leaf, crushed
½ level teaspoon dried thyme
2 medium onions
2 garlic cloves, chopped
1 medium celery stalk, chopped
½ pint (1¼ cups) dry red wine
1 tablespoon (1¼T) olive oil
4 bacon rashers (bacon strips), chopped
½ pint (1¼ cups) beef stock

serves 4

A superior beef stew from the extreme north east, slightly resembling the French Boeuf Bourguigonne.

Cut the beef into 1-inch cubes.
To make a marinade, put the salt, pepper, bay leaf, thyme, 1 sliced onion, garlic, celery and wine into a bowl. Add the cubes of beef, cover the dish and leave to stand in a cold place for 5 to 6 hours. Turn the meat about three times. Before cooking, lift the meat out of the marinade and drain each cube carefully.
Heat the oil in a pan, then add the second onion, finely chopped, and the bacon. Fry gently until soft and pale gold. Add the beef cubes and fry a little more briskly until well sealed and brown.
Strain the marinade into the pan, then add the stock. Slowly bring to the boil. Cover the pan and lower the heat. Simmer gently for 2 to 2½ hours or until the meat is tender and the liquid fairly condensed. Stir occasionally.

Stufatino di manzo alla Romana
Beef stew Roman style

Make exactly as given in the previous recipe but use marjoram instead of thyme and add 2 level dessertspoons (2T) tomato concentrate with the stock.

Mixed fried fish (above)
Grilled trout (below)
Grilled sole (right)
Beef stew (far right)

Braccioli Stuffed meat rolls

6 thin steaks
6 bacon rashers (strips)
2 large onions, finely chopped
2 oz. (¼ cup) butter
2 tablespoons (2½T) oil
6 oz. (3 cups) fresh
white breadcrumbs
2 oz. (½ cup) grated
Parmesan cheese
1 level teaspoon marjoram
1 oz. (⅛ cup) sultanas
1 oz. (⅛ cup) blanched
almonds chopped
1 level teaspoon salt
pepper
3 level tablespoons (3¾T)
tomato concentrate
½ pint (1¼ cups) beef stock
seasoning to taste
serves 4

Braccioli are tasty meat rolls filled with an unusual stuffing and then oven-braised in tomato sauce.

Remove excess fat from the meat, then stand the meat on a board and roll with the rolling pin until very thin. Fry the bacon gently for 1 minute on each side then place a rasher on each slice of meat. To make the stuffing, fry the onions gently in butter and 1 tablespoon (1¼T) oil for 3 to 4 minutes. Remove half the onions and keep on one side. Add the crumbs, cheese, marjoram, sultanas, almonds, salt and pepper to the remaining onions and mix well. Divide equally between the meat slices and press down. Roll up tightly and secure the ends with cocktail sticks (picks).
To braise, heat the rest of the oil in a large flame-proof casserole and brown the meat rolls evenly on all sides. Add the remaining onion, and tomato concentrate mixed with stock. Season to taste with salt and pepper and bring to the boil. Cover the dish with a lid, then cook in the centre of a cool oven (325°F, Mark 3), for about 1 hour or until the meat is tender.
Serve with freshly cooked pasta, tossed in butter.

Fegato di vitello alla Milanese Liver Milanese

serves 4

Make exactly as veal escalopes Milanese, using 4 large slices of the very best liver (calf's for preference). Cut to about ¼-inch in thickness. Fry for about 5 to 6 minutes, turning once.

Fegato di vitello al Marsala Liver with Marsala and sage

serves 4

Make exactly as veal scallopine with Marsala, but use 4 slices of calf's liver (¼-inch thick) instead of veal. Add 4 chopped sage leaves or ¼ level teaspoon dried sage at the same time as the Marsala.

Trippa alla Fiorentina Tripe Florentine

Tripe is a great favourite with Italians and it is, without doubt, a dish worth sampling when cooked in the Florentine style.

Prepare a Neapolitan sauce, as given in the recipe for spaghetti Neapolitan (page 176), but add 1 to 2 level teaspoons dried rosemary instead of the basil.
Boil 2 lb. dressed tripe in salted water for 10 minutes. Drain and cut into squares. Add to the tomato sauce and simmer for approximately 45 minutes to 1 hour or until the tripe is tender but still fairly firm—rather like pasta. Coat each serving liberally with grated Parmesan cheese and serve straight away.

Trippa alla Parmigiana Buttered tripe with Parmesan cheese

2 lb. dressed tripe
½ pint (1¼ cups) milk
½ pint (1¼ cups) water
1 to 2 level teaspoons salt
3 oz. (⅜ cup) butter
2 oz. (½ cup) grated
Parmesan cheese
serves 4

Cut the tripe into strips. Put them into a saucepan with the milk, water and salt. Simmer for about 45 minutes or until the tripe is tender but still firm. Drain.
Melt the butter in a clean saucepan. Add the tripe and fry gently for about 5 minutes. Add the cheese and leave over a low heat until it just begins to melt. Serve straight away.

Veal with tuna sauce (left)

Veal escalopes torinese (top)

Stuffed aubergines (above)

Polpette con sugo di pomodoro
Meat balls with tomato sauce

1 lb. raw minced (ground) beef
2 slices white bread
warm water
2 garlic cloves, chopped
3 level tablespoons (3¾T) finely
chopped parsley
large pinch of nutmeg
salt and pepper to taste
2 eggs, beaten
any of the tomato sauces given
in the pasta section
serves 4

Put the beef into a bowl. Cover the bread with warm water and leave 2 or 3 minutes. Squeeze dry then add the beef with the garlic, parsley, nutmeg, salt and pepper to taste and the beaten eggs. Mix very thoroughly by kneading with the hand. Shape into small balls and drop gently into a pan of hot tomato sauce. Cover and simmer gently for 15 to 20 minutes or until cooked through. Serve with freshly cooked noodles.

Petti di pollo alla Bolognese
Chicken breasts Bolognese

serves 2

Make exactly as veal escalopes Bolognese (page 209) using the raw breast from 1 medium sized roasting (broiling) chicken. To remove the breast, lift away the skin from each side of the breast bone then, using a sharp knife, cut away the flesh completely. Flatten by beating with a rolling pin.

Chicken cacciatora

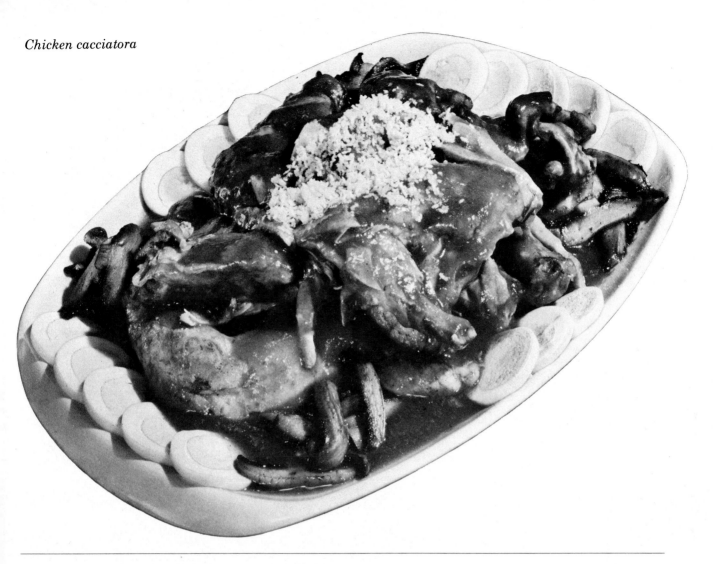

Pollo alla cacciatora Chicken cacciatora

**1 medium sized roasting
(broiling) chicken, jointed
flour
2 oz. (¼ cup) butter
1 tablespoon (1¼T) olive oil
1 large onion, chopped
2 garlic cloves, chopped
8 medium tomatoes, skinned and
chopped
3 tablespoons (3¾T)
tomato concentrate
1 level teaspoon sugar
¼ pint (⅝ cup) chicken stock
salt and pepper to taste
8 oz. (2½ cups) sliced mushrooms
4 tablespoons (5T) Marsala**
serves 4

Coat the chicken joints with flour. Heat the butter and oil in a large
pan. Add the chicken joints and fry until crisp and golden. Remove
to a plate.
Add the onion and garlic to the pan and fry gently until pale gold.
Stir in the tomatoes, tomato concentrate, sugar and stock then
season well to taste with salt and pepper. Bring to the boil.
Replace the chicken, cover the pan and simmer slowly for 30 to
45 minutes. Add the mushrooms and Marsala and continue to cook
for a further 10 to 15 minutes.
Serve with freshly cooked pasta.

Pollo Marengo Chicken Marengo

Meat balls with tomato sauce

Make as chicken cacciatora in previous recipe but use dry white
wine instead of the Marsala. Add 1 level tablespoon (1¼T) tomato
concentrate, 4 heaped tablespoons (5½T) parsley and 12 stoned black
olives with salt and pepper to taste. Use only half the quantity of
mushrooms.

Fried chicken (right)

Stewed shin of veal (below)

Meat balls with tomato sauce served with tagliatelle (far right)

Veal escalope Bolognese (far right below)

Pollo fritto   Fried chicken

A good way of cooking baby spring chickens which might otherwise be tasteless.

Cut each chicken into halves or quarters, depending on the size.
If liked, rub the pieces with a cut clove of garlic. Sprinkle with lemon juice then dust lightly with well-seasoned flour.
Cover a large frying pan with ½-inch of melted butter and olive oil.
Heat until hot then add the pieces of chicken, skin side up. Fry until golden, turn over and cover the pan. Continue to fry, turning twice, for a further 20 to 30 minutes or until the chicken is tender.
Remove from the pan, drain on paper towels then serve straight away with wedges of lemon.

Pollo al vino bianco   Chicken in white wine

1 roasting (broiling) chicken,
weighing about 4 lb.
flour, well-seasoned with salt
and pepper
2 oz. (¼ cup) butter
2 tablespoons (2½T) olive oil
1 medium onion, finely grated
1 garlic clove, finely chopped
2 medium carrots, grated
2 medium celery stalks,
finely chopped
1 slice lean ham, chopped
½ a small lemon
8 oz. (2½ cups) sliced mushrooms
½ pint (1¼ cups) dry white wine
¼ pint (⅝ cup) chicken stock
salt and pepper to taste
½ level teaspoon dried rosemary
or double the amount of fresh
serves 4

Divide the chicken into joints and dust well with seasoned flour.
Heat the butter and oil in a large pan. Add the chicken joints and fry until brown and crisp all over. Remove to a plate.
Add the onion, garlic, carrots, celery, and ham and fry over a low heat until soft but not brown. Add the lemon, mushrooms, wine, stock, salt and pepper to taste and the rosemary. Bring to the boil and lower heat.
Replace the chicken, lower the heat and cover the pan. Simmer very gently for 45 minutes or until the chicken is tender.

Chicken in wine

Coniglio al vino bianco
Rabbit in white wine

serves 4

Cook exactly as directed in previous recipe, using a young jointed rabbit instead of the chicken.

Petti di pollo al Marsala
Fried chicken Marsala

4 breast joints of roasting (broiling) chicken
3 oz. (⅜ cup) butter
1 dessertspoon (1T) olive oil
4 tablespoons (5T) chicken stock
salt and pepper to taste
4 tablespoons (5T) Marsala

serves 4

Wash and dry the joints thoroughly. Heat the butter and oil in a large frying pan. Add the joints, skin side up, and fry until crisp. Turn over and fry the other side until golden and crisp.
Pour the stock into the pan and then sprinkle the joints with salt and pepper. Cover and cook gently for 30 minutes or until the chicken is tender.
Pour the Marsala into the pan. Uncover and continue to simmer until most of the pan juices have evaporated. Serve straight away.

Pollo in padella
Fried chicken with tomatoes and pimentos

Cook the chicken as above.
After 10 minutes, add 4 skinned and chopped tomatoes, 1 de-seeded and coarsely chopped red or green pimento and ½ level teaspoon dried rosemary.
Cover the pan and continue cooking until the chicken is tender.

Chicken in wine (above)
Chicken cacciatora (right)
Roast duck (above right)

Pollo al barolo Chicken in wine

1 roasting (broiling) chicken,
weighing about 4 lb.
flour, well-seasoned with salt
and pepper
2 oz. (¼ cup) butter
4 tablespoons (5T) olive oil
1 medium onion, chopped
2 medium carrots, thinly sliced
2 medium celery stalks, chopped
chicken liver, chopped
¼ pint (⅝ cup) chicken stock
¼ pint (⅝ cup) dry red wine
1 level teaspoon dried basil
4 oz. (1¼ cups) sliced mushrooms
salt and pepper to taste
2 level tablespoons (2½T) finely
chopped parsley
3 tablespoons (3¾T) Marsala
serves 4

Slightly reminiscent of the French Coq au Vin, this Italian dish is deliciously flavoured and ideal for dinner parties. It teams well with pasta or buttered baby potatoes and a fresh green salad.

Divide the chicken into joints and dust each all over with seasoned flour. Heat the butter and olive oil in a large saucepan. Add the chicken and brown all over. Remove to a plate.
Add the vegetables and liver to the remaining butter and oil in the pan then fry slowly until pale gold. Add the stock, wine and basil then replace the chicken. Cover and cook gently for 30 minutes.
Add all the remaining ingredients then continue to simmer until the chicken is tender.

Arrosto di anitra Roast duck

1 duckling, about 4 lb. oven-
ready weight
2 fresh sage leaves or ¼ level
teaspoon dried sage
1 garlic clove, halved
salt and pepper to taste
5 (6¼T) tablespoons Marsala
serves 4

Wash and wipe the duckling inside and outside with paper towels, then put the sage and garlic into the body cavity. Place on a grid resting in a large roasting pan.
Prick the skin all over with a fork, then sprinkle with salt and pepper. Pour the Marsala into the pan. Roast in the centre of a moderately hot oven (375°F, Mark 5) for 1½ hours, basting at least twice.

Vegetables
and Salads

Fresh vegetables are much appreciated by the Italians and they go to some considerable trouble to make them appetizing and flavoursome. Aubergines (eggplants) and courgettes (zucchini) are frequently coated with flour and lightly fried; peas are braised with onions and ham; potatoes are fried with rosemary; mushrooms are stuffed or made into fritters; pimentos are stewed with tomatoes and onions; and very ordinary cabbage, braised with tomatoes, bacon and vinegar, is transformed beyond all recognition.

Italian salads, sometimes served as an hors d'oeuvre and sometimes as an accompaniment to a main course, are always simple, crisp, super-fresh, flavoured with garlic and lightly dressed with oil and vinegar or lemon juice. Of course one finds, all over the country, the green or mixed salad gaily festooned with strips of red and yellow pimento, tomatoes, onion rings and frequently olives. But there are also intriguing combinations of, for example, cucumber with fennel; lightly cooked cauliflower with anchovies, capers and olives; raw mushrooms with seafood. Clever and artistic touches demonstrate imaginative flair and masterly strokes of originality. An approach, in fact, which is very typically Italian.

Melanzane al forno   Baked aubergines (eggplants)

**2 medium sized
aubergines (eggplants)
2 garlic cloves, chopped
4 tablespoons (5T) olive oil
½ level teaspoon dried basil or
double that amount of fresh
chopped basil
1 level tablespoon (1¼T)
tomato concentrate
salt and pepper to taste**
serves 4

Wash and dry the aubergines (eggplants) and cut in half lengthwise. Score the flesh into a criss cross pattern with a sharp knife.
Beat all the remaining ingredients well together and spread on to the aubergines (eggplants). Transfer to a baking tray and bake in the centre of a moderate oven (350°F, Mark 4) for about 45 minutes or until tender.

Melanzane fritte   Fried aubergines (eggplants)

**2 aubergines (eggplants)
salt
flour, seasoned with pepper
deep oil for frying**

Wash and dry the aubergines (eggplants), then cut into ¼-inch thick slices. Stand on a rack, sprinkle heavily with salt and leave until the water has drained out. (Important to do this otherwise they may become very watery.) Wash and dry very thoroughly then toss in flour well seasoned with pepper.
Heat the oil until a cube of bread dropped into it turns golden in 1 minute and floats to the top. Add the aubergine (eggplant) slices and fry until golden brown. Remove from the pan, drain on soft paper towels and serve straight away.

serves 4

note: if liked, fried aubergines (eggplants) may be sprinkled with grated Parmesan cheese.

Zucchine fritte   Fried courgettes (zucchini)

serves 4

Prepare exactly as the aubergines (eggplants) in the previous recipe, using 8 medium courgettes (zucchini). Do not peel the courgettes (zucchini) and cut into ¼-inch thick slices before salting.

Sedano al gratin   Celery with cheese sauce

**1 large head of celery
1 oz. (2T) butter
2 level tablespoons (2½T) flour
¼ pint (⅝ cup) celery water
¼ pint (⅝ cup) milk
2 oz. (½ cup) grated
Parmesan cheese
salt and pepper to taste
a little extra butter for the top**

Wash the celery thoroughly and cut into 1-inch lengths. Cook in boiling, salted water until tender but still crisp. Drain, reserving ¼ pint (⅝ cup) water and keep the celery hot.
Melt the butter in a saucepan. Add the flour and cook for 2 minutes without browning. Gradually blend in the celery water and milk. Cook, stirring, until the sauce comes to the boil and thickens, then simmer for 2 minutes. Add half the cheese, then season to taste with salt and pepper.
Put the celery into a buttered heatproof dish then coat with the sauce. Sprinkle the rest of the cheese over the top, then dot with flakes of butter. Brown under a hot grill and serve straight away.

serves 4

Pisellini dolci al prosciutto   Braised peas

**1 oz. (2T) butter
1 medium onion, finely chopped
4 level tablespoons (5T) finely
chopped ham
2 lb. fresh peas
4 tablespoons (5T) water
salt and pepper to taste**
serves 4

A Roman dish, delicious made with early summer peas which are delicate and sweet.

Heat the butter in a pan. Add the onion and fry gently, without browning, until soft. Add the ham, peas and water with salt and pepper to taste. Cover tightly and cook slowly for 15 minutes. Uncover and continue to simmer for a further 15 minutes or until most of the liquid has evaporated. Serve straight away.

232

Crocchette di patate Potato croquettes

4 large potatoes
1 oz. (2T) butter
1 oz. (¼ cup) grated
Parmesan cheese
2 egg yolks
large pinch of nutmeg
salt and pepper to taste
2 egg whites
lightly toasted breadcrumbs
deep oil for frying

serves 4

Peel and wash the potatoes. Cut into quarters and cook in boiling, salted water until soft. Drain, stand the pan of potatoes over the lowest possible heat and mash finely.

Add the butter, cheese, egg yolks, nutmeg and salt and pepper to taste. When the mixture is cool enough to handle, form into croquettes or cork shapes. Coat with lightly beaten egg white and crumbs.

Heat the oil until a cube of bread, dropped into it, turns golden in 1 minute and floats to the top. Add the croquettes and fry until golden. Remove from the pan, drain on soft kitchen paper and serve straight away.

Patate fritte
Fried potatoes with rosemary

2 oz. ($\frac{1}{4}$ cup) butter
2 tablespoons ($2\frac{1}{2}$T) olive oil
4 medium cooked
potatoes, sliced
1 level teaspoon dried rosemary
serves 4

Heat the butter and oil in a frying pan. Add the potato slices then sprinkle with rosemary.
Fry over a medium heat until golden, turning frequently until all the potato slices are evenly browned. Serve straight away.

Fagiolini al burro
Butter fried beans

1 lb. (5 cups) sliced green
(snap) beans
1 oz. (2T) butter
1 tablespoon ($1\frac{1}{4}$T) olive oil
1 garlic clove, finely chopped
salt and pepper to taste
serves 4

Cook the beans in boiling, salted water until just tender. Meanwhile, slowly heat the butter, oil and garlic in a frying pan.
Drain the beans very thoroughly. Add to the pan of butter mixture and heat through for about 5 minutes, turning frequently. Serve straight away.

Fagiolini al pomodoro
Green beans in tomato sauce

Cook the same quantity of green (snap) beans as in the previous recipe, then combine with any of the tomato sauces given in the pasta section.

Cavolo stufato
Braised cabbage

4 oz. (1 cup) bacon,
(coarsely chopped
1 small onion, chopped
1 medium white
cabbage, shredded
4 tomatoes, skinned and chopped
$\frac{1}{4}$ pint ($\frac{5}{8}$ cup) water
salt and pepper to taste
1 tablespoon ($1\frac{1}{4}$T) wine vinegar
serves 4

In a large saucepan, fry the bacon slowly in its own fat until soft. Add the onion and continue to fry for a further 5 minutes or until soft but not brown.
Add all the remaining ingredients and boil for 5 minutes. Lower the heat, stir well to mix, then cover the pan. Simmer gently for 20 minutes, stirring frequently. Serve straight away.

Crema di spinaci
Creamed spinach

1 pint ($2\frac{1}{2}$ cups) spinach purée
5 tablespoons ($6\frac{1}{4}$T) double
(heavy) cream
pinch of ground nutmeg
salt and pepper to taste
serves 4

Put all the ingredients into a saucepan. Heat slowly, stirring frequently until most of the liquid has evaporated. Serve straight away.

Funghi in umido all'aglio
Braised mushrooms with garlic

4 tablespoons (5T) olive oil
2 garlic cloves, finely chopped
1 lb. (5 cups) sliced mushrooms
$\frac{1}{2}$ teaspoon chopped fresh mint
or double the amount of basil
salt and freshly milled pepper
to taste
serves 4

Heat the oil in a large pan, then add the garlic. Fry gently for 5 minutes.
Add all the remaining ingredients, cover the pan and simmer for 15 to 20 minutes.

A selection of vegetables

Peperonata   Peppers, Italian style

6 medium red pimentos
2 large onions
1 garlic clove
12 medium red tomatoes, skinned
5 tablespoons (6¼T) olive oil
salt to taste

serves 4—6

A famous stew of pimentos, tomatoes, onions and garlic which is a bit like the Mediterranean ratatouille in character, but less demanding of assorted vegetables and easier to make. It is one of those concoctions which improves on keeping and reheating and therefore it makes sense to double or even treble the quantities given below.

De-seed the pimentos and cut into strips. Slice the onions thinly. Chop the garlic and tomatoes.
Heat the oil in a large pan. Add the pimentos, onions and garlic. Fry gently for 15 minutes. Add the tomatoes and salt to taste. Cover and simmer for 30 minutes.

Fritelle di funghi Mushroom fritters

serves 4

Make a fritter batter as for fritto misto mare (page 202). Coat about 12 oz. (3¾ cups) sliced or whole mushrooms in batter and fry in deep hot oil until crisp and golden. Remove from the pan, drain on soft paper towels and sprinkle with salt and pepper. If liked, the fried mushrooms may also be sprinkled with grated Parmesan cheese.

Mushroom fritters (above left)   *Stuffed mushrooms (above right)*

Funghi ripieni   Stuffed mushrooms

16 large mushrooms
4 level tablespoons (5T) soft white breadcrumbs
1 medium onion, grated
1 small garlic clove, chopped
1 level tablespoon (1¼T) finely chopped parsley
3 anchovy fillets, finely chopped
4 tablespoons (5T) olive oil
beaten egg
freshly ground pepper

serves 4

A speciality from the Piedmont region.

Remove the mushroom stalks and chop finely. Place the mushrooms on a lightly buttered baking tray.

Put the chopped stalks into a bowl and add the breadcrumbs, onion, garlic, parsley, anchovies and 1 tablespoon (1¼T) olive oil. Bind with a little beaten egg, then season to taste with pepper.

Pile equal amounts on to the mushrooms, then spoon the remaining oil over each. Cover with foil and cook in the centre of a moderate oven (350°F, Mark 4) for 30 minutes.

note: aubergines (eggplants) can be stuffed in the same way, with the stuffing varied.

Asparagi alla Parmigiana
Asparagus with butter and Parmesan cheese

serves 4

Wash and scrape about 2 lb. of asparagus then cut off the tough part of the stalks. Tie in bundles and cook in boiling (unsalted) water for about 15 to 20 minutes or until tender.
Drain and arrange on a warm plate. Sprinkle with grated Parmesan cheese, then coat heavily with melted butter. Serve straight away.

Insalata verde
Lettuce salad

1 cut clove garlic
1 large lettuce
4 tablespoons (5T) olive oil
1 tablespoon (1¼T) lemon juice
1 tablespoon (1¼T) wine vinegar
salt and pepper to taste
serves 4

Rub the salad bowl with the cut clove of garlic. Wash the lettuce and shake the leaves dry. Tear into bite-size pieces and put into the salad bowl.
Sprinkle the lettuce with all the remaining ingredients. Toss thoroughly but gently and serve straight away.

Insalata di cavalfiore
Cauliflower salad

1 medium cauliflower
8 anchovy fillets, finely chopped
18 ripe black olives, stoned and halved
1 small onion, grated
1 level tablespoon (1¼T) capers
6 tablespoons (7½T) olive oil
2 tablespoons (2½T) lemon juice
1 tablespoon (1¼T) wine vinegar
freshly milled pepper to taste
serves 4–6

Break the cauliflower into florets and cook in boiling, salted water for 5 minutes. Drain and transfer to a bowl. Cool to lukewarm, then refrigerate for at least 1 hour.
Put all the remaining ingredients into a bowl. Add the chilled cauliflower and toss thoroughly. Chill for a further 30 minutes before serving.

Insalata di finocchi e cetrioli
Fennel and cucumber salad

1 clove garlic
1 medium cucumber
1 bulb of fennel
4 tablespoons (5T) olive oil
2 tablespoons (2½T) lemon juice
salt and freshly milled pepper to taste
serves 4–6

Rub the cut clove of garlic round the inside of a salad bowl. Peel the cucumber and slice thinly. Wash and dry the fennel and grate coarsely. Put both into the salad bowl.
Beat the remaining ingredients well together and add to the salad. Toss thoroughly and serve straight away.

Insalata mista Mixed salad

1 garlic clove
1 medium cucumber
4 medium tomatoes, skinned
1 medium carrot
1 medium onion
1 head of chicory
4 tablespoons (5T)
thick mayonnaise
2 tablespoons (2½T) olive oil
1 tablespoon (1¼T) lemon juice
1 tablespoon (1¼T) wine vinegar
serves 4

Rub the salad bowl with the cut clove of garlic.
Peel and slice the cucumber. Cut the tomatoes into wedges. Dice the carrot. Grate the onion coarsely. Discard the outer leaves of the chicory, then gently pull off the remaining leaves. Put all the prepared vegetables into the salad bowl.
Beat the remaining ingredients well together. Pour over the salad and toss thoroughly.

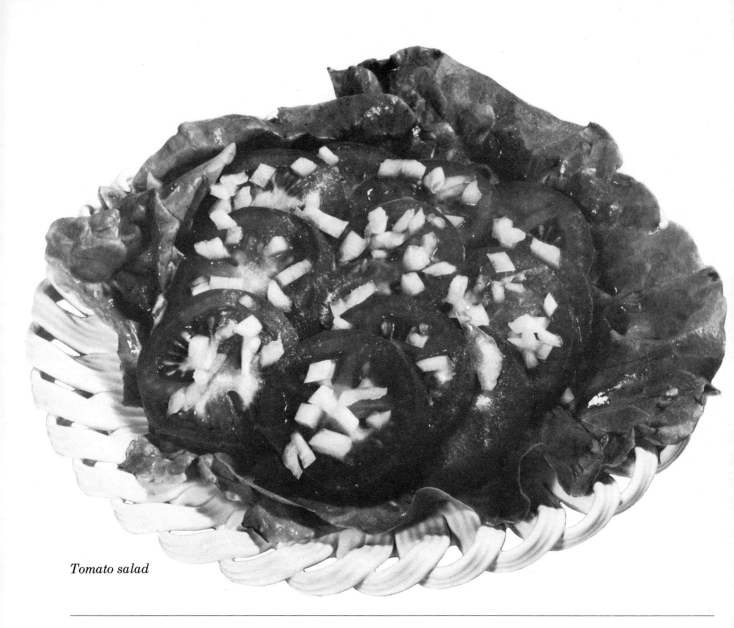

Tomato salad

Insalata di pomodori Tomato salad

8 large tomatoes, skinned
olive oil
salt and pepper to taste
2 heaped tablespoons (2¾T)
finely chopped fresh basil or
½ level teaspoon dried
1 small onion, finely grated
serves 4

Slice the tomatoes and arrange in a single layer on a large flat platter. Sprinkle with all the remaining ingredients and serve straight away.

Salad ingredients (previous page)

Seafood salad with mushrooms

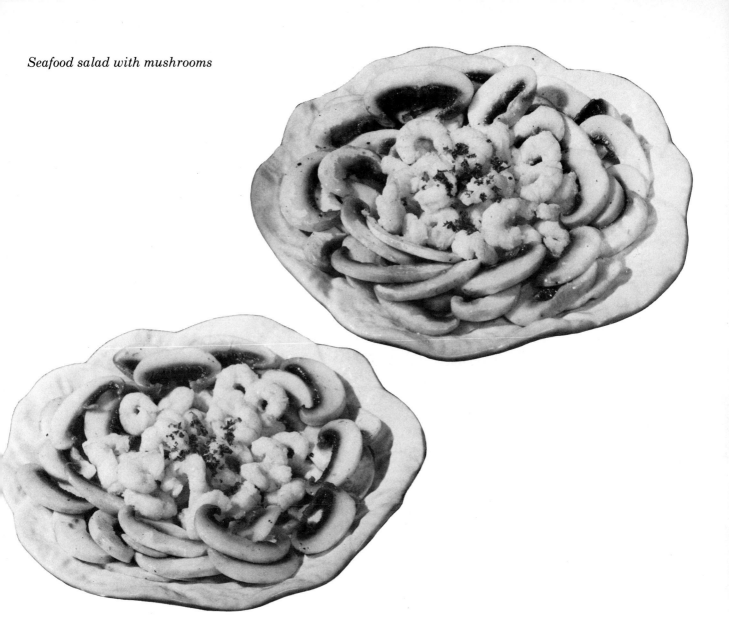

Insalata di fagiolini Green bean salad

1 garlic clove
1 lb. (2½ cups) sliced green (snap) beans, cooked
3 tablespoons (3¾T) olive oil
2 tablespoons (2½T) lemon juice
salt and pepper to taste
serves 4

Rub the inside of a salad bowl with the cut clove of garlic.
Add the beans, oil and lemon juice. Sprinkle to taste with salt and pepper, toss thoroughly and serve straight away.

Insalata di funghi e frutti di mare Seafood salad with mushrooms

1 garlic clove
8 oz. (2½ cups) sliced mushrooms
8 oz. (2 cups) chopped scampi or lobster
4 tablespoons (5T) olive oil
2 tablespoons (2½T) lemon juice
salt and pepper
2 level tablespoons (2½T) finely chopped parsley
serves 4

Rub the salad bowl with the cut clove of garlic.
Put all the remaining ingredients into the bowl and toss lightly together. Serve straight away.

Desserts

The Italian has, by nature, a sweet tooth and loves his rich, liqueur-laden, outsize wedge of cake accompanied by a miniature cup of heavy, black coffee. Or his giant portion of ice cream. Or his almond macaroons (an Italian invention), assorted biscuits and sweet pastries. But not after a meal. Indeed, the dessert course in the average Italian home consists of little more than fresh fruit or a piece of cheese, and the pie and pudding as we know it has never been appreciated by the Italians. For family festivities and special occasions, a cake will be bought from the local cake shop and served with Marsala or a liqueur at the end of a meal or Mama will make zabaglione, trifle, fresh fruit salad, water ice or a confection of puréed chestnuts with rum, vanilla, cream and chocolate. But this remains an occasional happening and, for the most part, the Italian is happy enough to enjoy his sweetmeats in any one of the restaurants or coffee bars to be found in every nook and cranny of the country.

Italian trifle

Zuppa inglese   Italian trifle

8 large macaroons
8 tablespoons (10T) Marsala
1 level teaspoon finely grated
orange peel
¾ pint (2 cups) milk
4 eggs, beaten
3 level tablespoons (3¾T)
vanilla sugar
¾ pint (2 cups) double
(heavy) cream
3 tablespoons (3¾T) milk
2 level tablespoons (2½T) blanched
and chopped pistachio
nuts or flaked and
toasted almonds
serves 6–8

An exceedingly sumptuous and rich trifle-de-luxe.

Break up the macaroons and put into a serving bowl. Moisten with the Marsala, then sprinkle with orange peel.

Bring the milk just up to the boil then pour, with the eggs and sugar, into a basin standing on a saucepan of gently simmering water. Cook, stirring frequently, until the custard thickens sufficiently to coat the back of a spoon, but on no account allow the custard to boil or it will curdle. Pour into a clean bowl (to prevent further cooking), leave the custard until cold, then pour into the dish over the macaroons.

Beat the cream and milk together until softly stiff, then pile over the custard. Scatter the nuts on top and serve straight away.

Zabaglione (left)

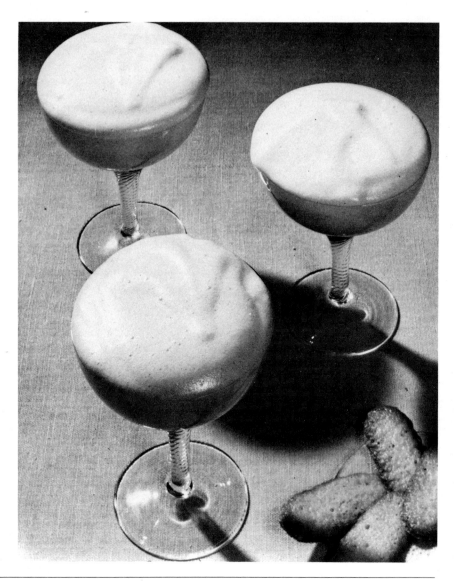

Zabaglione

Zabaglione Zabaglione

6 egg yolks **4 level tablespoons (5T)** **castor sugar** **1 large wine glass Marsala**	Put the egg yolks and sugar into a basin standing over a saucepan of very gently boiling water. Whisk until thick and white. Still whisking, add the Marsala gradually. Continue whisking until the zabaglione thickens and becomes light and foamy. Pour into glasses and serve straight away.
serves 4	**note:** do not allow zabaglione to boil or it will curdle.

Pesche ripiene in vino bianco Stuffed peaches in wine

4 large Italian peaches **1½ oz. (¾ cup) crushed** **macaroon crumbs** **1 oz. (½ cup) ground almonds** **½ level teaspoon finely grated** **orange peel** **1 egg yolk** **1 oz. (2T) butter** **1 large glass sweet white wine** **or Marsala** serves 4	Cover the peaches with boiling water and leave for 1 minute. Drain and cover with cold water. When cool enough to handle, lift the peaches out of the water and slide off the skins. Cut the peaches in half, remove the stones and place in a lightly buttered heatproof dish. Combine the macaroon crumbs with the almonds and orange peel, then bind with the egg yolk. Spoon equal amounts into the peach cavities, then dot with flakes of butter. Pour the wine into the dish. Cover and cook in a moderate oven (350°F, Mark 4) for 30 minutes. Serve while still warm.

Pesche alla cardinale
Cardinal peaches

4 oz. (1 cup) granulated sugar
¼ pint (⅝ cup) water
vanilla stick
4 peaches
1 breakfast cup (1 cup) raspberries, fresh or frozen
flaked almonds, toasted

First prepare a syrup by dissolving the sugar in the water. Add the vanilla stick, bring to the boil and boil steadily for about 5 minutes or until it becomes fairly thick and syrupy.

Prepare 4 peaches exactly as given in the previous recipe. Place the halved peaches, cut sides down, in a dish and coat with the hot syrup after first removing the vanilla stick. Cover and refrigerate when cold.

Before serving, crush the raspberries or blend to a purée in the blender. Remove the peaches from the syrup and transfer to 4 individual dishes. Coat with the raspberries, then sprinkle each with a few almonds.

note: the filled peaches may be served on ice cream as a Peach Melba.

serves 4

Macedonia di frutta
Fruit salad

4 large Italian peaches
12 ripe apricots
juice of 1 lemon
1 small ripe melon
8 fresh figs
sugar
2 tablespoons (2½T) brandy

Cover the peaches and apricots with boiling water and leave for 1 minute. Drain and cover with cold water. When cool enough to handle, slide off the skins. Cut the fruit into slices and put into a serving bowl. Sprinkle with lemon juice to prevent discolouration. Cut the melon and figs into cubes and add to the bowl. Sprinkle with sugar and brandy and stir well to mix. Cover and refrigerate for about 4 hours.

note: plums, pineapple and other seasonal stone fruits may be added to the fruit salad as well.

serves 4

Arance caramellate
Caramelized oranges

4 large oranges
8 oz. (1 cup) granulated sugar
½ pint (1¼ cups) water
1 tablespoon (1¼T) orange flavoured liqueur

Often served now in many Italian restaurants, these caramelized oranges are refreshing and sophisticated but at the same time easy to prepare and suitable for almost any occasion.

Peel the oranges carefully, removing all traces of white pith. Reserve the peel from two of the oranges and again cut away the white pith. Slice the peel into thin strips. Put the strips into a saucepan of cold water. Bring to the boil and boil slowly for 10 minutes or until tender. Drain.

Put the sugar into a saucepan with the water. Stir over a low heat until dissolved, then boil briskly until thickish and syrupy. Remove from the heat and leave to cool slightly. Stir in the liqueur.

Add the oranges to the pan of syrup and turn over and over until they are well-coated. Lift out of the pan and put on to a serving platter.

Add the orange peel strips to the remaining syrup in the pan. Cook gently until they begin to look transparent and the syrup itself turns pale gold. Pile equal amounts of peel and syrup on to each orange then chill thoroughly before serving.

note: these oranges are almost impossible to tackle with a spoon and fork so one is well advised to give everyone a dessert knife as well.

serves 4

(following page) Peach melba (left)   *Caramelized oranges (right)*

Crema di mandorle con ciliege
Custard cream with nuts and cherries

6 eggs
1 pint (2½ cups) milk
3 level tablespoons (3¾T) castor (superfine) sugar
¼ teaspoon vanilla essence
½ pint (1¼ cups) double (heavy) cream
2 tablespoons (2½T) milk
12 cherries, halved
1 level tablespoon (1¼T) almonds, chopped and toasted

serves 4

Beat the eggs well. Bring the milk just up to the boil and combine with the eggs.

Add the sugar and vanilla and strain into a buttered heatproof dish of 2 to 2½ pint (5 to 6¼ cups) capacity. Stand in a roasting pan containing 2-inches of cold water. Cook in the centre of a cool oven (300°F, Mark 2) for 1½ hours or until the blade of a knife, inserted into the centre, comes out clean. Leave until cold then refrigerate until thoroughly chilled.

Before serving, turn the custard out on to a serving dish. Beat the cream and milk together until thick, then pile on top of the custard. Stud with the cherries, sprinkle with nuts and serve straight away.

note: if liked, marinate cherries overnight in 1 or 2 tablespoons (1¼–2½T) brandy.

Alternatively the custard cream may be served without the whipped cream topping, and simply decorated with cherries and angelica.

Monte Bianco   Chestnut Monte Bianco

**12 oz. (3 cups) dried chestnuts, soaked overnight
6 oz. (¾ cup) castor (superfine) sugar
½ teaspoon vanilla essence
pinch of salt
2 dessertspoons (2T) rum
¼ pint (⅝ cup) double (heavy) cream
1 tablespoon (1¼T) milk
sifted icing (confectioners') sugar
2 level tablespoons (2½T) grated plain chocolate
serves 4**

Put the drained chestnuts into a saucepan and cover with cold water. Bring to the boil, cover and simmer gently until very tender; about 30 to 40 minutes. Drain thoroughly and mash finely with a fork. Stir in the sugar, essence, salt and half the rum. Press the chestnut mixture through a colander or sieve—with coarse holes—directly into a small serving bowl, allowing it to fall freely into a mound. Beat the cream and milk together until softly stiff, then stir in the rest of the rum and icing (confectioners') sugar to taste. Spoon over the chestnut mixture, then sprinkle with the chocolate. Serve straight away.

Granita al caffè   Coffee granita

**1 pint (2½ cups) very strong hot coffee
2 oz. (¼ cup) granulated sugar**

The granita is a cross between a sorbet and a water ice and during the height of summer—or after a heavy meal—is one of the most refreshing desserts in existence. Granita is, basically, half frozen crystals of ice, sweetened and flavoured to taste and served in small glasses. Easy and uncomplicated to make, any granita tastes impressive and does much to stimulate a flagging digestion.

Combine the coffee and sugar well together and stir until the sugar dissolves.
Pour into 1 or 2 empty ice cube trays and leave in the freezing compartment of the refrigerator until half frozen; between 2 to 3 hours. Stir the granita every hour while it is freezing to break down the ice crystals.
serves 4   Spoon into glasses and serve quickly as it melts fast.

Granita di limone   Lemon granita

**6 oz. (¾ cup) granulated sugar
¾ pint (2 cups) water
juice of 4 large lemons
peel of 1 lemon, finely grated
serves 4**

Dissolve the sugar in the water.
Leave until cold then stir in the juice of the lemons and the finely grated peel.
Freeze as directed in caffè granita but allow a little more time as the extra sugar slows up the freezing process.

Granita di arancia   Orange granita

**juice of 2 large lemons
juice of 2 medium oranges
peel of 1 orange, finely grated**

Make exactly as above.

Granita di agrumi   Mixed citrus granita

**juice of 2 large lemons
juice of 1 large orange
juice of 1 medium grapefruit
1 level teaspoon finely grated grapefruit peel**

Make exactly as limone granita.

For a subtle and interesting flavour, add a few leaves of fresh mint to the hot syrup but remove these once the syrup is cold.

Custard cream (left)

Chestnut Monte Bianco (following page)

Ice cream

True Italian home-made ice cream—doubtless the best anywhere—is based on an egg and milk custard, flavoured to taste with vanilla, coffee, chocolate or whatever, sweetened with sugar and then frozen. When whipped cream is added as well, the ice cream becomes sugar-smooth and utterly luxurious with a texture and flavour of remarkable quality. It would be unfair to say that this type of ice cream requires no attention. On the contrary, it needs loving care, a lot of patience and very fresh ingredients. But the effort is well worthwhile, for it is as different from commercially made ice cream as chalk from cheese. To prevent food in the refrigerator cabinet from freezing, turn the control back to normal setting once the ice cream is firm.

Gelato di vaniglia
Vanilla ice cream

¾ pint (2 cups) single (coffee) cream
6 egg yolks
6 oz. (¾ cup) vanilla sugar
¼ pint (⅝ cup) double (heavy) cream

serves 6

Set the refrigerator control to the coldest setting at least 1 hour before making the ice cream.
Heat the cream slowly, stirring continuously, until it just comes to the boil.
Remove from the heat and pour into a basin standing over a saucepan of gently boiling water. Beat in the egg yolks and sugar. Cook, stirring frequently, until the mixture thickens sufficiently to coat the back of a spoon, but do not allow the custard to boil or it will curdle.
Remove from the heat, leave until cool, then strain into 2 empty ice cube trays. Cover each with foil, then stand the trays in the freezing compartment of the refrigerator.
Leave until the ice cream has frozen about ½-inch round the sides of the trays, then tip into a bowl and beat briskly until the mixture is smooth. Return to trays, cover with foil and freeze until half frozen. Tip into the bowl as before and beat briskly until smooth.
Whip the cream until softly stiff then fold the custard mixture into it. Put into trays and freeze for about 2½ hours or until firm.

Gelato di caffè
Coffee ice cream

Make exactly as vanilla ice cream but heat the cream slowly with 2 level tablespoons (2½T) medium ground coffee and strain. Use ordinary castor (superfine) sugar instead of vanilla sugar.

Gelato di cioccolate
Chocolate ice cream

Make exactly as vanilla ice cream but melt 3 oz. (3 squares) bitter chocolate slowly in the cream. Include vanilla sugar but reduce the amount by 1 oz. (⅛ cup).

Gelato di nocciolini
Hazelnut ice cream

Make exactly as vanilla ice cream but stir in 2 to 3 level tablespoons (2½–3¾T) very finely chopped hazelnuts at the same time as the whipped cream.

Gelato di limone
Lemon ice cream

Make exactly as vanilla ice cream but stir in the finely grated peel of 1 medium lemon at the same time as the whipped cream.

Gelato di lamponi
Raspberry ice cream

½ pint (1¼ cups) double (heavy) cream
½ pint (1¼ cups) thick raspberry purée, made from frozen or fresh raspberries
4 oz. (½ cup) castor (superfine) sugar

serves 6

Set the refrigerator control to the coldest setting at least 1 hour before making the ice cream. Beat the cream and sugar together until thick, then gently fold the raspberry purée into it. Transfer to 1 or 2 empty ice cube trays, cover with foil and freeze for 1 hour. Tip into a bowl, break up with a fork and return to the trays. Freeze for a further hour. Tip into the bowl and beat with a fork until smooth. Return to the trays, cover with foil and freeze for about 2 to 3 hours or until firm.

Gelato di fragole
Strawberry ice cream

Make exactly as raspberry ice cream, using thick strawberry purée instead of the raspberry.

Gelato di albicocche
Apricot ice cream

Make exactly as raspberry ice cream, using thick apricot purée instead of raspberry. A level teaspoon of finely grated orange peel improves the flavour.

A selection of ice creams (left)   *(previous page) Chocolate ice cream (left)*   *Vanilla ice cream (right)*

Cheese

Italy offers us a surprisingly generous range of dessert and cooking cheeses which have their own distinctive characters. Regrettably many of the cheeses—some made in the countryside by local farmers, others produced on a commercial basis—must be consumed fresh and, therefore, are unsuitable for export. Those that are, however, are listed below in our small 'dictionary' and should give you some idea of what is generally available in Italian food shops and supermarkets.

I formaggi   Cheese

Bel Paese—or 'Beautiful Country'—is a very well known and popular cheese made in the north of Italy, near Milan. It is a gentle cheese with a delicate flavour and soft, creamy texture and makes an excellent table or dessert cheese. It keeps well and because of its melting properties, may also be used in cooking instead of Mozzarella.

Burrini is a firm, well-flavoured cheese from the south with a large piece of butter inside it. When cut, each slice consists of a ring of cheese encircling a round of creamy butter which, for some reason best known to itself, stays beautifully fresh. This cheese is fun to serve and eat and makes a good lunch or supper snack with crusty bread or rolls.

Dolcelatte: This is a mild, delicate and creamy cheese with green veining. It is less impressive, perhaps, than Gorgonzola, but well-liked by those who find stronger cheeses overwhelming.

Fontina: Used for the famous Piedmont Fonduta—the Italian version of Fondue—this is a rich and creamy cheese with a distinctive flavour. In appearance, it looks rather like Gruyère but has smaller holes. Sometimes it is served as a dessert cheese.

Gorgonzola is to the Italians what Stilton is to the British and Roquefort to the French. A superior and exquisitely flavoured fairly strong cheese with a soft, creamy texture and turquoise coloured veining. It is made in the North of Italy and was first produced in the 9th century.

Mozzarella: This is a soft, mild and pliable cheese, best eaten very fresh and still moist with its own whey. When dry, it serves best as a cooking cheese and is frequently used as a topping for pizza. At one time, Mozzarella was made only from buffalo's milk but, due to a shortage of buffaloes, cow's milk has tended to replace it. Connoisseurs claim that Mozzarella made with buffalo's milk has a better flavour, but this is a matter of opinion.

Parmesan: It would be hard to imagine a pasta dish without the

traditional hint of Parmesan, and indeed this famous cheese is
probably more widely used than any other in the cuisine of Italy.
It has an unmistakable, pungent flavour with a slight bite, is pale
creamy-yellow in colour and has a close, grainy and almost rocky
texture; hence the name 'Grana' by which Parmesan is known in
Italy. It is an age-old cheese produced in the Northern regions and
has been in existence almost 1,000 years, although the people of
Parma insist it is much older still. Certainly, Parmesan has always
played an important part in Italian cooking and when mature (at
least two years old), makes an excellent dessert cheese with a glass
of full-bodied red Chianti. Mostly Parmesan cheese is sold in tubs,
already grated and quite expensive. A more economical way is to buy
a piece of Parmesan and do it yourself, grating only as much as is
required for immediate use; like coffee, Parmesan loses flavour and
aroma if grated in bulk and then stored for any length of time. It is
useful to know that in the piece, Parmesan keeps almost
indefinitely and improves greatly with age.

Pecorino: This is a hard, fairly strong cheese made from sheep's
milk. It is found throughout Italy and is often used in cooking
instead of Parmesan. Table Pecorino is milder than the cooking
variety and makes an excellent dessert cheese either on its own or
accompanied by crisp apples or ripe pears.

Provolone: This is a flavoursome cheese made from buffalo's or cow's
milk and comes in various sizes and assorted shapes. When fresh and
still soft it may be eaten as a dessert cheese. When older and harder
it is excellent for cooking. Sometimes this cheese is smoked and is
then known as Provolone Affumicato.

Ricotta is a smooth white and bland cheese—mild and slightly
sweet—which could be bracketed with the Quark of Germany, the
Demi-Sel of France and the Cottage Cheese of the U.S.A. and
Britain. It is a by-product of other cheeses and, in Italy, is often used
as a sweet and savoury cooking ingredient and sometimes as a
dessert cheese.

Wines

In a country which flows with vast quantities of every conceivable wine imaginable—and fine wine at that—is it any wonder that those who have visited Italy come away with a feeling of La Dolce Vita and, in retrospect, the firm belief that 'In vino veritas!'* Sadly, not all the wines take well to travel and this is said with a measure of disappointment for many of the local ones—too sensitive to be moved far—are a poem and one would dearly love to enjoy them in the leisure of one's own home. Be that as it may, some excellent wines from all over Italy are exported and listed below are the ones that should be obtainable from wine merchants and supermarkets without too much difficulty.

*Truth comes out in wine—Pliny—AD 23–79

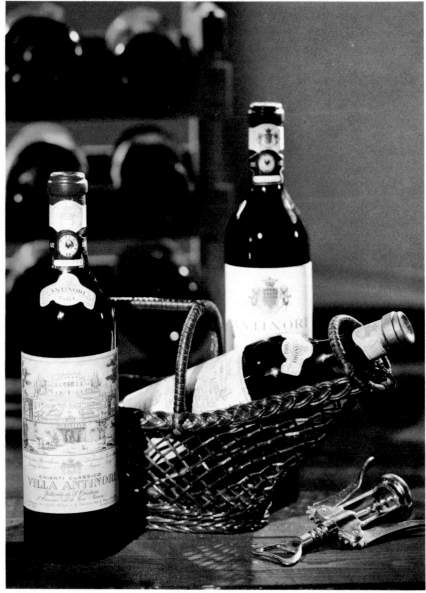

I vini italiani   Wines of Italy

Chianti: Everyone is familiar with Chianti, the famous red or white Italian wine in its raffia-covered bulbous bottle which is made, in enormous quantities, in north-west Italy, in the province of Tuscany. Chianti, usually drunk while still young (about six months), is an everyday table wine of reasonable merit and teams happily with robust and earthy foods, with coarse sausage, with strong cheese and crusty bread. Chianti Classico, however, is produced in smaller amounts near Sienna (and carries the official government stamp in the form of a yellow seal) and is a wine of greater character, quality and maturity than ordinary Chianti, primarily because it is produced more individually on specific estates and allowed to mature for several years before being sold. Most of the Chianto Classico is red, although a small quantity of white is also available.

Barolo: A wine from Piedmont in the extreme north-west of Italy. Full-bodied, red and heavy with a rich, aromatic bouquet, it is considered to be one of the finest wines in the world. Like vintage Burgundy, it should be reserved for beef roasts and grills.

Barbaresco: Also from the Piedmont region comes Barbaresco, a lighter wine than Barolo and less heavily scented. It, too, is a suitable wine for beef dishes and roasts in particular.

Barbera: Yet another wine from Piedmont is Barbera, completely different in character from the Barolo and Barbaresco and considerably less mellow. This is a lighter, slightly more acid wine, usually served open in the carafe. Barbera is a good quality wine but not in the same class as Barolo and Barbaresco.

Valpolicella: Valpolicella comes from the Venice area and is a light dry red wine with charm and character. It has a good bouquet and flavour and is at its best slightly chilled. Delightful, in fact, to sip during long summer evenings or to serve with simple pasta dishes.

Soave di Verona: This is an intriguing white wine, light, dry, fresh and pale. Usually bottled in long, green bottles which are similar to those used for the famous German Moselle, it is Italy's best wine and comes from the village Soave, north-east of Verona. It is excellent with fish.

Lacrima Christi: This is a wine which comes from the slopes of mount Vesuvius and is usually golden in colour and fairly sweet. Other varieties of the same wine are red and dry.

Orvieto: Orvieto is a white wine from the province of Umbria. It has a subtle sweetness which is neither cloying nor rich and is a smooth, light wine with a faintly aromatic bouquet. A perfect dessert wine, especially with nuts and summer fruits.

Frascati: Named after the town of Frascati which is close to Rome, Frascati comes from the Alban hills and is a full-bodied, strong white wine with a pleasant fragrance. It is honey-coloured and dry.

Asti Spumante: Asti Spumante—from the region of Piedmont—is a sparkling, sweet white wine which is the Italian equivalent of French champagne and German Sekt. It is a gay and heady wine, suitable for serving with the dessert course at the end of a meal. It also makes a pleasant drink on its own with sweet nibbles of biscuits, dates, glacé fruits and nuts.

Marsala: This is a Sicilian wine which has been enjoyed by the British for some two hundred years. It is a rich wine, similar in many ways to a mature sherry, and was first shipped to Britain in 1773 by an Englishman called John Woodhouse. Today there are three categories of Marsala available which vary in quality, price and flavour. Virgin Marsala is the least sweet, the best quality and the most expensive. Next comes Garibaldi and then Italia, which is highly commendable as a cooking wine and additive to clear soups. Marsala enjoys the reputation of being Italy's finest dessert wine—which it is—but also makes an excellent aperitif.

(previous page) Gorgonzola (left)   *Bordolino vineyards (above right)*
Chianti (right)   *Vats for Ruffino Chianti (right)*

Gli aperitivi Aperitifs

Vermouths The most famous Italian aperitif is Vermouth which is produced mainly in Turin but also locally in other parts of the country. It is a blend of wine made from Muscat grapes, fortified and distilled with an assortment of some fifty herbs, the principal one being wormwood (or the German Wermut, from which the drink is named). Vermouth may be either white (bianco) or red (rosso) and either sweet or dry.

Bitters Also popular as aperitifs are Italian bitters made from a secret combination of herbs, spirits and, in some cases, quinine. They are an acquired taste—too bitter for many—and include vivid red Campari—nearly always served with ice, soda and a twist of orange—Punt e Mes containing quinine, Cynar made from artichokes and also quinine and Chinato which has, as its base, Barolo wine and Fernet Branca.

Entertaining

Because there is a big selection of interesting and colourful dishes to suit almost any occasion and please even the most discerning palates, Italian food lends itself admirably to either informal or formal entertaining. The Italians themselves are hospitable and warm-hearted people and enjoy having guests, either to share their bowl of spaghetti or outsize pizza and bottle of Chianti or, at the other end of the scale, to sit down more formally to a three course lunch or dinner with all the trimmings and appropriate wines.

Below are our menu suggestions for winter and summer. Each consists of three courses and the quantities of ingredients listed in all the recipes should be doubled, trebled or even quadrupled depending on the number of guests invited.

Dinner or Lunch Summer

Rice salad (page 147)
Grilled sole (page 202)
Cucumber salad with fennel (page 258)
Fresh seasonal fruit or if cheese is preferred, Ricotta with biscuits and butter
Coffee
Wine: Frascati or Soave di Verona

Parma ham with melon (page 157)
Fried chicken with tomatoes and pimentos (page 227)
Green bean salad (page 243)
Apricot ice cream (page 259)
or fresh seasonal fruit. If cheese is preferred, Dolcelatte with biscuits and butter
Coffee
Wine: Frascati or Soave di Verona

Stracciatella (page 166)
Ham pizza (page 191)
Lettuce salad (page 258)
Strawberry ice cream (page 259)
or fresh seasonal fruit. If cheese is preferred, Bel Paese with biscuits and butter
Coffee
Wine: Valpolicella or Barbera

Egg and tuna mayonnaise (page 154)
Cannelloni (page 183)
Tomato salad (page 242)
Pesche alla cardinale (page 247)
or if cheese is preferred, table Pecorino with biscuits and butter
Coffee
Wine: Valpolicella or Barbera

Dinner or Lunch Summer

Garlic dressed artichoke hearts (page 151)
Fritto misto mare (page 200)
Mixed salad (page 259)
Arancia granita or (page 251)
fresh seasonal fruit. If cheese is preferred, Burrini with biscuits
Coffee
Wine: Frascati or Soave di Verona

Dressed beans (page 146)
Vitello tonnato (page 211)
Lettuce salad (page 258)
Fruit salad or if cheese is (page 247)
preferred, Gorgonzola with biscuits and butter
Coffee
Wine: Frascati or Soave di Verona

Dinner or Lunch winter

Artichokes with mayonnaise (page 150)
Chicken cacciatora (page 223)
Fried courgettes (zucchini) (page 232)
Zabaglione (page 246)
or if cheese is preferred, Dolcelatte with biscuits and butter
Coffee
Wine: Soave di Verona or Frascati

Semolina gnocchi (page 191)
Boiled fish with garlic sauce (page 203)
Boiled potatoes
Tomato salad (page 242)
Fresh seasonal fruit, or if cheese is preferred, Gorgonzola with biscuits and butter
Coffee
Wine: Barbera or Frascati

Dinner or Lunch winter

Hot cheese antipasto (page 146)
L'osso buco (page 211)
Risotto Milanese (page 186)
Caramelized oranges (page 247)
or if cheese is preferred, fresh
Provolone with biscuits
and butter
Coffee
Wine: Soave di Verona or
Frascati

Zuppa di lentecchie (page 162)
Beef stoffato (page 215)
Pasta al burro (page 172)
Green vegetables to taste
Zabaglione (page 246)
or if cheese is preferred, table
Pecorino with biscuits
and butter
Coffee
Wine: Barbaresco, Barbera or
Valpolicella

Milanese style minestrone (page 159)
Roast duck (page 229)
Crumbed potato cakes (page 233)
Green vegetables to taste
Fresh seasonal fruit or if
cheese is preferred, Burrini
with biscuits
Coffee
Wine: Barolo or Barberesco

Stuffed aubergines with egg (page 143)
Roast lamb with Marsala (page 212)
Fried potatoes with rosemary (page 234)
Creamed spinach (page 234)
Chestnut Monte Bianco (page 251)
or if cheese is preferred,
Bel paese with biscuits
and butter
Coffee
Wine: Barolo or Barberesco

Parties hot

Bagna cauda (page 155)
Seafood salad with mushrooms (page 243)
Cauliflower salad (page 258)
Tomato salad (page 242)
Cold escalopes (page 208)
Fruit salad and/or (page 247)
Chocolate ice cream (page 259)
Various cheeses, butter
and biscuits
Coffee
Wine: Valpolicella and
Frascati or Orvieto if sweet
white wine is preferred

Parties cold

Brodo con farfallo (page 166)
Risi e bisi (page 188)
Fried scampi with (page 200)
Salsa verde (page 205)
Small pizza (page 191)
Dressed beans (page 146)
Stuffed peaches in wine (page 246)
Various cheeses, biscuits
and butter
Coffee
Wine: Barbera and Frascati,
Asti Spumante if liked

Weights & Measures

All recipes in this book are based on Imperial weights and measures, with American equivalents in parenthesis.

Measures in weight in the Imperial and American systems are the same. Measures in volume are different, and the following table shows the equivalents:

spoon measures: level spoon measurements are used throughout.

Imperial	American
1 teaspoon (5 ml)	1¼ teaspoons
1 tablespoon (20 ml)	1¼ tablespoons (abbrev.: T)

liquid measures:

Imperial	American	
20 fluid oz.	16 fluid oz.	1 pint
10 fluid oz.	8 fluid oz.	1 cup

Metric measures

The following table shows both an exact conversion from Imperial to metric measures and the recommended working equivalent.

weight:

Imperial oz.	metric grams	working equivalent grams
1	28·35	25
2	56·7	50
4	113·4	100
8	226·8	200
12	340·2	300
1·0 lb.	453	400
1·1 lb.	½ kilo	
2·2 lb.	1 kilo	

liquid measures:

Imperial	exact conversion	working equivalent
¼ pint (1 gill)	142 millilitres	150 ml.
½ pint	284 ml.	300 ml.
1 pint	568 ml.	600 ml.
1¾ pints	994 ml.	1 litre

linear measures:

1 inch	2½ cm.
2 inch	5 cm.
3 inch	7½ cm.
6 inch	15 cm.

It is useful to note for easy reference that: 1 kilogramme (1000 grammes) = 2·2 lb. therefore ½ kilo (500 grammes) roughly = 1 lb.

1 litre roughly = 1¾ imperial pints therefore ½ litre roughly = imperial pints

Oven temperatures

In this book oven temperatures are given in degrees Fahrenheit with the equivalent Gas mark number. The following chart gives the conversions from degrees Fahrenheit to degrees Centigrade:

°F	°C	
225	110	very cool or very slow
250	130	
275	140	cool or slow
300	150	
325	170	very moderate
350	180	moderate
375	190	moderately hot
400	200	
425	220	hot
450	230	very hot
475	240	